HEY, MR BIG!

D0996156

HEY, MR BIG!

David Gasking

iUniverse, Inc.
New York Lincoln Shanghai

HEY, MR BIG!

iUniverse, Inc.

For information address:
iUniverse, Inc.
2021 Pine Lake Road, Suite 100
Lincoln, NE 68512
www.iuniverse.com

ISBN: 0-595-33091-6

THE JAMIE FUND

Hey, Mr Big! is an entirely non-profit making venture, with all proceeds from the sale of the book going to *The Jamie Fund*, set up in memory and celebration of the life of

JAMIE COLIN GASKING, AGED 11 YEARS

who died in an accident at the Falls of Bruar, Perthshire, Scotland on 11 July 2003, just eight days after completing his final year at primary school.

Hey, Mr Big! is written by Jamie's Dad, David. The book has been self-published by *The Mr Big Group*, a fully-constituted community group of unpaid volunteers, with the financial support of a Small Community Grant from Moray Badenoch & Strathspey Enterprise, together with matching funding from the Community Economic Development Programme of the European Union.

All money raised for *The Jamie Fund* will be used towards the improvement of facilities for young people in and around Jamie's home village of Carr-Bridge in the North of Scotland. To follow the progress of *Hey, Mr Big!* and other fund raising efforts, please feel free to visit our Mr Big website at:

www.mr-big.ik.com

where you will also be able to enjoy many of the pictures from the book in their original colour.

PROJECT PART-FINANCED
BY THE EUROPEAN UNION

Moray Badenoch
& Strathspey
ENTERPRISE

Europe and Scotland
Making it **work together**

for my Wee Man

with love from Dad

David Gasking has written a memoir which is both moving and positive. It is moving in that it speaks of a father's love for his son—a love that is beautifully described and which comes from the very deepest chambers of the heart. It is positive in that it shows us how to make something glowing and inspiring out of the darkest, bleakest loss. This is a book that enriches our moral landscape. It tells a story that is full of forgiveness and healing.

—Alexander McCall Smith, author of
The No. 1 Ladies' Detective Agency

WELCOME TO *HEY, MR BIG!*

For me, this book is not written down at all, but spoken aloud. If it helps, you may like to think of it as a conversation between Jamie and myself, with you—the reader—listening in. Over my shoulder perhaps.

Jamie's death prompted an enormous outpouring of goodwill and support in our local community and further afield. A similar response has been much in evidence in the generosity of every one of the many individuals and organisations who have contributed so willingly to assist the production of this book.

Jamie died on a single day in July 2003. But for the previous eleven years he was a boy who lived and who, in his own, childlike way, touched the lives of countless other people. You will not find this a book crammed with details of a tragic accident. Yes, inevitably, there is sadness and loss here. But if you choose to read on, I hope you will come to agree with me, that a short life does not necessarily have to mean a life that was lived in vain.

Hey, Mr Big! is my own, very personal account, based on extracts from the longer *Jamie Scrapbook* that I built up day by day over the six months immediately following Jamie's accident. Like so many children of his generation, Jamie was a boy who shared his time between two homes. In putting together the manuscript for this book, I have written to the child that *I* was privileged to know. At the same time, I have also sought to respect the privacy and feelings of others.

I take full responsibility for the content of *Hey, Mr Big!* My aim throughout has been to be fair and truthful and to avoid sensation. If I have erred at all, I suspect that it is most likely to be in the direction of leaving things out.

If I could have one wish for *Hey, Mr Big!*, it must surely be that my youngest son will have the chance to carry on touching the lives of others through this glimpse into the world of one eleven year old boy with so many dreams.

My thanks to you, the reader, and to all those who have given their help.

David Gasking (better known as Jamie's Dad)

SO VERY MANY THANK-YOU'S...

To the countless folk who helped to shape and enrich Jamie's life, not least:

- The pupils, parents and staff of Carr-Bridge Primary School.
- The youngsters and leaders of the Aviemore Cubs and Scouts.
- The members of the Carr-Bridge Village Music Club.
- The cast and organisers of the Inverness Gang Show 2001 and 2003.

To everyone who has consented to the use of their letters and writing:

- Rachel Sermanni from P7 for her song "Your smile" which she sang so perfectly to a packed hall at our *Jamie Weekend* in January 2004.
- Bryce Hope from P7 for his song "Changes" and for the three songs that he and Jamie composed together for their *Fast Food Boys* routine.
- Sarah McWilliam from P6 for the letter that she brought to our house just a day after Jamie's accident.
- Jasmine McInnes from P7 for the letters that she has written to Jamie.
- Wee George Rae from P2 for the kind message of the card that he drew and brought to our door.
- Richard McKendrick for the poem that he wrote for himself and Jamie's brother Kyle to read aloud at Jamie's funeral.
- Josh McKenzie of the Aviemore Scout Pack for the thoughtful words of his card from an "extremely caring Scout friend".
- Helen and David Banks for the uniquely personalised message of their butterfly and rhubarb card.
- Mary Kirk for her teacher and pupil letter.
- Eoghann's Mum, Sheila for her letter reminding us of tree planting
- The Forestry Commission's Glenmore Forest Park Visitor Centre for permission to use pictures and articles from *The Glenmore Times*.
- Alexander McCall Smith for agreeing to review the proofs of *Hey, Mr Big!* and for allowing us to use his words on the cover and as an epigraph to the book.

- Nick Park of Aardman Animations for sparing the time to write a letter whilst in the midst of filming the new Wallace & Gromit film and for allowing us to include a quote on the cover of *Hey, Mr Big!*

- IMP for permission to reproduce the words of the song "Saying goodbye" from *The Muppets take Manhattan* (lyrics and music by Jeffrey Moss; Fuzzy Muppet Songs (ASCAP)).

- Dana Dyer Pierson and Joel Pierson of Minds Ear Audio Productions, USA for their e-mail that planted the first seeds of *The Jamie Fund*.

To those who have helped to make this book a practical reality:

- Moray Badenoch & Strathspey Enterprise for a Small Community Grant to help with the costs of self-publishing and financing the first print run of *Hey, Mr Big!*

- The Community Economic Development Programme of the European Union for the provision of matching grant funding.

- The members of *The Mr Big Group* who have shared in the setting up of the finance for *Hey, Mr Big!* and in promoting and selling the book.

- Charles Muller of Diadem Books, South Laggan, Spean Bridge for his open-handed advice on the practicalities of self-publishing.

- iUniverse Inc, USA for doing the self-publishing business.

To those who have helped to make all the pictures possible at no charge whatsoever (as detailed in the Picture List below):

- The parents of Jasmine McInnes, Bryce Hope and Eoghann Adam for their kind permission to feature school photographs of their children.

- The Aviemore Cubs and Scouts for permission to use photographs from the album of special moments that they prepared.

- Aardman Animations and The Art Group for permission to use original artwork from the Wallace & Gromit card sent by Nick Park.

- "Uncle" Colin Leach, now of Philadelphia, USA and Janice Simpson of Inverness for a pair of absolutely incomparable pictures of Jamie.

- H. Tempest Photography, St Ives, Cornwall, for granting copyright release on Jamie and Bryce's P7 class pictures.

- The Strathspey & Badenoch Herald (the *Strathy*), the Inverness Courier and the Press & Journal (Aberdeen) for permission to use pictures that originally appeared in their respective newspapers.

- Wendy Price of Wendy Price Cartographic Services, North Kessock, Inverness for preparing a personalised map especially for Jamie.

- Alice Buttress of Carr-Bridge Artists Studio for the hand-made "Smile for Jamie" medals that she created as prizes for our "Draw a picture to make us smile" children's art competition on the *Jamie Weekend*, January 2004.

- Bob Grantham of the Spar shop, Carr-Bridge for saving all the various newspaper headline placards from the *Strathy* for me.

- Pavel Satny of the Aviemore Photographic shop for re-photographing my original 1985 slide of the Falls of Bruar.

I would like to express very individual thanks at this point to a man who came to hold a unique place in Jamie's private folklore, even though their two lives failed to overlap by a matter of one year. I refer to Karl Fuchs, the pioneer of Scottish skiing whose legacy is preserved in the Gaelic name of our house: *Seann Bhruth-ach*—Old Slope—for his historic dry ski slope that once stood on this site. It seems apt that while preparing the graphics for this book I should have been reading *Struan: the extraordinary story of Karl and Eileen Fuchs*, by Richard Brown, about the couple who previously occupied this piece of land and whose lives were also touched by tragedy. *Hey, Mr Big!* is a very different book but I am happy to share it now with the Fuchs family, as a postscript to their own story.

And last but by no means least I would like to offer a particularly BIG thank you to my family who have helped to see me through this difficult period in my life, and especially:

- Grandad who took on the task of reading the *Jamie Scrapbook*.

- Grandma who was always there with the same unwavering belief as Jamie—that there really would be printed words on the page, one day.

- And, most of all, to my other BIG son, Kyle, who has been my closest companion, not least in those hours of dog walking when we have debated together through the obstacles of publishing a book about someone who was, and always will be, so very special to us both.

OTHER ACKNOWLEDGEMENTS AND APOLOGIES

In places I have taken the liberty of including brief quotations from the works of other writers, notably:

- *The Little Prince* by Antoine de Saint-Exupéry
- *Out of the Silent Planet* by C.S. Lewis
- The *Harry Potter* books by J.K. Rowling
- *The Lord of the Rings* by J.R.R. Tolkien
- Songs from Peter Jackson's three films of *The Lord of the Rings*
- "Song IX" by W.H. Auden
- "Desiderata" by Max Ehrman
- "Hugs and cuddles" from the Speyside Heather Centre, Dulnain Bridge
- "The Fast Food Song" by the Fast Food Rockers
- "You'll never walk" alone from *Carousel* by Rogers & Hammerstein

Sources are credited as they occur and I hope that all concerned will feel that I have not exceeded the bounds of "fair use".

In a very few instances, despite all my best efforts, I have been unable to identify the exact origins of some material:

- The Jamie silhouette that I have used on the cover of *Hey, Mr Big!* and as a feature of the Mr Big website. Unfortunately no one could recall which of Jamie's classmates drew round the original shadow outline.
- The "Smiling" poem, which is widely cited on the internet as anonymous or author unknown.
- The "Friends" poem, which was passed to Rev David Whyte for his use in the Carr-Bridge Primary School Leavers' Service 2003.
- The poem "Love is love's own reward" given to me by Liz Bishop.

I am sorry that I have not been able to give full credit where it is due in these cases. And if there is anyone else whom I have overlooked, I hope that they too will accept my grateful thanks.

As for any errors or omissions—my sincere apologies.

THE PICTURE LIST

I acknowledge with thanks permission for the use of photographs, artwork and other materials as detailed below.

I have sought to put together a collection of pictures of the kind that I think Jamie would have enjoyed and approved of. All the scanning and composition is my own work and I apologise for any liberties in the use of the various images!

Front cover
Silhouette: traced around Jamie's shadow by one of his classmates in school.
Mr Big and his henchmen from the musical *The Piper*: a selective enlargement from the original newspaper report in the *Strathy*, December 1998.
"Glowing and inspiring…" quote: Alexander McCall Smith
"Smile for Jamie": hand-made by Alice Buttress of Carr-Bridge Artists Studio.

Back cover
Jamie's P7 school photo: Rhona Campbell for H. Tempest Photography.
"Jamie reminds me…" quote: Nick Park, Aardman Animations.
Wallace & Gromit: Aardman/W&G Ltd 1989, courtesy of The Art Group.
Jamie's map: Wendy Price Cartographic Services, North Kessock, Inverness.

Page vii: Frontispiece, Jamie, July 1994
The proper way to eat an ice cream: "Uncle" Colin Leach, Philadelphia, USA.

Page 8: Our Wigloo, January 2002
Newspaper article and placard: the *Strathy*.
The Wigloo: Frances Porter for the *Strathy*.

Page 13: Fun at Loch an Eilein, June 2003
Beside the Loch: Frances Porter for the *Strathy*.
Teaching everyone the "Fast Food Song": from the Cubs & Scouts album.

Page 22: The Inverness Area Gang Show
Programmes 2001 & 2003: The Inverness Area Gang Show.
The Keystone Cops, February 2003: Phil Downie for the Inverness Courier.
Accompanying newspaper article, February 2003: Inverness Courier.

Page 36: The Rising 5's go to BIG School
Jamie and Jasmine: adapted from Carr-Bridge Rising 5's/Primary School.
Drawing by Jamie, 18 June 1996.

Page 47: Animators at work!
Wallace & Gromit: Aardman/W&G Ltd 1989, courtesy of The Art Group.
Animation frames, April 2002: "Wallace" by Kyle, "Gromit" by Jamie.

Page 58: Andrew Dale
Placard, January 2004: The *Strathy*.
Award presentation, January 2004: The Press & Journal (Aberdeen).

Page 69: Carr-Bridge
Aerial view of the fire tower: Landmark Forest Theme Park, Carr-Bridge.

Page 83: The Jamie Fund
"Smile for Jamie": hand-made by Alice Buttress of Carr-Bridge Artists Studio.
Placard, September 2003: The *Strathy*.

Page 93: Costumes and activities
"Wow!" face: Janice Simpson, Inverness.
At the Soap Box Derby with Chil: from the Cubs & Scouts album.

Page 104: The grand Seann Bhruthach picture show
By Dad.

Page 111: Toys and making things
Artwork and the rest by Jamie, photos by Dad.

Page 128: Saying goodbye to primary school
Problem solving card: Carr-Bridge Primary School.
Music certificate: Helen Banks, Carr-Bridge.
Award certificate and medal: the Macdonald family/Carr-Bridge Primary School.
Jamie and Bryce's P7 pictures: Rhona Campbell for H. Tempest Photography.

Page 148: Sad Fwog and Dog
By Dad.

Page 163: Making music New Year 2003
"Australia", theme tune to the *Kangaroo Adventure* story by Jamie.

Page 177: Tree planting then and now
P2 story book, spring 1998, by Jamie.

Page 183: The Fwoggie Collection
By Dad.

Page 187: Housing protest
Placard, June 2004: The *Strathy*.
Pine marten: from *The Glenmore Times*, Forest Enterprise, 1998.
People power: Frances Porter for the *Strathy*.
Red squirrel: Landmark Forest Theme Park, Carr-Bridge.
"Say no" T-shirt design: Barney Mackie, Carr-Bridge.

Page 193: Landmark 1995
Landmark logo: Landmark Forest Theme Park, Carr-Bridge.

Page 198: "I like friends, don't you?"
Making a gingerbread house with Eoghann: Carr-Bridge Primary School.
Drawing and words by Jamie.

Page 212: The Dog Collection
By Dad.

Page 216: A year in the life of a BIG excavation
By Dad.

Page 226: At the cemetery
Scottish Crossbill from *The Glenmore Times*, Forest Enterprise, 1998.

Page 233: Lessons from Mr Big
Jamie at the pony trekking centre 1993/94: Carr-Bridge Playgroup.

Page 244: Our final week together
By Dad.

AN ORDINARY, SUNNY DAY
Friday 11 July 2003

It wasn't a bad ride home. There was a fair load of shopping on the bike but it was a fine day and I had no cause to rush. Up ahead, the rare prospect of three further nights on my own in the house. Plenty of time to sort out painting the playhouse and all the other jobs on the list before you and Kyle would be back on Monday morning.

I swung into the top of the drive and coasted down to the front gate. By the time I'd dumped the shopping in the house, and locked the bike away in the shed, the clock on the shelf in the office said ten past two. I know that because I remember checking it after I'd listened to the one message that was waiting for me on the answer machine.

The message was from Mum. I still have the tape but I don't need to listen again to remember what it says—the very last thing that I expected to hear at the end of a routine shopping expedition on just another ordinary, sunny day in July:

...there's been an awful, awful accident...

1. Our scrapbook
July 2003

Hi there, Jamie Man!

Mum was telling me about the conversation that the two of you had over breakfast before you set off for Perth that day. Remember? You said you'd decided you would have to start writing a diary of all the things you'd been up to.

It was the end of the first week of the holidays and you'd already been to so many different places, and done so many different things, that you were worried you might not remember it all by the time school started again in August. Such a busy time. So difficult to keep track of the who, what, where and when.

I wonder what kind of diary you had in mind. Not just words, I'm sure. Maybe not even a book at all. Something more like the Smiley Slug file you had for Music Club perhaps? I can picture you there so clearly now, with your collection of notes, and scraps of paper, and leaflets, and drawings, and photos, and maps, and souvenirs, and the rest—all spread out in your bedroom. Or more likely, across the lounge floor for everyone else to trip over!

Da–add…? You know those plastic pockets with the holes punched in them…?

And by the end of the holidays you would have had your bulging collection of facts and stories and treasures to remind you of these long, hot, dry days of July and August 2003. This most special of summers, when you were preparing to jump from being one of the big, grown-up P7 fish in Carr-Bridge Primary School, to a wide-eyed, eager, little fish darting here, there and everywhere in the magical new waters of S1 at Grantown Grammar School.

You know, I wonder whether *diary* is really a big enough word for it, Jamie Man. *Scrapbook* seems somehow closer to the mark, don't you think? I'm sure there would have been all sorts of things that overlapped. Bits and pieces that turned up in strange places and ran into one another—like with one of your watercolour paint sets. There'd be an outing in August that reminded you of a day in July. Then perhaps a list of jobs to be done later, when there was more time. Or some not-to-be-forgotten fun things to be enjoyed all over again, on one of those dull, rainy days that never came this year.

2. Scout games
Saturday 28–Sunday 29 June 2003

I'm reminded already of another day—I think it must have been just after the Scout's Soap Box Derby at Inverness Airport at the end of June—when you came home from school and announced that you needed a bar of chocolate.

Oh, yes, Jamie Man. What do you want a bar of chocolate for?

A prize for Scouts, it seemed. The Aviemore Pack had only just finished up for the summer and you were already planning your list of new games to entertain your friends when you all got back together again after the holidays. So I guess your diary might have recorded how you'd spent time on the computer at Mum's house that weekend, tapping out those new game ideas. And planning all the different things you'd need to make them work. Including that all-important bar of chocolate. Mum printed out those notes for me:

Games for scouts:

1. Torch and whistle Morse code

2. Treasure hunt

3. Daddy racing

4. Guard dog

5. Guess the building

6. Rob the robber

Need:

7 more Morse code sheets

1 chocolate bar

1 square and 4 AA batteries

1 map of Grantown Grammar

I'm sure that getting past the Guard Dog without setting him off barking would have been great fun, Jamie Man. As for "Daddy racing" I shudder to think what you had in mind there! Or what the batteries might have been needed for!!

I remember you bubbling away with enthusiasm about some of those ideas. But so much of the detail was still just shooting around in your head. Nevertheless, I'm sure that Stephen Macdonald—Skip the Scout Leader—and your friends in the Aviemore Pack will be able to imagine the sort of thing you had in mind. You were a great one for the games.

We—ell, perhaps we don't really need to rush out and buy a bar of chocolate quite yet, Jamie Man? Maybe better to wait and get a fresh one, a little closer to the time, eh? What do you reckon?

A big grin. A hug. Indoors just long enough for a quick bowl of Shreddies, change into the old clothes and then out again for the next home-made adventure in the garden.

Hey you! What about this school bag in the middle of the porch floor, just waiting for Kyle Man to trip over when he gets home...??

TO THE AX CLUB CO-ORDINATOR, SCOTTISH SPCA
(Scottish Society for the Prevention of Cruelty to Animals)
E-mail, Thursday 23 October 2003

Dear Maris

The latest edition of your AX Magazine has arrived in the post today, addressed to my son, Jamie Colin Gasking. Sadly, Jamie was killed in an accident on 11 July this year when he was out walking with his Mum at the Falls of Bruar in Perthshire. And so I have to ask you to remove his name from your membership role and circulation lists for the SSPCA.

As you will probably appreciate, this is just one of so many little tasks that have arisen over the past three months. I know that Jamie enjoyed receiving his magazine and taking part in the various challenges. The hedgehog haven that I still have as a permanent feature of my garden is just one that springs immediately to mind. And it was only earlier this year when he attended one of the open days at the Inverness centre and came home as the proud winner of a barking dog, which he was planning to use as part of a game he was making up for the new session of the Scouts following the summer holidays.

So although this is a painful note to write, I would like to take the opportunity to thank you and your colleagues in the SSPCA for the pleasure that your organisation brought to my son's life.

David Gasking

3. Holiday plans
Sunday 6–Friday 11 July 2003

We make plans. But things don't always work out the way we expect. The holidays were here. Nicola was off to Glasgow for the summer with Scottish Youth Theatre. Kyle was going to be in Perth all that week at the Basketball Scotland training camp with his friend Richard. So it would be just you and me in the house, Jamie Man. At the time, merely a few days of fun together. Looking back, moments to treasure.

Originally the idea was that you'd be staying here in Carr-Bridge till the Friday morning. Then Mum would pick you up in the car on the way down to collect Kyle and Richard. But for some reason those arrangements were changed. You went up on the bus to Inverness at lunchtime on the Thursday instead. Yes, the plan was altered. But the calendar on the wall in the kitchen never quite caught up. For Monday, when you were coming back from the ride to Glasgow with Nicola, I'd written:

Jamie comes.

And for the following Friday, 11th July 2003, it still reads:

Jamie goes.

Those two simple words that will never fail to send a chill of ice through my veins.

4. An unexpected turn of events
July 2003

So our summer holidays took a new course. And now I need to believe that you've been called to follow a different calendar—to write a different diary. I know that a very important part of you is still here with me. And perhaps, in your own way, you'll be there to lend a hand with our *Scrapbook* when the going gets tough.

So much of the time now, the everyday world seems to be rushing along too fast—too sharp, too bright, too loud, too harsh. It's all so hard to understand. Even harder to keep pace with. The best I can hope for, is to cling on to all these notes and quirky reminders, against a future time when I might come closer to catching up.

At first it's hard to know what to do. Everything passes like a dream. More like a nightmare really. The house seems full of echoes and nobody wants to move a thing, for fear of making it all come true. Nicola and Kyle walked round the garden with me and I told them the story of my week with you in the sunshine. They've been taking photos to remind them of the places you went and all the things you were up to, outdoors and in.

Nicola is gathering cuttings and pictures and other reminders for her own special collection. I suppose you could say that I'm doing the same here, Jamie Man, in words. Trying to hold on to all the happy echoes that you've left behind for us to remember you by. I close my eyes and try to imagine myself inside your head as I ponder what *you* might have chosen to write about a summer that didn't turn out according to plan.

A CARD FROM JOSH
July 2003
With warmest thoughts and deepest sympathy.
This card is to prove
I CARE xxxxx

To Mr & Mrs Gasking

I am a friend, Joshua, from Scouts. I was completely heartbroken to hear about Jamie. He was funny, kind, polite and so enthusiastic at everything he did. He would NEVER be horrible to anyone. He always took the bright side of things. At every Scouts meeting Jamie came bright and cheery, and there was never a dull moment with him. I never thought of him just as another Scout but as a great, trustworthy companion. Once again, I'm so sorry for you and Jamie. I'm sure it is hard to cope and I know that we all wish it never happened.

From extremely caring Scout friend,

Joshua xxxxx

---

5. One month on
Monday 11 August 2003

If that truly is the date, then it must be a whole month since that Friday morning when you set off for Perth. And a month yesterday since I said goodbye to you at the bus stop, down by the school here in Carr-Bridge. I wonder if anyone else will notice?

The man from the Highland Folk Museum is coming this afternoon to have a look at the timbers that we discovered down the hole in the garden. I know you'll want to be around then, Jamie Man, listening in to what he has to say. You were so desperately keen to be here when he came to inspect our very-own, home-made archaeological mystery.

The last photograph I took of you is that one when we finished for lunch the day before you left. You're sitting on the grass in front of the hole, wearing one of my tatty old gardening T-shirts and looking hot. We'd been working hard: me on my knees reaching down with the spade, and you carting away the bowls of earth to tip them on the ski slope. We were planning to record our progress over the summer in pictures.

6. What a summer!
Monday 11 August 2003

They said on the radio this morning that there was a new temperature record in England yesterday: 38.1C, or 100.6F, at Gravesend in Kent. A whole degree C higher than the previous record. Much too hot for you, Jamie Man—or for me! In fact, I don't think I like this summer very much at all. The brightest and warmest days for years just seem to mock me when I wake up in the morning. So often I've looked out at the sunshine and simply longed for it to have been a thoroughly cold and wet and nasty day on the 11th of July. A day fit only for huddling inside the car and bemoaning the fact that you'd missed the chance for a fun walk, exploring the Falls of Bruar.

7. Remembering our Wigloo
Saturday 5 January 2002 & Thursday 17 July 2003

It was quite a different matter in January last year, when we were building our Wigloo in the garden, wasn't it, Jamie Man! So many people have admired Frances the Photographer's picture up on the wall in the lounge, remembering when it was first in the newspaper. It's strange to be thinking of shovelling snow, and going out cross-country skiing with you in the woods, in the middle of a summer heatwave. But the *Strathspey & Badenoch Herald*—the *Strathy*—reprinted the Wigloo photo again this week, alongside my interview the day after the school launched the Book of Condolences. The paper got the name wrong this time though. They called it an *igloo*! But we know what it was, don't we. The snow wasn't right for building a proper Eskimo-type, rounded top. And so we went for the more pointed, wigwam look. Definitely a *Wigloo*. No question about it!

I came across an old e-mail where I was telling my friend Andrea in Germany about what we'd been up to:

Jamie has been a star at school since the picture appeared in the paper. Everyone has been asking him about the Wigloo.

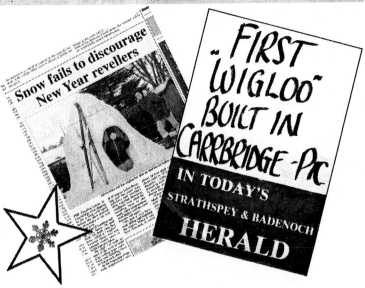

8. Saying goodbye
Thursday 10 July 2003

I paid the bus driver and passed the ticket to you, just like normal. You sat near the front, as usual. Kyle always preferred to be up the back. What a sociable pair you made when you were the only ones on the early bus to Inverness on a Saturday morning—sitting fifteen seats apart!

But then I call to mind other flashes of the two of you together. They come like a slide show in my head. I'm watching you both out of the kitchen window, shovelling up the first pile of snow for the Wigloo. Now you're playing cricket on the same piece of lawn in the summer sunshine—forever hunting for lost balls in the long grass of the Crannich Guest House next door! And I know that I'm not the only one who's struggling to know what to do with an enormous empty hole in his life. Poor Kyle.

Do I remember the words of my goodbye? I can make a pretty good guess. Like the usual bedtime routine. Or setting off for school. Or just another bus ride.

Whatever extra touches there may have been on that particular day, what I hear in my head now are the same old words from all those other countless, everyday little partings:

> *Bye bye, Jamie Man. Have a good time…See you on Monday.*

Did you think it silly that I always went to the front door to wave goodbye when you set off for school, or anywhere else on your own? Or that I came to say goodnight and turn out the light each night when it was time to settle down for sleep? Do you smile at those simple patterns of our life?—Dad and his predictable old routines? I wonder, is it too much to hope that it might be something you will always look back on now with fondness…?

WRITING ABOUT YOURSELF IN P5
2000–2001

The things I do…*play on my own a lot*
The things I say…*jokes and funny stuff*
The way I look…*funny clothes*
The things my parent says about me…*you are so dreamy*
The things my friends say about me…*funny and kind*

Jamie Gasking is a boy of 9. He has black hair and brown eyes. His Mum and Dad said that he was so dreamy that if he didn't stop dreaming so much he'd stay in one. He is very funny and he plays the guitar. My friends say I am funny and I have good jokes.

---

9. Margaret the dinner lady
Thursday 10 July 2003

We found Margaret the school dinner lady already waiting at the bus shelter. You'd had your hay fever tablet that day and you weren't doing too badly, but poor Margaret was suffering terribly with the pollen. Nevertheless, we chatted with her about the busy week you'd been having. And how you'd just had to dash through your lunch while I was washing out your paint brush in the kitchen. You explained to Margaret about the bird table you'd made for the garden. And how you'd left the tin of varnish out in the playhouse, all ready to put the second coat on when you came back next week.

You were wearing your black sports trousers. I remember that because I'd paused at the gate to double-check that you didn't want to change into your new jeans? No, these were one of your best pairs. They would be fine for the long weekend at Mum's.

You sat on the left side of the bus, giving me one of your usual beamy smiles and a wave through the window as the driver pulled away. Then, as you swung out of the car park, there was the chance for one more final wave from the other side before you headed off up the road towards Inverness.

It wasn't the usual one night away. But otherwise it seemed just like any other day as I carried on up the road towards the Spar to pick up the paper. Then it was home, wandering up between the cemetery and the war memorial, through the woods and out past the woodland maze and the giant waterslides of the Landmark Centre.

It'd been an exhausting week with you. I really don't believe we could've squeezed a single thing more into our time together—busy days that brimmed to the top. Naturally there were loose ends. And leftovers to be taken up once more the following week. But no unfinished business. You went away in sunshine and I know with absolute certainty that we parted with a smile in both our hearts. That was the gift you left me.

10. Spring cleaning and varnishing
Thursday 10 July 2003

You were delighted when we came across the old can of wood preservative in the shed that week. You'd been telling me for ages that the playhouse and the shed were starting to look rather faded. A great wee man you were for organising your old Dad's list of jobs!

> *Well, it does depend on the weather, Jamie Man. And of course the playhouse will need a bit of tidying out first...*

No sooner the word than the deed! You might have been all set to go to Inverness at lunchtime, but on Thursday morning you decided it was time to hit the playhouse...

A few weeks earlier, when Bryce was round to play, the pair of you had gone crazy, filling the place up with all sorts of scrap wood from the stick pile—old fence posts, broken planks and so on. Now all that clutter had to come out again. But of course, in the Jamie Man Manual of Doing Things, every job needs to bring a friend. And so, in the process of spring cleaning the playhouse, you decided that the small table in there was getting a bit shabby as well.

> *Okay, fine, Jamie Man. I'll get you some sandpaper. And while you've got the varnish out, you'll be able to put the first coat on your bird table too.*

So you disappeared off with your sandpaper and I occupied myself going round the house sweeping down the windows and doors with the broom. After so little rain all year, the whole place was covered in pollen from the woods. Not good for the hay fever, eh!

When you were ready, we swept out the playhouse together and I found you some paper to spread out on the floor inside. Then you got going with your brush and varnish while I went round the back to see about clearing away some of the junk from around the shed, so that I'd be able to get in with the wood preservative later on.

Thus we passed our final hours together, contentedly occupied, shuttling back and forth, checking on one another and calling for an extra pair of hands where needed. Come lunchtime, you had the first coat of varnish completed on both the playhouse table and the bird table, and I'd got the decks all cleared ready for the big re-staining campaign.

It was a close run thing. Or put another way—not a moment wasted.

11. Now for that wood preservative
Thursday 10 July 2003

We debated Dad's big work plan on the way up to the bus. If it stayed dry, then it would be okay to paint the shed. But if it looked like rain, then the playhouse would be more sheltered under the big sycamore tree. So what had Mr Weatherman had to say?—Maybe a few showers in the afternoon. Big help!

After a late lunch, the sky still looked pretty blue, so I decided to risk it and go for the shed. I saw the new neighbour over the fence as I went round to get started and I joked about how that this wasn't my favourite job, squeezing down between the shed and the old corrugated iron fence on a hot day with a pot of wood preservative under my nose! He chuckled sympathetically and agreed it probably wasn't much fun.

It was approaching seven o'clock when I finally came to the end of the job, racing against the droplets of a shower that threatened and then decided to move on elsewhere instead. At this time of year it wouldn't be dark for several more hours yet. Should I press on with the playhouse? No. More than three hours of painting was enough for one day. Time enough to carry on tomorrow…

12. A surprise for when you got back
Friday 11 July 2003

We'd wondered about cycling down to Aviemore on the Wednesday afternoon. There was going to be the first of the *Reading Maze* events at the library that day. But the pollen was very high and in the end you decided you'd rather stay at home and potter around with other things. I could always catch up on the jobs in Aviemore on Friday, when you'd be on your way down to Perth with Mum.

I wasn't rushing myself that Friday morning, however. I sat down with a cup of coffee and picked up the *Strathy* for a browse before setting out. And there to my surprise was a photograph of you on page two! Taken on the evening of your sponsored walk and barbeque with the Scouts at Loch an Eilein. You'd said that Frances had been there that night but that was a whole month back. We'd given up hope of a photo in the paper. It was a wonderful picture of you with Skip and a bunch of the Cubs and Scouts beside the Loch. Everyone relaxed and happy. The bigger ones like you looking forward to camping out on a fine summer's night just a week before the longest day of the year.

Fun at Loch an Eilein, June 2003

"A Pizza Hut, a Pizza Hut…"—teaching everyone "The Fast Food Song".

I thought to myself at the time, if we hadn't been so very busy with everything else that week, we might have gone to pick up the paper when it first came out on Wednesday afternoon. And then you could have seen the photo before you went up to Inverness. But never mind, it would be a nice surprise waiting for you when you got back on Monday...

13. Talking to the press
Saturday 12 July 2003

A mere twenty four hours later, I was sitting in a car on the drive talking to a pair of freelance journalists for the Sunday Papers, no more than a few steps away from the playhouse—still unpainted. Indoors, the *Strathy* was lying out on the table where I'd left it the day before, still open to the picture on page two, waiting for you to come home. In that short space of time, the whole of our quiet little world had changed forever. I was surrounded by evidence of the everyday and ordinary but nothing was the same anymore.

These men were seeking to turn our loss into their story. My task was to shield Mum and Kyle and Nicola from their prying. I spoke to them about the things you loved to do. About stories and make-believe and about how every corner of the garden was a reminder of all the things that you and I had been doing together that first week of the holidays. I talked about how much you loved the Scouts and how you'd rehearsed for six months to be in the Gang Show, first as a Cub in 2001 and then again at Easter this year. I told them the story of the camp at Loch an Eilein and the conversation that you and I had afterwards, about how accidents can sometimes happen. And I told those men in the car that morning that what had happened the day before was nobody's fault.

14. Accidents can sometimes happen
Saturday 14 June 2003

Once upon a time, it truly seemed as if we might come to look back on 2003 as rather a good year in our lives. You were all fired up for secondary school. Kyle was happy with his subject choices for Standard Grades in S3. My script for *The Valhalla Triangle* series was in production in America. And Radio Scotland had even been making enquiries about some possible sketch writing.

I wouldn't call myself a superstitious person. Nevertheless, looking back now, it might almost seem as if Friday the 13th of June marked a turning point in the year...

That was the evening you went to Loch an Eilein with the Beavers, Cubs and Scouts. You kicked off with the sponsored walk. Followed by a barbeque. And then the overnight camp for the Scouts. You were thrilled at the prospect and off you went with your sleeping bag, rucksack, suntan lotion, hay fever tablets, midgie repellent and a proper spring in your step. But what was the one thing we forgot to pack? That's right, your Scout shirt! You didn't mention it and I never thought of it. Which is why you weren't wearing it when Frances came to take the picture for the newspaper that evening.

Saturday morning, Kyle was away to Mum's and I was outside fighting the weeds, not expecting you back for another hour. Then, all at once, there you were coming down the drive with your bags of kit and looking rather glum. What was up? Had something gone wrong? You nodded. Right at the very end, after all the fun, Skip had slipped over playing rounders and broken his ankle. What a sad end to such a great time together.

We came back into the house and had baked potatoes and talked about the way that unfortunate accidents like that can sometimes happen. Ninety nine out of a hundred times Skip would have got up, dusted himself off, grinned and said, "What a silly fellow am I!" And then you would all have had a good laugh and carried on with the game. Unfortunately for Skip on this particular occasion, it didn't turn out that way.

15. A picture for the paper
Saturday 12 July 2003

The journalists were asking for a photograph of you. I tried to point them to the Scout picture from Loch an Eilein. That's how I will always remember you, Jamie Man—one step away from the wee lad at primary school. You'd grown up so much in those last few months. But they weren't interested in the picture that Frances had taken. They wanted one of their own to sell on to the newspapers. We let them copy your P6 school photo that was up on the wall in the lounge. It's only afterwards you think to yourself that you could have said no…

It's a sad fact that some newspaper people seem to believe that your face belongs to them as soon as they've got hold of it. And they measure your worth by sensation and circulation figures. In one or two of the Sunday Papers they'd even flipped the photo over left to right to make it look different. Presumably it's easier for the freelancers to sell it that way. I suppose we just have to be thankful they didn't print your picture upside down in any of them, eh, Jamie Man!

16. Captured on film
Sunday 13 April & July 2003

We've been having all the old packets of photographs out in the past few weeks, passing them round for everyone to see. Little did I guess how important that last film was going to turn out to be, when I put it in the camera back at Easter. It wasn't just that final picture of you in front of the hole where we'd been digging. There was the whole sequence I took of you in the kilt that Mum hired for you to wear for the Gang Show as well. That was the afternoon of Palm Sunday, the day after I brought Grandma and Aunty Iris up in the bus with the Cubs and Scouts and Brownies to see you in the matinee performance. After all the months of rehearsals, the Gang Show was finally over for another two years. You were weary, but happy—and already talking eagerly about next time.

The pictures show a bright April day out in the garden beside the drystone wall, with the daffodils at their very best round the bottom of the pussy willow tree. And there's you in your green Scout shirt, with the special Gang Show necker. You were wearing that same bright red necker with the leather woggle when we came to say goodbye to you at the church, the night before the funeral.

17. The wonders of wood
December 2002–July 2003

There were photographs too of the wooden elephant that you carved for Nicola last Christmas. And everyone was amazed all over again that you'd made something so fine when you were just eleven years old. On the shelf in your bedroom I found the fish and the begging dog that you and I made together when you were first learning to use the knives and the files. And there was the big totem pole with all the weird and wonderful animal heads in there as well—something which very conveniently doubled as a microphone stand in your make-believe recording studio.

I reckon wood must be catching in this family. Splinters in the blood, perhaps? Or something in the genes? I picked up the habit from Grandad. And I suppose there was always something wooden going on around you from your earliest days: carving, making shelves, building the playhouse, chainsawing, chopping and stacking fuel for the stove.

That final week you looked at logs in the shed and bits of wood in the loft and you dreamed aloud of things you might do with them one day. You'd just started making up your own tunes. You couldn't wait to get stuck into all those exciting labs and workshops at the Grammar School. It was just one of those stages in your life when the horizons were expanding off in all sorts of directions. The future was beginning to take shape…

18. Special pictures
April & September 2003

When I was taking those photographs of you in the kilt after the Gang Show, I hardly imagined that one of the first copies would be going to the *Strathy* to accompany an article on the launching of a memorial fund in your name, Jamie Man. I just thought I was snapping off pictures so we'd have plenty of prints to send out to all those people who didn't get the chance to see you very often.

And now? Where do you start with making up such a list? Family, friends, school, Music Club, Cubs and Scouts, the Gang Show…? And then actually handing them out. I had no idea how difficult a task *that* was going to turn out to be.

I got some cards to mount the pictures in. Some I wrote a message inside. With others, like to your friends at school, it seemed better just to leave them blank. But whichever way it was, the mere process of selecting a picture and deciding on a few simple words, or nothing at all, turned out to be one of the hardest of all the jobs I've come across during these past few months. I could manage about three or four in a day, crying most of the way through and trying not to smudge the ink, or to drip onto the picture.

Delivering the cards was an exhausting business too. As far as possible, I tried to hand them over in person. For the school alone, that meant three or four separate visits to find all the different people on their various days. Hard going. But then let's face it, Jamie Man. For the most special people—how could it possibly have been otherwise?

19. Out of our control
July–August 2003

Precious little survived of our original plans for the summer. Events simply took over. Grandma and Grandad did come to stay, but not when the calendar said. Uncle Bob, Aunty Pam and Cousin Alan were here too. The second half of July conjures up images of endless meals, beds and travel arrangements—phone calls, letters, cards, visits, appointments and meetings. A non-stop flurry of words and faces. Meanwhile all the ordinary jobs we'd earmarked for filling the spaces in our summer were simply left to multiply.

But, sooner or later, Kyle and I were going to have to think about life with just the two of us. Family and friends had places of their own to go back to. And with the best will in the world, there were tasks that we couldn't even begin to think about before we finally had the house to ourselves again. Under control? Hardly.

20. Dog therapy
August 2003

August arrived and the house went quiet. Kyle and I listened to the forecast on the radio each morning for signs of a break in the weather, but heard only talk of more sunshine and still hotter days to come. When we weren't playing games and reading stories, or watching videos, it was easier to be outside and away from the house. I rang up Mairi Robertson, your old head mistress, suggesting that her Monty Dog might like to come out to play. And she was delighted to lend him to us for a spot of dog therapy.

The first afternoon, we took the camera with us and before we set off I used up the remaining three pictures on the film with snaps of Kyle playing with Monty on the front lawn. Jolly pictures with an excited dog in the sunshine. At the same time so very aware that the previous photo would be that one of you sitting on the grass in our own garden.

Kyle and I walked and talked while Monty galloped all over the place with logs in his mouth—crazy dog! I'm sure it did all three of us a lot of good, each in his own way. Kyle's now got the job of official dog walker one day a week. I meet him up at Miss Robertson's house after school and it makes a regular appointment for the two of us to look forward to. Monty certainly never says no!

21. Mr Big aka the Jolly Postman
Christmas 1997 & Friday 27–Saturday 28 November 1998

So many people have spoken of you on stage, Jamie Man. Some of them look right back to the Jolly Postman, at Christmas in P2, with your big bag and the jacket and the hat and that broad, beamy smile. You looked so much at home. In a way maybe that is where it all began. The first glimpse of a new Jamie who had not been revealed before.

Then the following year we had *The Piper*. You were in Rising 5's when I started sketching out the first rough storyline and the words of a few songs. And you watched it grow all the way through P1 and P2. Did you catch something there perhaps as well? There's no doubt you loved the whole process of putting together a home-grown musical, as we accelerated up to our two grand performances in Carr-Bridge and Nethy Bridge. There were Rats and Children from the two Primary Schools. Teenage Bullies from the Grammar School. And John Batty from Eden Court Theatre in Inverness as our Drama and Technical Director. Not to mention all the other actors, singers, musicians and helpers from up and down the valley who joined in to make it a real community event.

It was quite a family affair too, wasn't it. Big sister Nicola was the narrator—local newspaper reporter Annie Vent. Big brother Kyle was a rat. Mum was one of Mr Mayor's wicked cronies on the Town Council. Dad was the Piper. And you, Jamie Man, at just seven years old, were the silent, shady Mr Big, the villain of the piece. Yes, everyone remembers you in your big bowler hat and the fancy waistcoat, with your two sinister henchmen (Hilary and Shirley) to do all the dirty work for you. Did I say it was a silent part? That didn't stop you piping up at one of the dress rehearsals to suggest to John how he could improve his performance as Mr Director! Do you remember this verse from the henchmen's song?

> *Mr Big, what a guy! He's our main man*
> *Sorting out each contract according to plan*
> *Satisfaction guaranteed with customer care*
> *Problems resolved with benefits for all to share*

The original song was all very ironic, of course. But now, I'm constantly coming across people who speak so warmly of what we might call your *customer care*. Mr Big—a character worth remembering. You gave me so many reasons to feel proud.

22. Good friends missing you
July 2003

The first call I made after I heard that there'd been an accident was to Mr and Mrs Banks. And, as things worked out, the first of the kilt picture cards that I delivered went to Helen and David as well. I took it down after school one day when Mrs Banks was teaching. They've known you all the way through primary school, plus Music Club, of course. It was Mrs Banks who taught you and Kyle and Nicola to play the recorder and the tin whistle, as well as all her supply teaching in the school. And then she was our Musical Director for *The Piper*, with Mr Banks as the Stage Manager.

It's going to be tough when Music Club starts up again after the October holidays, isn't it. Friday evenings were always such a regular fixture on our winter calendar. You and I staggering down to the school together with the piano accordion for me plus whatever variety of instruments you had on your menu for that particular week.

Mrs Banks told me that she cried again recently when she went to a concert where someone was using percussion egg shakers. It made her think of all the times you borrowed hers. I've given her one of your home-made eggs: a wee souvenir of that night when you took them along to Music Club to show her and then dropped one on the floor. What fun we had chasing those little, round fishtank stones all over the place in the school hall!

23. In the first dark hours
Saturday 12 July 2003

The day after your accident I sent Mrs Banks this song. It was something I'd written a few years ago but it just seemed to sum up so much of how I was feeling at the time. The memories we shared. Yes, sometimes you did drive me up the wall. But there is no doubt about it, the sharp words are indeed the first to fade.

THE DARK WEDGE

Time alone forced the dark wedge between us
Only the years had the power to tear our lives apart
Snatching the solid photographic pages that recorded the days of our sharing

> *Pictures, dreams and recollections*
> *Secretive signs and missing connections*
> *Colours, shapes, bring subtlest echoes*
> *Doubts revealed, insecurities whispered*
> *Burdens shared and weaknesses pardoned*
> *Accepting each load with no question of payment*
> *Love preserved, so tenderly painted*
> *In shades from the warmest of red to bitter cool violet*

>> *I cling to this open ended album of our incomplete relationship*
>> *That was so unexpectedly concluded, arbitrarily dividing*
>> *The black and white*
>> *Of yours and mine*

Faith alone spans the dark wedge between us
Only our love has the power to soothe the wounds of grief
Finding the stolen photographic pages of the days that preceded our parting

> *Pictures, dreams and recollections…etc*

I leaf through the old and cherished memories of our undiminished partnership
That is just temporarily suspended till the time we reassemble
Those sleeping hues
Of you and me

    Yes, perhaps sometimes there were sharp words
    But, as I recall, they were always softly forgiven
    And now they are long forgotten

---

24. Gang Show 2003
Wednesday 9–Saturday 12 April 2003

You've come a long way since Mr Big and The Jolly Postman, Jamie Man. And I know I'm very fortunate to have so many of the different performances on video. Scenes to go back to…when the time is right. School Fun Days, pantomimes, the Talent Show. It was a busy and exciting road that led you to the stage of Eden Court Theatre in Inverness—the only boy from the Aviemore Pack in the Gang Show, twice over.

I had a long talk with Iain Macdonald, the Gang Show Director, when we all went back to the Carr-Bridge Hotel after the funeral. He was one of the six Cub and Scout leaders who held the cords with Kyle and I as we lowered your coffin down into the grave. Taking part in the Gang Show demands a big commitment. Rehearsals every week for six months, leading up to the five performances in the Easter holidays. By the time that's all over everyone involved is like one of a family. All feeling the loss.

My abiding image of this year's Show will always be that build up to the Grand Finale, when every single member of the cast paraded across the stage waving to the audience. And there you were, in the kilt that Mum had hired for you and smiling all the way. No wonder you won one of the *Best Smile* awards each time you were in the Show, Wee Man. So happy to be part of the team. Already looking forward eagerly to next time…

Like you wrote in class after your first Gang Show:

The best place I've ever been…*behind stage at Eden Court*

When I was a star…*when I was in Eden Court*

Yep,
    they even put you in the
        newspaper to promote the Show!

Members of the 'Gang'
have their collars felt

The Inverness Area Gang Show 2001/2003.

THE INVERNESS AREA GANG SHOW
Your P5 class report, 2001

In October 2000 Jamie Gasking, a boy from Aviemore Cubs group started to go to the Inverness Area Gang Show rehearsals in Inverness. On the first day they practised some of the songs and learned some of the actions for them.

By the second rehearsal more people had joined and they started to do some of the actions and the Cubs learned some of their sketch The Wizard of Oz.

As it went on all the sketches got better and better. One night a man came from Moray Firth Radio and recorded them. The night before they went into Eden Court, Alan the keyboard player said to the Cubs and the people who were new, "we're going to make this show the best ever."

When they got into Eden Court they got shown to the dressing rooms and they got their costumes handed out. Derek the Director took the whole cast up on stage to show them the stage. At the first performance Jamie was really excited.

On the Friday night at the Finale the curtain got stuck up and the same thing happened at the interval the next night.

---

25. A poetry workshop
Friday 11 July 2003

The evening of 11th of July was pencilled in my diary for a workshop in Dornoch with the Scottish poet Rhoda Dunbar. I'd been invited by someone from the on-line writers' group. You were going down to Perth with Mum that day so it looked okay. I'd even embarked on a big sort out of all my own poems and songs in honour of the event. It came to around two hundred and twenty in all, some going back as far as when I was at school. With a week to go, I sent an e-mail to check on the arrangements:

> *…as of yesterday I'm into summer-holidays-Dad mode, which tends to mean I follow where the wind blows and try to fit in with everyone else's last minute changes of plan! One son is away playing basketball in Perth all this week and the other is being picked up by his Mum on Friday morning to drive down to collect his brother. Then both of them will be back to hers for the weekend. So…unfore-*

seen events, accidents and deadly diseases aside, the evening looks fairly clear at this stage.

I can report that my "homework" is finished—the marathon poems and songs review is complete. I wouldn't want to do that again in a hurry! Transport remains the BIG issue. Did you hear of anyone who might be passing this way?

The reply that came back was rather a disappointment after all my preparations:

I have been asking around and unfortunately there is no one else coming from as far south as yourself. In fact I get the feeling it may be a rather small affair compared to what was originally intended. As far as I can tell there are only around six people coming to the one in Dornoch. I wouldn't like to drag you all the way up here for something that (what's the buzz term…ah yes…does not meet your expectations). Perhaps it isn't meant to be this time.

Well. As things turned out, I wouldn't have been going to a workshop in Dornoch, or to anywhere else on the planet that night. The entire evening was spent in a fog of ignorance, not knowing whether I might have to jump into a police car at any moment to go down to Bruar. It just wasn't meant to be this time? That's an understatement!

26. A visit to the dentist
Thursday 3 July 2003

At the end of the afternoon on the last day of term we all went to the dentist. We arrived in Grantown with five or ten minutes to spare, so you and I popped into the Coop to pick up a few bits of shopping beforehand. You set off hunting for breakfast cereals while I dealt with the potatoes and vegetables. Do you remember how the lady at the till sent you to see if there were any more of the special-offer boxes of Rice Krispies down by the front door? And you came back grinning so smugly because you'd got us the very last one.

The weather was bright as we carried the bags along the Square to the dentist's and you had a more-than-average spring in your step. After all, it was a once-in-a-lifetime day. No more primary school. You'd had your trial days the week before and Grantown Grammar beckoned. You seemed to have grown up so much in just a few, short months.

Now Mr Wylie examined your teeth and congratulated you that you would be the only one in the family who would never need to have a brace. And of course he was quite right.

27. Hooray for Pooh!
August 2003

So often it can be the simplest and most everyday things that are most painful. Cupboards stocked up with picnic rations for the summer holidays ahead. A freezer full of just the right size portions for *two* boys. Winnie the Pooh on that box of Rice Krispies.

No, you didn't really need another novelty bookmark. But Pooh Bear was always one of your favourites. (You and Grandad both). I'm sure you'll remember when we first got the morphing software for the computer and we had fun switching your head and shoulders with a picture of Winnie the Pooh. A matching pair of cuddly smilers.

That big box of Krispies from the Coop hung around in the cupboard for a long time with the mystery packet buried deep in the bottom. It might have been a Piglet. Or a Tigger. Or just another glum Eeyore like we got in the previous packet. But, of course, what I *really* wanted was to find Pooh Bear himself down there under the Krispies. That's what would have happened in the fairy stories. And everyone would have lived happily ever after too. But like we've said before, things don't always turn out the way we'd like, do they Jamie Man. Consequently I now have *two* plastic Eeyores sitting up on the shelf in the lounge.

28. And hooray for you too!
Tuesday 5 August 2003

We did think about going down to see the cousins on the farm in Wales this week. But in the end Kyle's decided he'd rather just stay at home. Perhaps it's for the best. There's been lots of talk on the radio about trains being delayed because the rails are buckling in the heat. And even if they did run on time, the journey would still take about 14–15 hours door to door. Not much fun in temperatures of 35C and more!

So we didn't need to go to buy train tickets. Somehow though we still ended up cycling to Aviemore. We went down to Christopher's house and Kyle stayed there playing games on the computer, while I carried on for the usual round of tin bank, library, and Tesco's—a painful, slow-motion replay of the day you went to Bruar. Locking up the bike in the same place outside. Stepping inside the door of the shop. Pushing a trolley up and down the aisles. Mooching aimlessly. Staring blankly at meaningless shelves and packages.

And still there are fresh encounters—a long chat with Dr Irvine this time, up by the milk. Further round and there's Mrs Banks at the checkouts with her wee granddaughter, up from England for a summer holiday visit. Outside and I've just finished packing the shopping into the panniers on the bike when...

Hello, you probably don't know who I am, but...

It's Gregor's Mum. She's anxious to tell me about how you spent time looking after her wee boy when he was unhappy going into the nursery. The difference you made. How Gregor came home with stories of his new-found hero. In any other circumstances I guess I would never have known about that at all, Jamie Man. But it made me feel good inside when I heard what Mrs Richards had to say. Hooray for you!

29. The last day of term
Thursday 3 July 2003

School was due to finish at midday on the last day of term but it was quite a while after that when you finally arrived home. You came in and gave me a twirl to display your tatty old Carr-Bridge Primary School sweatshirt in all its new glory—covered in signatures and writing, front and back. Looking at it here now, I can see Bryce and Thomas and Sarah McWilliam and Zoë and Gemma and Cailin and Fergus. Then there's best wishes from Sandra in the Nursery. And a big "Bye!" from Mrs Rennie who taught you in P4. But the crowning glory is on the back, signed by Mrs Banks and Mrs Kirk.

I gave you a hug and told you it was great. Now I had the perfect excuse never to wash that jumper again, didn't I! You were the youngest and you'd put up with all the hand-me-downs. But now primary school was a thing of the past and there was a brand new sweatshirt hanging in the wardrobe ready for the Grammar School after the holidays.

A LETTER FROM MRS KIRK
July 2003

[Jamie]...was always last out of class on a Thursday, and he would have a wee chat about his out-of-school activities, about the Gang Show activities, or what he

was going to do at the weekend. I was very fond of Jamie and I think he knew that, and was able to bridge the Teacher–Pupil gap so that we talked as friends…

---

30. Your friend Mrs Kirk
Tuesday 7 October 2003

Mrs Kirk was unquestionably one of your special people. She goes into school on a different day now. That caught me out and it meant that hers was the very last of the kilt photo cards to be delivered. It's strange how these things work out. That was the day the stone masons brought the headstone to the cemetery, so Mrs Kirk was the first to hear.

I talked to her too about how pleased you'd been with your sweatshirt on the last day of term. She said that it had been a spur of the moment idea. You were the first. She'd got Mrs Banks and the other children who were still around to suggest words to go with the letters of your name. And after that, of course, all the other P7's had been clamouring to have the same on *their* sweatshirts too.

Jolly

Amazing

Marvellous

Incredible

Excellent

What more can I say?

31. Sorting out the school work
Thursday 3 July 2003

Here's another strange thing. Your immediate thought that first afternoon of the holidays, was to settle down and sort through the entire carrier bag full of P7 classwork that you'd brought home with you that day. That was unusual. In previous years you would have put it aside as a job for another day. I suppose that finishing primary school does only happen the once though, doesn't it. Anyway, you seemed to think that the occasion merited picking out the special pieces of work that you particularly wanted to hold on to.

All the written work went on one side for us to look through together later—we had all the time in the world for that. The thing you really wanted to show us then was the artwork that you'd sorted out to add to our collection on the wall in the lounge. There was one picture in particular that Kyle and I both agreed was especially good and you said you wanted to give that one to Mum. She has it in a frame now as you go up the stairs at her house, for everyone to see as they come along the hall.

The really sad thing is that I don't seem to be able to find the jotter with all your stories and other creative writing from P7 now. I can't believe you would have thrown that out. Perhaps it got left at school? I guess I just have to hope it'll turn up somewhere, one day.

32. A weekend of comings and goings
Sunday 6 July 2003

The first weekend of the holidays was a complicated affair. You all came back to Carr-Bridge with Mum in the car on Sunday, plus Kyle's bike on the trailer. You were going to be here that week, but Kyle was the one who was staying on Sunday night. The most immediate problem that afternoon was how to fit the bike into the shed. That was when I remarked that the place was in need of a good sort out. Did your eyes light up? Is the sea wet?

We'd certainly be wanting to get the three bikes in and out more easily than that over the holidays, with all the trips we had in mind. No doubt we'd be out and about in the woods. And the seven miles to Aviemore was well within your grasp these days. We were starting to look further afield now. The new Sustrans off-road cycle track along General Wade's Military Road and over Sluggan Bridge to the Slochd perhaps? Or maybe even all the way over Dava Moor to Lochindorb? Each time the holidays came around, the horizon was just that little bit broader and more exciting. So it was with a summer of adventure in prospect, that Kyle and I waved you and Nicola and Mum off again, as you set out on the first stage of the drive down to Glasgow and Scottish Youth Theatre.

33. Greetings from the London Eye
Thursday 18 July 2002 & Thursday 14 August 2003

I had to clear off the mantelpiece when the chimney sweep came. There was the postcard from the London Eye. A souvenir from the time when you and Kyle and Nicola went down for the day with Mum from Nan's house. I turned it over to refresh my memory:

> *Dear Dad*
>
> *Yesterday we went to London and got* Time stops for no mouse *whitch is the book I have been looking for ages. We also whent on the London Eye and I took some good photos of London. On Monday we went toe Whitby and saw the real yende-ver and bought a poster.*
>
> *From Jamie.*

It took me a while to work out "the real yendever" but I got there in the end—it was Captain Cook's exploring ship, the *Endeavour*. The postmark says 3.00pm on 18 July 2002. A year away. A lifetime away. How can such a few, simple, short lines carry so many tears?

34. One more order to amazon.co.uk
Tuesday 27 May & Sunday 6 July 2003

Back in May, you were giving me instructions on new books to add to my Amazon Wish List. Or perhaps I ought to say *your* Amazon Wish List, since it was mostly all the ones that you fancied! We started off searching for the *Series of Unfortunate Events*, by Lemony Snicket. You'd enjoyed reading the first two stories and now you were keen to track down the rest of the titles in the set.

Then, to your delight, we discovered that the follow-up to your beloved *Time stops for no mouse* book was due out in July. I could recall so many occasions standing at the bus stop waiting to go down to Scouts and you telling me with such eagerness about the adventures of Hermux Tantamoq the mouse. You were so keen to read more that I said I would order the new book so you could have it as soon as it was published. We could call it a welcome-to-the-holidays treat. Of course, that did mean I had to find something for Nicola and Kyle as well.

The much-awaited *Harry Potter and the Order of the Phoenix* was coming out just then, so that went on the list too. Amazon sent Harry straightaway but the rest of the order was being held back waiting for *your* book, due out on the very last day of term. I got to counting down the days. Would Nicola have her choreography book in time for Glasgow? Saturday morning came and with not a single day to spare, the parcel arrived!

So there was a special package for each one of you when you came on that Sunday afternoon. Michael Hoeye's second Hermux Tantamoq adventure, *The Sands of Time*, for you. *The Discworld Companion* for Kyle—Terry Pratchett, of course. And the *Intimate Act of Choreography* for Nicola to take with her to Scottish Youth Theatre. It wasn't exactly a surprise for you, of course. But you took your new book along with you in the car with no less delight for that. And when you arrived back the next day, you told me that you'd read the first chapter to yourself in the Youth Hostel before you went to sleep that night.

35. Back from Pitlochry
Monday 7 July 2003

You reappeared on Monday, brimming with excitement after the big ride to Glasgow. A night in Pitlochry on the way down. Followed by lunch with all Nicola's new summer drama friends. I think the very first thing you asked me when you came in through the door, was whether we could get the projector out one night that week and see all the old slides of Pitlochry again. Back when Nicola was a baby. Highland Perthshire—I guess if my job hadn't changed, we might still have been living there now. But then I might never have had the good fortune of knowing my Kyle and Jamie Men. Who can say what *might* have been? We just have to look ahead and deal with what we get. Not behind.

In fact you'd arrived back earlier than expected that afternoon. So you and Mum had stopped for a pizza at some place in Aviemore before coming on up to Carr-Bridge. You fixed me with that earnest sort of look that said I was about to get some wise advice and told me that you never wanted to go back to eat *there* again. My home-made pizza was far better. What higher praise could I ask for?

But now, if only you could go back…Keep looking forward. Not behind.

36. Plus one go-kart
Sunday 6 July 2003

I'd quite forgotten. Kyle's bike *wasn't* the only thing that you dropped off on the way to Pitlochry, was it, Jamie Man. There was the front end of a go-kart too, the one that you'd "rescued" at the end of the Soap Box Derby the previous weekend. I'd been hearing all about it but it was still a surprise to see just how fancy the whole thing was. The steering mechanism looked like it must have come from a proper motor go-kart.

By the time I got to see it, you'd already done a lot of work stripping it down at Mum's house. You'd got the front cowling off and you'd cleaned it up and decorated it with new plastic tape spelling out *AV*, for the Aviemore Scout Pack. Now you wanted me to help you dismantle the rest in preparation for next year's race. I took a quick look and cautiously suggested that *maybe* we should wait and see how it matched up with what Skip had left over from this year's kart building attempts in Aviemore. What you had here was so good, you might be able to use it just as it was for next year's entry...?

How about we stick it up in the loft for now?

It's still up there in the loft. Waiting for next year. Looking for a new home.

37. The Soap Box Derby
Saturday 28 June 2003

Yes, that final Saturday of June was the famous Scouts annual Soap Box Derby at Inverness Airport. You'd always looked forward to building and racing the go-karts with the Cubs and now this year was going to be your first chance with the Scouts. But then the whole thing was thrown into doubt after Skip broke his ankle at the camp at Loch An Eilein. How could he manage to get go-karts finished with a leg in plaster and only two more Scout nights before the big event? The first week was definitely out. But Skip was still hopeful that he'd be fit enough to hobble in for the second Thursday. It would be cutting it fine, but he was determined to get the work completed in time.

We came to the start of that week still with hopeful fingers and toes crossed for the race on Saturday. And everything was looking fine right up until late on Wednesday evening. Then I had a call from Stephen to say he'd been to the hospital for a check-up that day and the doctors had found that his ankle wasn't setting properly! Poor Skip had had to have the whole break reset and now he was under strict instructions not to move around at all for at least a week. Scouts was off the next day. And so that seemed to be it for any Aviemore entries for the Soap Box Derby this year...

38. A get-together with the Cubs and Scouts leaders
Friday 3 October 2003

Skip (Stephen Macdonald), Chil (Heather Preece) and Arkela (Hazel Hamilton) invited Mum and me out for the evening at one of the hotels in Aviemore. They brought along an album of messages and pictures for us that the Cubs and Scouts had helped to put together. Reminders of so many special occasions. Like the Millennium Camp at Moy and the Pack Weekends at Tomintoul. Snaps of you in the Gang Shows. A Wizard of Oz Munchkin. An American marching bandsman. In rehearsal and up on stage at Eden Court. And of course how could I possibly forget the Cub-Scout Scottish Conference in Aviemore in 2001, when you and Anders treated them to your Laurel (him) and Hardy (you) routine? That's another fine mess you got me into, eh, Jamie Man!

I really like the picture from the barbeque at Loch an Eilein. It's the one where you were teaching everyone the words and the actions for the "Fast Food Song" and they're all laughing and singing along with you.

My other favourite is the action photo of you pushing Chil in the go-kart. Yes, that's right. You *did* get to compete in the Soap Box Derby this year after all, didn't you. Mum dropped you off at the airport so you could go and watch the races and cheer the teams on. But then there was a spare go-kart, so you were able to make up a scratch team with Chil plus one of the lads from Inverness. And I got a cheery phone call telling me how you'd even made it through to the semi-finals. What a bunch of stars!

Arkela told us that they'd organised a special, joint evening for the Cubs and the Scouts at the start of the new session after the summer holidays. And they let them pick the games and activities that they thought *you* would have enjoyed most, Jamie Man. Chil said they got one of the old go-karts out and everyone had a ride, pushing one another around the car park at the Aviemore Centre. I'm sure it must have been a sad evening at times. But I'm glad that they chose to remember you by the fun things. And that the whole pack was involved in putting together the words and pictures in the album.

I gave each of the leaders one of your Gang Show kilt pictures, as my thank you for all the years of joy that the Cubs and Scouts had given to you. And there was one for them to pass on to Iain Macdonald and all your other friends in the Gang Show too.

39. Uncle Bob: almost a go-kart champion
Tuesday 22 July 2003

Go-karts came up again when Uncle Bob, Aunty Pam and Cousin Alan were here the week of the funeral. There are so many jobs that just have to be done at a time like that. And going to see the Registrar the day after you were buried was unfortunately one of them. While Mum and I were doing that, Uncle Bob took Kyle and Alan on the go-karts in the Aviemore Centre, just over the road from the Scout Hut. Kyle was grinning when we met up with them again later on. Evidently Uncle Bob had gone wide on the final bend, allowing Kyle to nip past and beat him to the line. Ha, ha! Uncle Bob likes to win. But so does Kyle. Uncle Bob got a go-kart Fwoggie card from me for his birthday this year. I wonder why…?

40. Hugs and cuddles
Thursday 24 July 2003

Later in the week, Uncle Bob and Aunty Pam took Cousin Alan and Kyle out for a drive round Loch Ness and Urquhart Castle. Once upon a time that was to have been our Thursday and Friday with the hire car to take Grandma and Grandad out sightseeing. Loch Ness had even been mentioned as a possible destination. But now it seemed that the *Oldies* were in need of something rather less tiring at the end of such a difficult week.

The alternative we came up with was afternoon tea at the Speyside Heather Centre with Mr and Mrs Banks. Everyone had a rest and a chat, followed by a gentle browse around the shop and the garden centre. Don't tell her I said this, but I think it's still quite a novelty for Mrs Banks being a grandmother. She was full of *oohs* and *aahs* over all the kids' stuff. But then, it was so easy to imagine a certain wee man I know, going round and falling in love with all the models and gadgets and giant cuddly toys in the shop there…

Just before they went home the following week, Grandma and Grandad brought out three little *Granny Clootie* posters that they'd bought at the Heather Centre that day. One for Mrs Banks and one for Denise Robertson—who'd both been helping out so much that week—and one for me. I've got mine blu-tacked up on the wall in the kitchen now. It helps to remind me of one of the things that you were always so very good at, Jamie Man. I'm sure you'll have seen it there, but this is just to remind you how it begins:

> *There's something in a simple hug that always warms the heart;*
> *It welcomes us back home and makes it easier to part.*

A hug's a way to share the joy and sad times we go through,
Or just a way for friends to say they like you 'cause you're you...

41. Off to the Highland Wildlife Park
Monday 30 June 2003

At the beginning of the final week of term, the whole of Carr-Bridge Primary School went down to see the wolves and the wildcats and all the other animals at the Highland Wildlife Park by Kincraig. It took me back to just such outings when I was your age, Jamie Man. Where did we go? All sorts of places. The Natural History Museum in London. Whipsnade Zoo.

I wonder what little memory snapshots *you* would have put by for your diary, to smile at in years to come? Whatever they were, I'm sure quite you would have linked them up with the day later in the summer when we were planning to take Grandma and Grandad back to the Wildlife Park in the hire car, with you as the expert guide.

Just as you were about to leave the house that Monday morning, I suddenly realised I hadn't given you any money to take with you. You tried to insist you didn't need any more—you'd already had your pocket money that week. But I said not to be silly. This was a special day that deserved a little extra. And anyway, no one was forcing you to spend it—you could always bring it back again! I half expected you to do just that. But in the end, you did buy yourself a couple of small souvenirs from the shop.

The first was a kind of mini-microscope, for examining wee beasties and the like. I showed this to Grandad when he was here and he's taken it home with him as one of his special keepsakes. Maybe he'll be able to use it with Cousin Alan one day.

And then there was the long, stripy snake, who now spends his time woven in and out of the bars on the back of my bed. We had a debate about his name, didn't we. You said you were going to call him Ben. But I said I thought he looked more like a Sid to me—more hissy. Well, whatever you choose to call him, it seems only right somehow that a character like Ben-Sid the snake should have turned out to be one of the very last little treats that you bought for yourself. You never could resist a new soft toy or puppet, especially if it did something to make everyone laugh. Like the Talking Toucan on your desk, who records what you say and then chirps it back to you in a funny voice. Or the famous Barking Dog. And who could forget the bright yellow Millennium Man with his black top hat, who *would* keep on waking us all up in the middle of the night with yet another countdown to the Year 2000 each time you rolled over on top of him in bed?

42. Tying up the loose ends of Primary School
Wednesday 25 June 2003

The Wednesday before you went to the Wildlife Park, I walked up the road for a big occasion of my own. It was twelve years since Nicola started in P1 at Carr-Bridge Primary School. And now here I was on my way to my last ever "Parent Consultation".

Mind you don't step on the wee ones!

That became our chorus as you progressed further and further up the school, didn't it, Jamie Man. It was amazing how the new P1's got steadily wee-er and wee-er every year! Funny, for so many years starting "big school" means moving up from Playgroup and Rising 5's. Then all at once here we are talking about each one of you in secondary school!

Going in to talk about your progress in P7 seemed a bit of a formality, with the end of primary school so close in sight. Well anyway, Mrs Offord was full of praise for your efforts to improve your presentation, which had always been on the...original and creative side? Your class had been having assessments for reading and writing. Spelling was still a bit of a struggle but you'd done okay for your age. Reading comprehension was quite a surprise though. According to the test results, you'd come out at over 15 years old!

Well, I don't think that any of the teachers at Carr-Bridge Primary School had ever found you reluctant to take part in a discussion in class, or to ask questions. And I guess something might have rubbed off from all those hours that we spent reading stories together at home. All in all, Mrs Offord and I agreed that there seemed to be nothing to be concerned about with the move up to the Grammar School. You were ready for it.

43. Going to Big (Primary) School
Tuesday 18 June 1996

Sorting through the bags of work that you brought home from school over the years I came across a drawing marked 18/6/96. Big round body and head, sausage arms, stick legs. A self-portrait?? I don't know. But, from the date, it must be the picture you drew on the day when your group of Rising 5's went in for a first taste of life in "Big School". That seems a long time ago now, Jamie Man—and yet, in another way, just like yesterday.

Jamie and Jasmine go to visit BIG School!

Rising 5's 1996

18 June 1996.

44. Going to Big (Grammar) School
Tuesday 20 May & Wednesday 25–Thursday 26 June 2003

You got your first nibble of secondary school in May. One of the teachers from the Grammar School came to meet the P7's in the morning. And then you all went back over to Grantown in the minibus for a few hours after lunch. But the real adventure came at the end of June. Two whole days. Catching the school bus at eight o'clock in the morning. Lessons, lunch and learning your way around. Meeting all the new teachers and classmates that you'd be working with after the summer holidays.

You were up and ready with half an hour to spare that Wednesday morning. And it was one of those true, lump-in-the-throat moments when I stood at the door and watched the pair of you setting off up the drive to catch the school bus for the first time together. Okay, Kyle would probably go and sit up on top and you'd be somewhere downstairs. But I know it was a special occasion for the two of you as well.

You saved a seat for when Bryce got on at Duthil. The weather was fine and warm. The day was full of wonder. And the timing that afternoon couldn't have worked out better. I was just making my way up the road from my meeting with Mrs Offord, when the school bus arrived back in the village. Which meant that I got the unexpected bonus of walking along the street and down the drive with you as you bubbled over with all the things that you'd been up to. Mr Malcolm next door told me afterwards that he'd overheard our conversation through the fence that day and it was so clear how much you'd enjoyed your first experience of secondary school. I think you made an impression on a lot of the folk over in Grantown too, Jamie Man, even in those two, short days. So many people who tell me how they remember seeing you there so happy and full of enthusiasm.

45. Porridge Day
Sunday 14 September 2003

Today we've had the 10th World Porridge-Making Contest here in the Village. It's grown to be quite an event over the years, with a great deal more than just porridge on the menu these days. This year there's been sideshows, and a car boot sale, and dog races, and—for the first time ever—chainsaw carving. What about that, Jamie Man! Sawdust and shavings a-plenty. The competitors started at eleven with sections of tree trunk nearly as tall as themselves. And they were sawing and shaping until three o'clock. It was great for the spectators because you could keep popping back to see how they were getting on. I met Councillor Black down there and he agreed that chainsaw carving was just the thing for Carr-Bridge, with all the forest round about. The Landmark Centre sponsored the competition and it sounds like they plan to make it a regular event from now on. I could just imagine you there, right at the front of the crowd, watching every move and dreaming of the day when you could have a go yourself.

There were four men taking part. First prize went to a bear cub climbing up a tree. At the end—after the racing dogs had finished trying to eat one another—the carvings were auctioned off and the winner went for £230! The runner up was a girl's head with long hair, and that went for £160. Not bad for four hours work, eh, Jamie Man!

Councillor Black told me he remembered you as the wee lad who stood up and spoke out at the public meeting in the Village Hall last year, when we all got together to discuss the proposals for building houses in the woods. He said how very impressed he'd been by the clear and sensible way you talked about the things that mattered most to you.

46. The famous fifty ton all-terrain crane
Sunday 14 September 2003

Few toys ever managed to rival the broom or the hoover when you were small. I told Councillor Black how you were always fascinated by tools of any kind. That got me on to the story of when they were building the new water slides at Landmark back in 1997, when you were in P1. Remember, we went over the road to see how they were getting on and we met one of the engineers who was in charge of the job? He was very proud of his giant, fifty-ton, all-terrain crane that they were using to do the work on the wet, boggy ground. Your eyes couldn't have been any bigger, or brighter.

Fifty tons!

I could see the cogs working in your head. What more could you ask for? You could build anything, anywhere with a fifty-ton, all-ter-rain c-rane. From that moment on the name slipped into the word book of family folklore. Blu-tack or cellotape might not always work, but with a famous fifty-ton, all-ter-rain c-rane at your disposal, *anything* was possible—you simply couldn't fail to get the job done, could you, Jamie Man!

47. Back in uniform
Tuesday 8 July 2003

The first morning back from Glasgow you were up and raring to go with a hatful of ideas for the week ahead. So what was it going to be to start with, on our first full day together? A big bike ride? Exploring in the woods? A picnic perhaps? Or…

> *Landmark!? Again?? Ok–kay. If that's what you want. I think we know the way by now. And no doubt it won't be the last trip across the road this summer…*

Yes, at the time it may have seemed like a very unexceptional start to the week. But then, things can appear different later, looking back. What price do you put on a last ever visit? It's difficult to avoid the feeling now, that in the course of those final, few days, some strange instinct led you to revisit every single place that had come to be special or important to you in one way or another: in the house, in the garden, around the village, in the woods. And retracing the route to Landmark that Tuesday morning was the first step. Then after lunch? What was next on your agenda? You got it—that shed!

> *Well, fair enough. If you're sure that's what you want to do, Jamie Man. It certainly could do with a good clear out. And a bit more space for getting the bikes in and out would be useful. But if we're going to do that, then you'll need to go and find some old clothes that won't matter if they get spoiled…*

It was quite amusing really. You went off into the bedroom and then reappeared a few minutes later wearing…yes, your old Carr-Bridge Primary School uniform! And you were quite right of course. You certainly wouldn't be needing *that* any more! We'd been eking out those tired old joggers and sweatshirts to the end of term. But now they'd more than reached their sell-by date. We had a little laugh about it together as we went round the back of the house to set about emptying everything out of the shed.

48. Echoes and earliest memories
Summer 1993–summer 2003

You were always so proud that your earliest memory went right back ten whole years to the summer of 1993, when the builders had just started work on our new house here. We were staying down near Kincraig then, but you didn't remember that. Nor the dry ski slope and the big trees that were here on the site before. What you remembered was the weekend when we drove up with a picnic to see how Macleod Building were getting on. And you thoroughly enjoyed yourself wobbling along the top of the foundations. It's strange how your first memory—of builders at work—so closely echoes my own. That was the summer of 1958 when I watched with my big brother—Uncle Bob—as the men came and built a new motorway across the end of our road. Now they call it the M1.

There wasn't a word in Gaelic for ski slope. They didn't have such things back in the old days. So we called our new house *Seann Bhruthach*—old slope—so that people wouldn't forget that it was built on a site that was previously used by one of Scotland's earliest skiing pioneers, the Austrian Karl Fuchs. That was when our garden was still part of the Struan House Hotel. It's good to think we live on a piece of land with all those echoes and memories of the past. So your story will be in good company, Jamie Man.

49. Clearing out the shed
Tuesday 8 July 2003

Welcome to a magic cave between the stick pile and the log pile. Part of that constant cycle of winter fuel. Chainsawing and chopping. Sacks of sawdust and kindling. We're still burning wood from before the house was built. Anything at all that will help to see us through the cold months. Who knows when it might go down to minus 25C again?

I passed the things out to you, and you organised them all in your own, highly-individual way round the back and along the side of the house. It calls to mind one of those school reading books from P1 or P2 days. The type that's basically just one big, long list of marvellous and intriguing objects. You had parking spaces to find for three bicycles and the garden trolley that I made for shifting rocks when I was building the drystone wall. There were bits of plank and old fence posts to be sorted out and arranged. The lawn mower, the strimmer and garden tools of all descriptions. A hosepipe that was most reluctant to unwind itself from the comfortable shape that it had settled into since the last time we needed to water the garden—several summers back. Wood preservative, white spirit, chainsaw oil, motor oil and an ancient tin of grease. Sacks of kindling for the stove and those bags of sawdust not to be wasted. And then there was the fence wire and all sorts of other sneaky junk that had crept away into the corners over the years. Before we finally got right down to the big sycamore logs at the bottom of the pile.

What an empty and unfamiliar sight! And what a museum of your lifetime arrayed outside. No wonder we fell to reminiscing about days spent toddling around the foundations. Or that I had to rack my brains to recall where those sycamore trees had been. It's always a shame to see trees cut down. And we did try to keep as many as possible. But there were some of the big pines overhanging the ski slope that simply had to go to make room for the house. And they'd been hacked around so much over the years that they weren't in very good shape anyway. Unfortunately, when Ramie Taylor got to work with his JCB and started to excavate the ski slope, we found there were other trees, like the sycamores along the back fence, that were left with their roots sticking out two or three feet above the ground! And so they did have to come down too.

But we replanted more new trees than we cut down. So now, almost ten years later, the garden's more leafy than before we started. And of course I certainly wasn't going to let all that good timber and firewood go to waste, was I! The giant pine trunks and branches went on the wood pile to be chopped up over the years for keeping us warm. But I found a special place for those sycamore logs, away at the back of the shed, when you were still that wee toddler. And I always promised myself that *one day* I'd find the time to make use of them for some really *big* wood carving.

Well, of course, time moves on faster than our daydreams. But now here you were getting into the wood carving for yourself. And we talked about how, even if I never got round to it, those logs would still always be there for you to make use of when you were a bit older. Your eyes shone at the thought of such a juicy prospect for the future.

50. A week is a long time
Tuesday 8 July & Monday 28 July 2003

A week since the funeral.

Two weeks since the Book of Condolences.

Three weeks since you arrived back from taking Nicola to Glasgow.

Four weeks since you came home from the Wildlife Park with Ben-Sid the snake.

On my way back through the woods alongside Landmark today, I came across a log left over from the recent tree felling. One tiny part of the work on the new road to the overflow car park they're building out into the woods at the back behind the fire tower. I picked up that lump of wood and carried it home as a keepsake of our first and last trip across the road to Landmark these summer holidays.

We started with a quick run down one of the water slides. The middle one with the bumps, I think it was. The *Wildcat*. But the Scottish schools were all on holiday by then, and the queues were quite long, so we didn't bother to wait to go on the steep drop of the *Falcon*, or the spirals of the *Otter*. Plenty of time for that later in the holidays. We were more curious to see what was going on in the woods out the back. We thought it must be something to do with the new car park. And we reckoned we ought to be able to get a better view from the top of the fire tower. In fact, at that time there really wasn't much more to see, even from up there. We could hear the chainsaws hard at work down in amongst the trees. But it was still too early to tell what the final shape of things was going to be.

There was a family up at the top of the tower at the same time. The Dad was asking the kids how many steps they thought they'd climbed to get up there. After they'd made their various, wild guesses, you gave them the correct answer: one hundred and eight. Ten flights of ten, plus four more up to the final viewing platform and a further two on either side to the top balcony. I wonder whether that family would remember the conversation now? Or how the Dad suggested it sounded like we must go up there quite often? I had to agree with him, we did. But in all those countless visits to Landmark, I can't recall a single occasion when I went down the water slides in one of the boats on my own. I always used to tease you that you made a good shield for catching the water splashes. And now I don't think I want to go down a water slide without my shield.

51. The new car park takes shape
Wednesday 23 July & Monday 27 October 2003

Of course, those chainsaws didn't stop work just because our world came to a halt, Jamie Man. And it was quite a different scene there just two weeks later, when I returned for my one and only other climb up the Landmark tower this summer. This time it was with Kyle and Cousin Alan, two days after your funeral. By then the beginnings of the first, big clearing were plain to see. And now, with the October holidays behind us, you don't need to go up the tower at all to be able to inspect the enormous new car park that they've created to deal with all the extra visitors who've been coming to Landmark since the water slides were opened.

I guess that might sound bad, cutting down all those trees. Actually though, I'm not too upset about it. The cars were spilling out all over the village in the summer. And if they had to make a new car park anywhere, then better up the back there than somewhere more obvious. The place where they've put it was once an old waste tip for the village and the ground there was full of glass and metal and all sorts of other rubbish. Quite dangerous for dogs and for the wild animals. So you could almost say it's an improvement.

I'm not going to burn that log from outside Landmark. I've left it in the porch to dry out slowly and one day maybe I'll have the chance to carve it into something special to keep in the house. Not necessarily anything recognisable. Perhaps just a very smooth surface that will feel good to the touch. A solid reminder of some of those small and unremarkable moments that went to make up the shape of our time together.

52. Wood in the porch
Tuesday 8 July 2003

There was no need to take the big sycamore trunks right out of the shed. Shifting them around was enough to allow a good sweep up of all the sawdust and everything else that had wormed its way down between them over the years. That was dusty, sneezy work, eh, Jamie Man! But what a difference afterwards when they were wrestled back into place. Then all that remained was to deal with the catalogue of stuff outside…

What an assortment of wood! Joiners' leftovers from when the house was built. My off-cuts from the playhouse. Posts, poles, planks and other scavengings from round and about. We sifted through the pile to pick out some of the better pieces that were worth putting up in the loft with all the other "building supplies". And you carried those round to the front door for me, while I got on with stacking everything else back inside the shed.

It was only when we were finished outside that I discovered that we could hardly move in the porch for wood! We had a smile about that and agreed that it could all just stay there till the next day. It might give Ian the postman a bit of a problem if he came with any parcels in the morning. And it wouldn't be the route for an emergency evacuation in the night. But otherwise, it wasn't going to be in anybody's way. Thank goodness for back doors, eh!

53. Making dinner and make-believe
Tuesday 8 July 2003

We came in from the shed creaking and groaning, and you disappeared off into the lounge for a wee rest. You were working your way through the *Muppets* videos, yet again. Two minutes later, however, you were back…

> *Da–add…Can I go and unlock the shed and get trolley out again?*

So while I fixed dinner, there you were outside once more, gathering up all those scrap fence posts and planks that we'd just dumped out on the stick pile!

And bit by bit you trolleyed them round the house to construct yourself a new make-believe "road" across the patio and along the path to a checkpoint by the back gate. You and that trolley—love at first trundle!

When I look out of the kitchen window these days you are still there, pacing up and down the course of your road, balancing from one rock to the next along the line of spare stones that were left over from building the wall. And, as always, you're talking and waving your arms, recounting the whole story to yourself as you go. I can't catch the words, but I still hear the murmur of your voice. It's the same wherever I turn to look—the patio, the path to the gate, the ski slope, the stick pile, the shed, the playhouse, the lawn, the playpark over the fence, or out and about in the woods—there is nowhere that is not touched by the echo of your voice and the mark of your footprints, my Jamie Man.

TO NICK PARK OF AARDMAN ANIMATIONS
A letter, Tuesday 29 July 2003

Dear Nick,

I am writing this by way of a thank-you letter though, as you will see, the circumstances are far from joyful.

Just over two weeks ago my youngest son Jamie, aged 11, was killed in a fall while out walking at the Falls of Bruar in Perthshire. For a few days the story was headline news in the media and then the press moved on.

Whenever Jamie was asked what he wanted to do when he grew up there was never a moment's doubt or hesitation in his response—he was going to be an animator like Nick Park. If it came to a choice of his favourite videos, I guess that only Jim Henson and his puppets could be considered a serious rival for Wallace & Gromit, Morph *and the Aardman Classics.*

During the final week that Jamie and I spent together while his older brother and sister were away on their own summer activities, we talked (as so often before) of the animation studio that he and I would build in our loft one day when he was grown up. Even now, I still find myself surrounded by evidence of the make-believe that was so much a feature of Jamie's life, right down to the half-finished cardboard theatre that he was in the process of building on my kitchen floor, for use in his plasticine rehearsals.

One of my happiest memories will always be of one rainy day some time in the school holidays when Jamie had made his "Gromit" and his brother, Kyle, had made his "Wallace" (complete with two lolly stick skis on his shoulder). We set up the camera on the tripod and ran off an entire film of simple 35mm shots that we planned to morph on the computer to produce their first little simple "film". It is hard to think of an occasion when so much pleasure was generated all round from such simple things.

It is sad fact that accidents do happen, and sometimes with tragic results. My Jamie will never have the chance now to grow up and realise his dream of making a career in animation. Nonetheless I would still like to take this opportunity to express my thanks to you and your colleagues at Aardman for the joy and magic that you brought to my son during his short but busy life.

A few days ago I was putting together a list of thoughts under the title of What is "okay"? and the final poem included the following line:

"Okay, is a homemade Gromit…and plasticine in the carpet"

Which, to me, seemed to sum up the working priorities of an 11-year old, aspiring animator.

So, once again, my thanks for all your work.

Yours sincerely,

David Gasking

---

54. Up in the loft
Wednesday 9 July 2003

Well, the very first task on Wednesday morning was to do something about that heap of wood in the porch, of course. I set up the stepladder, you did the fetching, and little by little it all disappeared up into the loft, followed by your go-kart bits from the Soap Box Derby. When that was all done—surprise, surprise—you wanted to go up for a look yourself. I extended the ladder so you could climb up and we perched together on the boards in the middle to survey the scene.

A jumble of timber and boxes. Old costumes and equipment from past School Fun Days. The cross country skis. All the old carpet and lino offcuts. And Uncle Tom Cobbley and all. Where would we put all the stuff if we ever got the money to finish building up there, you wondered? I grinned and said something about finding a spot for it all…*somewhere*. For now it remained a giant playground for the imagination.

We talked about go-kart designs for 2004. Ideas for the summer holidays. How different this big, open barn might look one day with walls and a floor. A new bedroom for each of us? A shower room? Another upstairs living room perhaps? It's all there on the plans and waiting to happen. Or maybe, we dreamed, that animation studio that we'd talked so often about...? One thing was so clear in your conversation: you never pictured yourself living anywhere else when you were grown up, but here in this house...

A WALLACE & GROMIT CARD FROM NICK PARK
Saturday 11 January 2003

Dear David

You wrote to me in July '03 about the tragic loss of your son Jamie. I apologise for this late reply. I have often meant to write but with shooting the latest Wallace & Gromit film—I hope you will understand.

Like many, I'm sure, I was very saddened to hear of Jamie's accident and I wanted to offer my condolences too. You also told me of his life and interests and I was encouraged to hear how our work had inspired him. I felt honoured to think that Wallace & Gromit had become such a part of his world.

Jamie reminded me a lot of myself at that age—so prolific and enthusiastic about life and with so many hobbies and interests.

Thank you for sharing something of Jamie's life and your memories with me and for your encouragement. Very much appreciated.

Very best wishes.

Nick Park

Caution, animators at work!

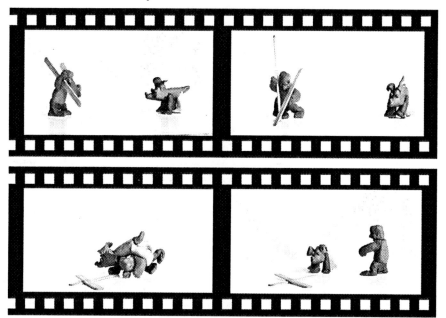

The card from Nick Park, with scenes from your own "film", April 2002.

55. Thanks for the memory
Wednesday 30 July 2003

At the end of July, I wrote a letter to the *Strathy*, to thank all the people who'd helped us out in so many different ways since your accident. It was one of those times when it felt like everything was crowding in on me from all sides. Problems to sort out. Constant telephone calls. Arrangements to be made. The day the *Strathy* came out I needed to escape for a while and be with you. I sat up on the grass at the cemetery and looked at the letter in the paper. I'd included a copy of the "okay" poem that I told Nick Park about, along with a brief explanation of how it came about:

> *At times like this we find ourselves repeatedly asking one another "are you okay?" A few days back my Dad—Grandad—posed me the question in reply, "what is okay?" I suppose each of us would have a different answer, but this is what I eventually came up with for him.*

WHAT IS "OKAY"?

Okay, is a touch of bitter amidst a field of sweet
Okay, is going for gold and coming home with a sticker
Okay, is time with you in the garden and the housework left undone
Okay, is "Dad...have you got...?"—that's another trip to the loft
Okay, is some old bits of wood and a feast of make-believe
Okay, is a homemade Gromit...and plasticine in the carpet
Okay, is "how does that work?" and "can you mend this?"
Okay, is those creaks and groans after saying goodnight to you
Okay, is walks in the woods and stories read aloud
Okay, is the odd wrong note and a happy, smiling face
Okay, is two, whole days at Grantown Grammar School
Okay, is shedding tears in the arms of loving friends
Okay, is not losing you even when you're out of sight
Okay, is no regrets for a short but busy life...well done

---

56. The touch of bitter
Saturday 6 September 2003

When I look back on the eleven years I was privileged to share with you, my Jamie Man, I find that it's the small incidents—the trivial, the odd, the crazy—that spring most readily to mind. These are in every sense the bitter-sweet memories. Carrying with them the most joy and at the same time the most pain. When the tears flow and the waves of sorrow roll over me for the times ahead that should have been and now can never be.

I opened up my heart to my children. There were choices. And when it came to weighing up what really mattered, it seemed to me that the most valuable gift I had to offer was my *time*. I built my castle with simple stones. I set up the strongest defences I could muster to keep you safe from the world and all its perils. But ultimately none of that was enough. We found ourselves confronted with a future that was beyond any power of my imagination to anticipate, or to protect you from. I am constantly reminded of the final verse of the Streetsweeper's song in *The Piper*, when he sings about his daughter:

> *My child is the future*
> *And (she) is the promise*
> *That makes it all worthwhile*
> *Though some folks might say I have little to offer (her)*
> *The treasure we have is not measured in gold*
> *For we share a life that's built on the precious stones no one can steal*

I came across something you wrote about me in your homework back in P6:

> *I admire my Dad because he does lots of things with me and he is very funny. He is very kind. He plays lots of games with me and gives me lots of presents.*

Were there truly so very many presents? Or was it really just "being together"?

57. The famous Loch Vaa bike lock incident
Monday 15 October 2001

One of the crazy little memories that has often come back to me in these recent, bleak months, is the case of the famous Loch Vaa bike lock incident. You know those occasions when we grit our teeth and tell ourselves, we really will look back on this and laugh in years to come. As with all such tales, we're familiar with the mythology. But is that *really* how it happened? Or has the story grown with the telling? Well, I found the e-mail I sent to Andrea in Germany that same evening, so I think this ought to be fairly reliable.

It was the beginning of the October holidays. The week before, the doctor had given you your first asthma inhaler. But there was something wrong with it and by the first weekend it was empty. So we needed a trip to Aviemore to pick up a replacement…

> …*after lunch the sun came out and we all set off on our bikes. The boys rode with me as far as Loch Vaa, a beauty spot about 6–7km along the road. I was going to go on from there to Aviemore (another 4–5km) to collect the prescription and then pick up a few bits of shopping. We locked up their bikes and they went off for a walk alongside the loch, skimming stones, etc.*
>
> *By the time I set off from Aviemore, with the shopping in the panniers and the rucksack, the rain had returned. The sky was black and all the cars were driving around with their headlights on. Back at Loch Vaa the boys were sheltering under the trees and they had moved their bikes under cover too, locking them up to a handy tree. Which was fine…until we discovered that Kyle's bike lock was jammed and we couldn't get it unfastened! And no, I wasn't going to uproot a full-sized birch tree to carry it home with us!*
>
> *Then, still worse, the key broke off in the lock while I was trying to get it open! Double stuck!*
>
> *So, in the end all I could do was to leave Kyle there, ride back home with Jamie in the pouring rain, dump all the shopping out of the panniers, leave him to have a hot shower, pack up some tools and then ride back down to Loch Vaa to cut the chain off and bring Kyle home!!!! Fortunately the clouds blew away and we were just able to make it back here before it started to get dark.*
>
> *All this means that my "simple" little trip to pick up an inhaler, turned into a marathon ride of about 35km and by the time everybody had put the bikes away, got out of their soaking wet clothes and had a hot shower, we didn't get dinner until 8.00pm.*
>
> *After a weekend of chopping more wood and restacking the log pile, I had been thinking of a nice, peaceful day to rest my aching bones. Huh!! Soaked to the skin, frozen, stiff, creaking—what fun the holidays can be!*
>
> *So, tell me. How was your day, my dear?*

58. Just another routine trip to Aviemore
Friday 11 July 2003

I'd been pottering through my Friday morning. I got the bike out. The tyres were a bit soft, so I paused to pump them up. Half past eleven came and went. Suddenly I realised I'd need to get a move on if I was going to make the library before they closed at 12.30. But it was a fine day. Perfect conditions for a quick zip down the road to Aviemore—pedalling past Loch Vaa, scene of our famous bike lock incident.

I fastened the bike up outside Tesco's and puffed into the library with ten minutes to spare. Helen the library lady greeted me with her usual, cheery smile and we chatted away the remaining minutes until closing time, just like all those other occasions when you came in with me to take the books back before Scouts.

Those Cubs and Scouts nights were the fixed centre of our week. A hurried dinner—bacon rolls, hot dogs, scrambled eggs on toast, or some such—then dashing out to catch the bus. And you always enjoyed popping in to the library to say hello before going over to meet up with Skip and all your friends at the Scout hut. I'm sure we must have kept Aviemore library going single-handed with all our book requests. Helen had only just told me that they'd decided to buy all the rest of the *Jennings* series that you'd been enjoying so much. I think we'd read about fourteen of them already.

So many regular, everyday people who got to know you over the years: bus drivers; Helen in the library; the staff in Tesco's; drivers from the Community Car Scheme who gave us a lift back each week with the shopping. So many folk who all say now how much they miss the sight of your familiar, cheery face.

59. Playing the time game
July 2003

It's many years now since I wore a watch. Every day is twenty four hours long. Every hour has sixty minutes. Yes, of course we checked the clock for catching the bus, or setting off for school, or getting to the library before it closed. But for so many other "important" things, plus or minus ten minutes—what did it really matter? The time game was one more of those little bits of fun that grew up with the three of you over the years.

The other two are a bit big for stories in bed these days. But you still liked to come and climb in for another chapter before breakfast. *Swallowdale* by Arthur

Ransome was our latest book. And on school days, you still enjoyed playing the same old game: I had to guess the time and you would check the clock radio:

> *No, I am not cheating, Jamie Man. I can't even see the radio without my glasses on, can I!*

A minute either way signalled a good day. Four to five minutes...so, so. Ten minutes was a pretty good indication that Dad wasn't quite on the ball yet. On average, what do you reckon? Plus or minus two minutes? Three perhaps? Who needs a watch!

Recently though, hmmm...I've ventured into some strange and unfamiliar territory. I don't know how well I would score on the time game these days, Jamie Man.

60. Somewhere in Tesco's
Friday 11 July 2003

It seems like you'll always bump into someone from Carr-Bridge wandering around the aisles in Tesco's. Sometimes it'll be a leisurely chat. On other occasions, more like a frantic wave and "I should have been somewhere else ten minutes ago." That particular Friday lunchtime, there was Foster McGowan up by the meat and fish counter, exchanging a few words in passing. My library panic was over and there was no particular rush anymore. The playhouse was not going to run away!

Shopping on the bike is all about sizing up what'll fit into the panniers and the rucksack. Like the time game, it comes with practice. The list that day? Nothing special. The usual suspects. But I can't ever forget the punnet that went in on the top—a treat for my big plum fan to enjoy when he came home on Monday. I see them again every time I approach the fruit counter, Jamie Man. To say nothing of every time I pick up a plum. It's the same with the vegetables. I wonder if you were the only eleven-year old boy in the world who would always give *cucumber* as his favourite food?

Yasmin Harrower from P6 and her Mum Caroline were at the next checkout. It's not the easiest place to talk but we managed a smile and a few words. From what I've learned since from the Procurator Fiscal, that must have been just about the moment...

It would have been around half past one by the time I set off up the road on my well-laden ride back to Carr-Bridge. Pumping up the tyres had made all the difference. Lunch would be late yet again. But with the long summer evenings, there was still plenty of time for playhouse painting. Or if not today, certainly before you came back.

61. Your first ever text message
Thursday 10 July & Wednesday 3 September 2003

Painting jobs may have been uppermost in my mind as I rode home from Aviemore that day. But it was not until nearly two months later that it came back to me that I'd sent you a text message on that very subject the night before. From the computer to Mum's mobile phone. Just a wee newsflash on my progress with the shed after you'd left on the bus. I asked Mum about it afterwards and she said that the message had arrived in time for you to read it just before you settled down to sleep that night.

When I clicked *SEND* that Thursday evening, I was sure I could picture the joy on your face when you received your first ever text message. On this morning in September, I stood under the shower and wept yet again for a happy memory suddenly recalled to mind, but now burdened with the overwhelming weight of sadness. How could I possibly have imagined that your first ever text message, was destined also to be your last?

62. One message on my answer machine
Friday 11 July 2003

…there's been an awful, awful accident…

I think Mum had left the message about twenty minutes earlier. Somewhere around the time when I would have been on the road coming past Loch Vaa. I sank back in the chair and took several deep breaths. Just how bad was an awful accident?

Had there been a crash while the two of you were driving down to Perth?

Were you in hospital?

Was it Nicola down in Glasgow?

Or Kyle at the basketball camp?

Someone else?

I picked up the phone and rang the number of Mum's mobile, telling myself all the while that there was no sense in fearing the worst. Whatever it was that had happened, things were bound to sort themselves out.

63. My dream
Tuesday 26 August 2003

You came into my dreams for the first time last night, Jamie Man. I was on the track that runs up between the Church and the Village Hall. There was a line of tables with telephones and one of them was ringing. I picked up a phone but it wasn't the right one. Nor was the next. When I tried the third, I heard your voice at the other end. You said "hello" in a jokey sort of way and then gave a little giggle. But before I got the chance to hear what else you had to say, the buzzer on my clock radio went off. Ten to seven, time for the start of another day. I lay in bed, half way between awake and asleep.

I felt frustrated. But at least you had sounded happy. Dreams can sometimes come back again, can't they, Jamie Man. Do you think one day I might get the chance to hear what it was you were calling to tell me last night...?

The strange thing is, I do have a recording of that same little voice saying "hello" like that and then cutting off. It's the only thing on the answerphone tape before Mum's message from Bruar. It must have been a leftover from one of your weekend calls sometime. I can't explain, however, why just that one, tiny snippet should have survived, when the rest of the message was recorded over...?

Hello...

I'm looking forward so much to your next call, Jamie Man.

64. You and Kyle on tape
Friday 31 May 2002 & Thursday 31 July 2003

There are photographs. There are countless hours of video from all the various stage performances. But apart from that brief, chance snippet on the answerphone, I didn't seem to have any other recording of you speaking, Jamie Man. Is that strange? The world loves pictures. But that's no substitute for the sound of your voice. It never struck me before, but you were always filmed when you were doing something in a group—never alone. Such a simple thing to sit you down in front of a microphone...But then, which of us ever imagines that the voice of the child that greets us so cheerily in the morning, might be switched off forever by the evening...?

Then suddenly at the end of July it came to me. A vague memory of recording you and Kyle playing snatches of music on all the different instruments. And *talking* in between. I racked my brains. Kyle had had the saxophone...so it must have been...sometime last year...? Slowly the pieces came together in my head.

I'd recorded some programmes off the radio for Grandad. Melvyn Bragg on Chaos Theory, of all things. There'd been some space left on the end of the tape and we'd decided to give Grandma and Grandad a surprise treat. So we spent a whole Friday afternoon filling up the rest of the cassette with a mixture of music and your commentary.

Grandad's hunted the cassette out and posted it up to me. I have it here in the drawer in my bedroom now. Like all the other recordings, I haven't listened to it again yet, but I will...one day. I see that it's dated just before the School Fun Day last year. There's a recording of the tune for the "Going for gold" song that I'd written for you all to sing that day, with World Cup year and the Queen's Golden Jubilee much in the news.

GOING FOR GOLD
Carr-Bridge Primary School Fun Day 2002

When you run the race
Or you shoot for goal
Spare a thought for others
You can try your best
You can aim to win
But don't lose sight of your neighbour

> *Gold, silver, bronze are one sort of treasure*
> *But first, second, third are not all that matter*
> *Win, lose or draw, there's always the pleasure,*
> *The game and the team and working together*
> *Gold, silver, bronze are one sort of treasure (rpt)*

With your sights set high
You can run, jump, throw
Faster, higher, further
But remember there
May be other things
That count as much as a medal

> *Gold, silver, bronze are one sort of treasure...etc*

---

65. An afternoon of uncertainty
Friday 11 July 2003

When I came off the phone from talking to Mum, I still didn't really know what had happened. I told myself to stay calm. You'd had some kind of fall. That much was clear. But what did that...?

DON'T FEAR THE WORST! Wait for news.

And meantime be ready to...to what? Broken bones would mean hospital. I'd have to get down to Perth somehow. I'd probably have to stay overnight too, like when the school bus went off the road and Nicola was knocked unconscious.

So what about Kyle then? Where would *he* go if I had to be away? That's when I picked up the phone and tried to call Mr and Mrs Banks. They were out. What could I say to their answerphone? No point in worrying people unnecessarily.

Hello, Helen and David. Something's come up. I'm not sure of the details yet, but it looks like I might need some help with the boys...

Mum had said to talk to Chris in Cromdale. Richard's Mum. By the time I spoke to her, she'd already been in touch with the basketball people about getting Kyle and Richard back from Perth. Neither of us had transport and we were both working totally in the dark. No clear idea what had happened, or what arrangements we were supposed to be making. All we could do was to wait for more word and agree to keep in touch...

I drifted round the house, working on automatic. I put the shopping away and got something ready to eat. I've no idea what time it was when I finally sat down for lunch. Well after three o'clock, certainly. It was the first of many meals eaten with wooden jaws and tasting like cardboard. I was completely in limbo. My legs were wobbly from the cycling. Trying to get hold of anyone else would only block up the phone for incoming calls.

Where were you, my Jamie Man? In an ambulance with flashing blue lights? Chatting breezily with some doctor in casualty at Perth Royal Infirmary? Or maybe just getting patched up at the surgery in Pitlochry? Cuts and bruises, or broken bones would soon mend. Knocked unconscious? They'd sort that out too...wouldn't they?

JUST DON'T FEAR THE WORST! Wait for news...

66. Andrew Dale: the hero
Friday 11 July 2003

Andrew Dale was the man who went all on his own to try to rescue you. There's no question about it, he was a genuine hero, putting himself at risk for you, Jamie Man.

Andrew just happened to be visiting the Falls of Bruar with his family that day. It could have been anyone. Who would believe that the first person Mum came across when she ran for help would be a member of the Galloway Mountain Rescue Team? He didn't have all the usual gear with him, of course. But he knew what was needed in an emergency. And he didn't hesitate.

Andrew sent his wife, Pamela, to call for the emergency services and his daughter, Nicola, to fetch the first aid kit from the car. Then he set about trying to climb down the side of the cliff to find you. He started at the place where you fell but he couldn't get more than half way down there. So he had to climb back up and try again further along for an alternative route. Once he'd found his way down to you, he moved you to a safe place, wrapped you up in his jacket and did all the important first aid checks before going back to guide the emergency teams in when they arrived. But even then, when the mountain rescue people were there with all the proper equipment, he still refused to leave your side through all the remaining hours it took to get you back out.

Andrew Dale didn't hesitate to put his own life in jeopardy to try to help you. I know I've wished so many times that I could have been there with you myself, Jamie Man—and yes, that it could have been me instead of you. But quite honestly, I know that we could not possibly have asked more from anyone than Andrew did for you that day. It is a great comfort to know that you had the company of such a fine and brave person.

67. Courage recognized
Monday 13 October 2003

When I heard what Andrew had done, I felt the least I could do was to make sure that his courage did not go unrewarded. I remembered how Claire's brother Ross got an award for bravery when he jumped into the river to rescue the ladies whose car had gone off the road. In my opinion, Andrew Dale deserved no less.

Today I had a call from the Royal Humane Society to say that my nomination has been accepted and that Andrew is to be awarded what they call a *Testimonial on Vellum*. That's a very fancy certificate that has to go all the way to Buckingham Palace to be signed by Princess Alexandra. I was so pleased. When the certificate is ready, I'm hoping we can invite Andrew and his family up for a very special weekend, to show that they'll always be admired and welcomed by everyone who knew you here in Carr-Bridge.

Andrew Dale—another BIG guy—with the Royal Humane Society Certificate.

You know, Jamie Man, when the Royal Humane Society called this morning, I was in the middle of playing "Highland Cathedral" on your big whistle. The same tune that Mr Barnes your chanter teacher played for us at the graveside on the afternoon of your funeral.

68. A harsh and rugged land
Tuesday 21 October 2003

It must have been some fifteen years since I last visited the Falls of Bruar—when we were still living in Pitlochry and Nicola was just a wee toddler. Back then, you simply pulled off the road and wandered up the path past the old hotel on the way to the Falls. It was all very different when I went back there last week. The old Bruar Falls Hotel is long since demolished and in its place there's the brand-new House of Bruar, with its giant carpark, bringing the coach parties and passing tourists flocking in by the hundred.

Now, a week later, and three months to the day since we stood at your graveside and Mr Barnes played "Highland Cathedral", I've been speaking on the phone with the Factor of Atholl Estates, the landowners at Bruar. Yesterday there was a similarly-long talk with a man from Perth & Kinross Council, who manage the paths there for public access.

I've had all sorts of conversations these past few months. It's impossible to know what to expect. In fact, as a parent of young children, I found the Factor deeply shocked by what had happened. In the end I think we must have talked for about two hours or more.

There are risks in all walks of life. Scotland is a beautiful but harsh and rugged land. You can't put a cage around the countryside. What you can try to do, is to teach people how to treat the land with respect, to be aware of the dangers, and to know how best to protect themselves from harm. Your death was a tragic accident, Jamie Man. There's nothing to be gained from a witch-hunt, or seeking to point the finger of blame. That will not help to bring you back. The closing words of my conversation with the Factor today were concerned with positive action for the future, not recrimination.

69. A call from the doctor
Friday 11 July 2003

What's worse? The phone that stays silent when you're waiting for it to ring? Or the sudden shock of the sound that tells you there's no longer any escape? Did I look at the clock? Maybe. But if so I don't remember what time it said. I guess it must have been after half past three. Four o'clock perhaps? Who knows? Another deep breath and I picked it up.

A woman's voice. She gave a name, Dr Jan Calder from Edinburgh. At the time it didn't register at all. She began by telling me that Mum had asked her to call.

Keep calm. That doesn't mean anything. Mum was upset when we spoke before. She's had a shock. It's all quite sensible. That's what doctors are there for…

Was I alone?

Yes.

Was there anyone else nearby?

No.

Then she gave me the news. She said that you had "passed away".

She apologised for having to tell me over the phone like that. The alternative would have been a policeman knocking on the front door. It was simply unreal. She asked if I was alright. I said I was…*okay*. In fact I was totally numb. Cold right through. I felt…nothing whatsoever. Like I was cut off from arms, or legs, or any other part of my body. I was totally…empty. She assured me that that was quite natural, quite normal.

Natural? Normal? How can <u>anything</u> ever be natural or normal again?

I don't think we talked for very long, though at the time it seemed like forever. The one thing that I do remember more clearly than anything else:

This is probably a very stupid question, but…are you quite sure?

I wasn't shouting, or screaming, or complaining, or crying, or any of those other things that people are always supposed to do on TV. It just came out, slow and quiet. Like I was Hermione Granger asking Professor Lupin a question about grindylows…

The doctor assured me it wasn't a stupid question to ask. No, she hadn't been able to reach the place where you were. Not herself. But she could see you from a distance. And she knew from the man who was down there with you, that there was…"no hope".

70. Safe Highlanders
Wednesday 8 May 2003

Back in May this year your class went up to Inverness to take part in the *Safe Highlanders* day, with children from other schools all around the Highlands. You were looking forward to the day out. The one disappointment was that your best friend Bryce had to miss the trip. I couldn't believe it when you told me. Bryce hadn't been able to go to *Safe Highlanders*...because he'd fallen off of one of their horses the day before and broken his arm!

He certainly did look a bit sorry for himself when he returned to school with his arm in a sling. But you did your best to help him get by in lessons and it wasn't long before he was back round here to play again. As I recall, that was the day the two of you went wild filling up the playhouse with all those planks and posts, before dashing out into the woods with your explorers' tea. Plaster, what plaster?

When I was clearing up in your bedroom for Grandma and Grandad, I came across the yellow and white *Safe Highlanders* bag. I didn't know whether to keep it and treasure it. To use it as a bin bag. Or simply to tear it up into the smallest pieces I could possibly manage. But if visits to *Safe Highlanders* can help some other family to avoid having to walk this same dark road, then that has to be a good thing, doesn't it, Jamie Man.

71. Calling people
Friday 11 July 2003

It's hard to remember the order of events after I'd finished speaking to Dr Calder. And certainly when I picked up the phone again to make the first call, I had no idea that this was the start of something that was going occupy the greater part of my time for the following three weeks or more. Talking everyone through what had happened—family, friends, the press, people who came up to me in the street, perfect strangers even.

I guess I must have tried to get hold of Grandma and Grandad first:

Oh, God! Not BT Answer!

What can you say to an answering service at a time like this? And the two of them more than 500 miles away. Keep it calm. No panic in the voice. Nothing to alarm them.

Hello, it's me. Something's come up. Can Dad ring me as soon as you get in?

Would it have been Pam Hope next?—Bryce's Mum? I think it might have been. As far as I knew, Bryce was away at his Granny's for the next four weeks. How would they find a kind way to tell a son of eleven that he won't ever be able to see his best friend again?

At some point it was back to Richard's Mum, Chris. Confirming the worst fears that each of us had so desperately been trying to pretend would never come about.

Every parent's worst nightmare.

How many times did I hear *that* particular phrase repeated in the weeks to come?

The phone rang again. Mrs Banks returning my call. Oh, for those simplistic images of a visit to casualty when I'd left the message on her machine earlier on.

I'm sorry, Helen. It's worse than I thought when I rang you before. Jamie's had an accident...I'm afraid he's dead.

And then Grandad calling back. Concerned but similarly unprepared. What can you do to soften the blow, when the worst nightmare has indeed come true?

72. The second six months
Tuesday 11 May 2004

Does it get better when "life goes on" and everyone is "getting over it"? Seven months? Eleven months? The numbers no longer have the magic ring of one, three, six. Or of that first anniversary which is yet to come. No, it doesn't get better. There are just fewer people at the door. A pain that is harder to explain. And a garden with no one to share it.

I've been waking up to music again. Colours with no meaning outside the confines of my own head. One tune is familiar but it's taken me some days to recognise its origins. You called it "Australia": the theme you made up on your guitar to go with the *Kangaroo Adventure* story that you were writing. Who else does that matter to, ten months on?

73. Living in two separate worlds
Saturday 20 September 2003

It seems almost like I'm living in two separate worlds at once. There's the one that continues to dash along just like normal. Everybody's going about their usual, hectic business as if nothing out of the ordinary has happened. But in the other world everything moves in slow motion. Every job take ten times longer than it did before. Things that might once have been important in the previous life hardly seem to matter at all now.

In the fast world, it's the head that rules. Logic and clear thinking are in charge. Everything has hard edges. A clear price. A precise value. Image and appearances matter. In the slow world, somewhere off in the corner of your eye where it's more difficult to see, there's more time to look into the heart of things. Follow your feelings. Ignore the wrappings. Concentrate on the content. Close your eyes and allow your thoughts to drift.

I suppose it must be more difficult to reach out into that slow world, because so many people don't even seem to realise it exists. But it must be there, Jamie Man, because I'm sure that's where all the stories must come from. And the music. And the ideas for the next pet project. And everything else that doesn't simply come out of a tin, or get knocked up from a ready-made kit. Perhaps you could call it the Land of Make-Believe and Making Things. I think I've been going there for as long as I can remember, and I'm sure that's where *you* must have gone visiting too, Jamie Man, all those times when you were striding your way along the stones, and reciting aloud to yourself as you went.

It's a special treat when you get the chance to meet someone else who knows the way to that Land of Make-Believe and Making Things. And now each time I walk along that same path to the back gate, I am reminded that there will always be a part of me that's going to remain eleven years old, with you for company, for the rest of my days.

74. Grandad's summer projects
Tuesday 22 July 2003

According to those original summer plans, Grandma and Grandad should have been arriving for their visit today. Whereas, in the revised version of the script, this becomes the day after your funeral. So of course they are here already. But you are away.

Poor Grandad. We'd talked so much on the telephone. For weeks he'd been squirreling away all sorts of exciting bits and pieces to bring with him in the suitcase. Everything for those summer projects with you and Kyle. All swept aside now.

And you had your own list of little jobs to keep Grandad occupied too. I don't remember them all now. There was definitely the broken African stringed gourd up on the top of the bookshelf waiting to be fixed. And your smoke machine question of course—how to make a fine spray of heated glycerine. Hmm...?

Grandad had promised to bring one of those old perfume sprays with the rubber puffer bulb so we could try some experiments.

75. Grandma's treasures
Wednesday 30 July 2003

Grandma's not terribly impressed by smoke machines, or cat's whisker radios, or computers, or anything else "technical" like that. Grandma has her own special treasures. Like her collection of photographs of you and Nicola and Kyle. And all those drawings and paintings that the three of you have done for her over the years.

Now that it's time for Grandma to go back home on the train, I've given her Winnie the Pooh to take with her in the suitcase. I felt sure that there wasn't anyone else in the whole world who would treasure your hot water bottle cover as much as Grandma, no matter how worn and thin he's grown after so many years of night-time hugging. I've also given her Big-E the bear, who's been cuddling up in bed with her while she's been here. And Aunty Iris has his brother, Little-E, to take back home with her to London tonight.

I guess as I work my way through the mountain of stuff that remains to be sorted out, there'll be other things that seem to have *GRANDMA* written all over them. I know she'll be missing her wee talks with you on the telephone, Jamie Man. And it'll be a comfort to her to have things of yours there. Treasures to help her hold onto the good and happy memories.

76. First tears
Friday 11 July 2003

So many calls to make. So many people to comfort, even as events still unfolded down at Bruar. So much remaining unresolved. And yet the one thing that mattered most of all that day had already been determined beyond any power of mine, or anyone else's, to influence or change. That decision had been made before I even rode back in through the gate with the shopping. Nevertheless the relentless sequence of events carried on. Far away. Out of my hands. Out of my reach. Through the afternoon and on into the evening. So many people giving of their very best to bring you back home to us.

With the first flurry of phone calls complete, I found myself standing by the lounge window and gazing out at your road of fence posts and planks from just two days before. And it was only then that I cried the first of the many tears for my lost Wee Man. I still didn't believe you were gone, It wasn't real. But some part of the anaesthetic was starting to wear off and the first of the pain was beginning to creep through.

77. No time for suffering
Friday 11 July 2003

I've spoken to many parents. I've followed the sadness and distress of your friends and classmates. I've suffered for poor Bryce, whose Mum and Dad wanted to tell him face to face—only for him to stumble across your school photograph in his Granny's Sunday newspaper. I cannot bring you back, Jamie Man, though that would be my dearest wish, for myself and for everyone else who held you in their affections.

When I listen to those parents recounting the words and reactions of their children, I recognise so much of the disbelief and insecurity that they express. They echo the feelings that I myself experienced at the age of eleven, when one of my own classmates, Keith, was killed in a road accident during the summer holidays, just weeks before he should have moved up to the Grammar School with our small group of leavers.

> *If it could happen to him…then what's to stop it happening…to* me*…? Perhaps life isn't as safe as you made us think it was…?*

Up to a point, it is true. There is an element of risk in everything we do. Accidents *can* happen. Mercifully, they remain very rare. Especially for those of us fortunate enough to live in a place like the Highlands of Scotland, far from so many of the dangers of busy city life.

To parents, teachers, children and everyone else I tell the same story. Jamie went for a walk and he slipped and he fell. In other circumstances, he might have been lucky. He might have got away with bumps and bruises. Or perhaps just a few broken bones. But on this particular occasion, things didn't work out that way. Jamie was unfortunate.

But that does not mean that there need be nightmares of pain, or prolonged suffering. You got a bang on the head as you fell. The doctors assure me that you must have died instantly. You wouldn't have felt a thing. I imagine that it must have been like all those many times when I turned off the light at bedtime.

> *Night, night, Jamie Man. Sleep well. See you in the morning.*

78. Help is at the door
Friday 11 July 2003

Not long after I'd finished the first round of phone calls, just at that point when I was starting to teeter on the edge, the door bell rang. It was Mr Whyte, the minister. News travels fast. He'd dropped everything when he heard from Mr and Mrs Banks.

How long did he stay? Six o'clock? Later maybe? I really don't know. That was the dark and hopeless time when the whole of my world was crumbling into despair.

You know how good Mr Whyte is at getting down and talking to the children at school and taking the time to listen, Jamie Man? Well, now he did the same for me. And before he left, he gave me the first of the many, many hugs of comfort that were to become such a feature of Carr-Bridge life in the days that followed. I think the events of this summer have reminded many people how very important it can be when friends come together and put their arms around one another. The other, abiding memory that I know you left with so many of those who met you?—the everlasting power of a smile.

SMILING
Handwriting practice in P5 (author unknown)

Smiling is infectious, you catch it like the flu
When someone smiled at me today I started smiling too
I walked around the corner and someone saw me grin
When he smiled I realised I had passed it on to him

I thought about that smile and then realised its worth
A single smile like mine could travel round the earth
So if you feel a smile begin don't leave it undetected
Start an epidemic quick and get the world infected

---

79. A Bridge to the future
Saturday 6 May 2000

Talk of bringing people together makes me think of *Bridge to the Future* in the year 2000. That was our next big musical event after *The Piper*, wasn't it, Jamie

Man. You and I even had the T-shirts to prove it! The Millennium and the 10th anniversary of the new school building gave Carr-Bridge the perfect excuse for a double celebration that year. Planning started right back in February or so. The idea was to put together a programme of new music and old Scottish tunes, with each class in the school acting out a part of the story of the village—past, present and future. That was when I came up with the idea of writing an anthem for all the children in the school to sing together at the end of the afternoon.

Kyle and his class were the clansfolk—Jacobites, the Clearances and all that. I remember a session down at the school one weekend, chopping up sacking for the kilts. That was tough stuff. I'm sure they must have been very itchy to wear! Meanwhile your class was doing the Old Bridge and the River Dulnain. Music Club were booked to provide the backing for that, so I couldn't watch you much on the day. But I saw it all on the video afterwards.

I particularly liked the way that each group of actors and musicians had their own spot, with the audience progressing around the school field from one show to the next. We had little marquees for all the electrical equipment, just in case it rained. But as I recall, the main problems on the day were reading the music in the sunshine, and persuading the sheets not to blow away in the breeze!

And at the end you all sang "Building Bridges".

BUILDING BRIDGES
School anthem for Bridge to the Future, 2000

If you think of weaving rainbows
Or imagine you can fly
Why not turn your dreams to bridges
And then hang them in the sky?

> *Building bridges*
> *Building bridges*
> *Silhouettes across the water*
> *Shining paths that never die*

You can sail across the river
Like an eagle flying high
Why delay until tomorrow
When the years are rushing by?

> *Building bridges…etc*

There's a promise of forgiveness
Love and hope for healing wounds
Joining paths that ran to nowhere
Turning strangers into friends

> *Building bridges...etc*

One small step is all that's needed
Take the chance and don't ask why
Reconciling past divisions
Let's join hands across the sky

> *Building bridges...etc*

---

80. Something to come back to
Saturday 6 May 2000

Bridge to the Future was only one of countless Millennium events taking place across the Highlands that summer. Later we went up to Inverness to join in with the combined celebrations for the *Pan Highland Festival*. And Mrs Banks was there with the video camera that day as you and Kyle and I set off to march in the street parade.

So I have the whole of *Bridge to the Future* and our part in *Pan Highland* on video. But I think it may be a while before I'm ready to go back and watch that particular tape again. I remember so sharply the tableau that your class did that sunny summer's afternoon. Acting out the story of the old stone bridge that was built to allow funeral processions to cross over the River Dulnain, even when the flood waters were at their highest. You wore a black shirt and a tall black hat and played the part of one of the coffin bearers...

The Old Bridge and the Landmark fire tower.

81. Sharing your waistcoat
Thursday 11 September 2003

I'm cold today, Jamie Man. Our two month day. The year is moving on. The temperature fell to just a few degrees above freezing last night. But this is not simply the weather. This is the cold that comes from within and runs through my veins like ice, threatening to freeze the soul itself. It's so difficult when the body gets its messages confused, unable to tell good news from bad, hot from cold, excitement from dread.

I've just been into your bedroom and fetched the fleece waistcoat that Grandma and Grandad bought you for your birthday last year. And now I'm sitting here with the zipper pulled right up under my chin and snug around the back of my neck to fight off that creeping chill. You know, sometimes our most off-hand words can return to haunt us. What did I say when you and Kyle got those waistcoats in the large size last year?

Well, at least I know they'll still fit me, when you two've finished with them!

It's just a shame they don't have something as good to bring the warmth back into my fingers while I type these words. Or something to bring *you* back with it too...

82. Cut off from the world
Friday 11 July 2003

After Mr Whyte had gone, the evening drifted on through a meaningless sequence of all the sensible and practical actions, while my thoughts continued to lurch between states of total numbness and knife-edged awareness. I climbed out of the shower and cried all over again as I dried myself on your yellow bath towel that still hung on the rail where you'd left it the morning before. What did anything matter anymore? Common sense rather than appetite pushed me through another tasteless meal. Then more drifting. Expecting any moment to have to drop everything and be whisked away in a police car down to Bruar.

I needed to keep the telephone free. I was sending e-mails all over the world while neighbours here would still be going about their everyday routines blissfully unaware. Did people ring up? I suppose they must have done. Don't ask me who, or when.

No, no more news. I'm just sitting here waiting to hear what I have to do.

Uncertainty. Dribbles of information, slowly filtering through. The rescue teams were still working to get you out. What on earth was going on? I shouldn't be wasting my time sitting here doing nothing. I should be down there with you.

Confusion. Kyle has arrived at Bruar and Mum has broken the news to him. He's upset, blaming himself. But it's not his fault, it's mine. I should've done a better job of keeping you safe, Jamie Man.

More waiting. Nicola is being ferried back across three different police districts in a relay of squad cars. She still doesn't know what's happened but it must be obvious that the news is very bad.

Waiting for someone tell *me* what's going on.

E-MAIL, 7.24PM
Friday 11 July 2003

There is no easy way to tell you this.

This afternoon I was told on the phone that Jamie has been killed in a fall during a stop off with Pam on their way down to Perth to collect Kyle from his basketball week.

It looks like I will need to go down there, but I am still waiting to hear more.

The world is very dark today…

---

83. Headline news
Friday 11 July 2003

Why did it never occur to me to turn on the radio? For all the talk of reporters besieging the House of Bruar, it never once entered my head to listen to the news. I know now that you were the headline story by late afternoon, Jamie Man. Uncle Bob heard the reports but never once imagined it might be his own nephew they were talking about. By the late evening news, people near and far were hearing your name on the radio and television. You even had your own page on the BBC website. And in the meantime, I still didn't have a clue what was happening, or even where I was going to end up that night.

84. How do we tell the children?
Friday 11 July 2003

One thing kept going round and round in my mind in all the confusion of that day. What about the children, Jamie Man? It was barely nine days since we'd sat in the church here for the end of term Leavers' Service. When Mr Whyte had reminded us all that friends don't stop being friends just because they're moving on to a new school.

Many of your classmates would be away on their holidays by now. Scattered far and wide. How would they hear the news? How would they feel when they did? We couldn't ring round every family. Mr Whyte promised to track down the head teachers for the two schools. That would be a start at least. We were making up the rules as we went along.

What next? The Scouts and the Cubs? I couldn't get an answer from Skip but I did manage to get hold of Chil. Your old Cub Leader, who went to the Soap Box Derby and the Gang Show with you. Needless to say she was horrified. As I suspected, Skip was away on holiday, but Chil would deal with everything for the Scouts and the Cubs.

Be prepared? I guess it's hard to think of a more dreadful situation to prepare for. I've wondered since, Jamie Man. How would we have handled it, if we'd been the ones to receive that call, telling us that one of your friends from school, or from the Scouts, or wherever, had died in an accident like that? I can only hope that we would have done as well as all those who rallied round that day and in the weeks to come.

85. Going…nowhere
Friday 11 July 2003

Eventually, late into the evening, I got the call from Mum saying they'd left Bruar and were on their way back up the road to Carr-Bridge. Amanda from Scottish Youth Theatre, who'd travelled across from Glasgow with Nicola, was driving them up in Mum's car.

But you, my Jamie Man. You weren't coming home. You were heading in completely the opposite direction. Left in the hands of strangers. Going all the way to Ninewells Hospital in Dundee. It felt like I was being slowly torn down the middle. One half that longed to dash straight down to Dundee and be with you. And the other half that just wanted to gather Nicola and Kyle into my arms and never let them go.

When I got out of bed that morning, I'd been expecting nothing more than a further three quiet nights in the house here on my own. Now all of a sudden, at eleven o'clock at night, I was making up beds, when I couldn't even think straight enough to know one end of a pillow case from the other. Mum and Nicola would have to sleep in your room. But of course, there'd been much more important things than housework, or tidying up to think about that week, hadn't there, Jamie Man. I'd always known that you would have the room sorted out before Grandma and Grandad were due to arrive the following week. But in the meantime, while the sun was shining, so what if the place was in a mess when you went away for the weekend? Call it simply…work in progress.

Unfortunately now though, there was just so much stuff spread around: on your bed, on the spare bed, all across the floor. I could hardly get in the door. I'm sorry, Jamie Man. At the time when I didn't want to disturb a single thing, all I could do was to push the whole lot to one side. I couldn't let myself think about it. There was no other way.

When they arrived, I stood on the drive outside the front door and held Nicola and Kyle tightly in my arms. What words of comfort can you find at a time like that?

Amanda came in for a few minutes and then went off to stay the night with an aunt in Aviemore before going back to Glasgow on the train in the morning. I thanked her for everything she'd done, closed the door, and locked out the world. Now it was just the four of us, no longer five…ever. We were walking round in a daze. Desperately wishing we could wake up to find that it was all just a horrible dream.

E-MAIL, 1.00AM
Saturday 12 July 2003

One o'clock in the morning. Pam, Nicola and Kyle are all in the house in bed. Tomorrow? Who knows?

A tragic accident. So many "what ifs" but ultimately such things do happen. Somehow I have to find a meaning and a future in it all. There are still two other children and I have to find it in myself to go on for their sakes. I wish it was not real, but this is no joke.

And everywhere I turn in the house is the trail of clutter and make-believe that remains from our Monday to Thursday this week with just Jamie and me, doing

HIS things. Like the tin of varnish that he left out in the playhouse telling me that when he got back next week he would need to put another coat on the bird table that he had made.

This is pain…

---

86. Sleeping and waking
Friday 11 July 2003

If there is any up-side to being plunged into the midst of events that are beyond your control, it must surely be that certain benevolent and helpful things do tend to happen all by themselves. That is to say, people assume that you're no longer capable of making normal, rational decisions and they step in to take charge. Okay, the occasional toe might get trodden on. Or the odd nose put out of joint. But on the whole, it's well meant and it's certainly better than being left to flounder without any lifebelt to cling onto.

I suppose doctors must be used to this kind of thing. All part of the routine of life, and death. Before I'd even considered ringing the Health Centre, there was Dr Mangham, the duty doctor from Aviemore, standing on the doorstep. The grapevine at work again. Somebody ringing through from the surgery in Pitlochry this time, I believe. I've no idea how many times she was in and out again over the next few days. It must be difficult to know *how* people will react in such circumstances. I guess almost anything is possible.

It was pretty late by the time I'd checked everyone else off to bed that first day. By then the responses were starting to come in on the e-mail. Shocked. Disbelieving. Was it a joke? I sat up typing replies. Yes, I could've taken the doctor's sleeping tablets. But what was the point? There was no running away from the monster that was pursuing me that night. And as Dumbledore says to Harry Potter towards the end of *The Goblet of Fire*:

Numbing the pain for a while will make it worse when you finally feel it.

Eventually I suppose I got to bed some time after two o'clock and slept till about six. That pretty much set the pattern for the weeks to come. Three, four maybe five hours deep sleep, no dreams. As with the meals, a regular routine of just enough to get by.

For about half a second when I started to surface on Saturday, it seemed like a fine morning, with sunshine peeking in between the curtains. That was before reality kicked back in. Then I lay there in the bed, crying for my lost Wee Man.

E-MAIL FROM INDIANA, USA
Friday 11 July 2003

Oh David,

We are both stunned to learn this, and so very, very sorry. We can't even begin to comprehend what you are feeling at this moment, but know that our thoughts and prayers are with you and your family during this tragic time.

I am working on Valhalla post production now, and of course, you are most welcome to dedicate it to your Jamie…

…Please let us know if there is anything else we can do for you in this time of such tragedy. I'm thinking, and this is just off the top of my head, that we could include a link to any charities he was involved in/fond of…sort of an on-going tribute spot on the Valhalla pages. Again, it's early, but know that we would be happy to honor his memory in some discreet and respectful way on the page for the show we'll now dedicate to his memory. Perhaps we can even set up a Valhalla per-unit sold donation to his favorite zoo, or theatre, or community club, or charity, or whatever else might be appropriate? Think about it.

The life of one so young, and one blessed with such a loving, creative and talented father, deserves some creative tribute and we'd be honored to help create that with your participation and blessing.

We send you our best wishes and a heartfelt prayer that the joy of Jamie's life will soon replace your pain at the loss of it. May your friends and family bring you comfort and hope.

We're so sorry, David.

Love, Dana & Joel

---

87. How does he know?
Saturday 12 July 2003

Like it not, one of the very first things I had to do on Saturday morning was to go to the shop. How many years have I walked that familiar route through the woods to the Spar? Never before with such painful steps. Over the road and in beside Landmark. Was it only four days since we climbed the tower there together? It was impossible to hold back the tears as I followed the familiar path amongst the pine trees and back down to the road between the cemetery and the War Memorial.

> *Death and my child.*

They were two pieces of a puzzle that simply did not fit together in my mind. I met someone coming up into the woods from the road. One of the usual, familiar faces going about the normal, comforting routine of morning dog walking. How could she possibly know that such things were over? All routines were cancelled. There had been life with you before. And now there was only life without you. Nothing could ever be the same again. I stumbled on by, turning away to hide the tears, and carried on down the road, reminding myself that no one would be aware of what had happened yet.

I put a bottle of milk down on the counter. Instant coffee for Mum. A bag of food for Corrie Dog. Then I attempted to fumble for some money. My fingers were twice their normal size. I didn't know what a pound coin was. All at once I could feel the tears threatening again. In the end I simply pulled out the first coins that came to hand, hoping I didn't look like too much of an idiot. Bob took the money and counted out the change. His words caught me completely off guard:

> *I'm so sorry for your loss, David.*

I struggled for a reply. I couldn't see a thing for the rising tears. All I could do was to nod stupidly and lurch out of the shop. I blundered home, racking my brains for some explanation how Bob in the Spar could possibly know about what had happened already? From someone I'd spoken to the previous day maybe? I still had *no* idea how our small, private, family tragedy was already propelling us into a completely new spotlight.

―――

E-MAIL TO INDIANA, USA
Thursday 31 July 2003

Dear Dana and Joel

It's taken a while to get here, but now I think is the fitting time to follow up your kind message of support…

…I have to thank you for contributing, albeit unknowingly, to one of the rays of hope that has carried me through the last couple of weeks. In your message you spoke of tributes and charities and so on. And from your little inspiration came the first seeds of "The Jamie Fund". This morning I got to the stage of filling in all the forms…and now the fund has its very own bank account, which already contains a fair sum collected from donations on the day of the funeral.

In due course I hope that our young people will also have cause to thank you for providing the first spark that may have set "The Jamie Fund" alight for a long time to come. We live in hope, which is infinitely better than despair.

David

―――

88. Open season
Saturday 12 July 2003

Beyond the obvious, a further down-side of being caught up in a tragedy like this, Jamie Man, is the way it attracts people whose only real interest is in selling newspapers and promoting sensation. As far as the media were concerned, it was open season. One minute, quiet obscurity. The next, public property. Fair game.

Mum had said there were reporters at Bruar the day before. In fact, it sounds like the first ones must have been there practically before I even knew that anything had happened. The police wouldn't let Mum go outside the House of Bruar to see to Corrie Dog all afternoon because the press were queuing up out there with their cameras. So I suppose we did sort of expect there might be *something* in a few of the papers on Saturday morning…At that time we still had no inkling of what'd been going on with radio and television the previous afternoon and evening. Naïve or what, Jamie Man!

Now that I think back on it, I suppose I must have walked past a whole line of national newspapers at the Spar. Yet it never once occurred to me to take a glance. No wonder Bob in the shop knew all about what had happened. He could hardly have missed the story—full front page of the *Daily Record* and all. I wonder if their headline writers ever pause to reflect on how *they* might feel if it were their own child, or some other loved one, that they were screaming out in their cheap, thoughtless words? Their "kid" was my son. But I guess none of the other tabloids were any better. The *Record* merely happened to be the one that Mum and Nicola brought in later that day. I cast my eyes over the cover. But it didn't make me want to read any of the rest on the inside pages.

Your name in the national papers? Lurid headlines? None of it made any sense whatsoever, Jamie Man. Not then, and not now. When Nicola was quoting bits aloud, I wasn't even sure I recognised the people they were talking about. Not amongst all the errors and inaccuracies…Pick a story, any story and don't let me see it.

89. Telling the news, your way
July 2003

The one thing I can never know, Jamie Man, is how *you* would have told this story in your summer holiday diary. How *you* might have dealt with nosey journalists and rescue teams and policewomen and doctors and everything else that was to follow?

The thing that turns each and every child into an individual, is that unpredictable spark—the "Wrong Trousers" train of thought that lays its own tracks as it goes along, and isn't averse to leaping off up some unexpected sideline whenever the fancy takes it.

Oh yes, I'm sure there would have been some tears in your account. But I like to think that there would have been things to bring a smile to our faces too. Like your *Slug Story* that Nicola read for us at the funeral. Or the sad plight of the wolf at the bottom of the pack that you thought about in a thank-you letter to the Highland Wildlife Park. I suppose all that I can really do here, is to hazard a few guesses and try to pick out some of the more obvious heroes and villains of the piece. Hoping thus to do you justice. Can it be the whole picture? No way. Just a brief glimpse through our little window on the world.

90. Fun Day 2003
Saturday 7 June 2003

Talk of telling tales, puts me in mind of this year's Carr-Bridge Primary School Fun Day. June is always a busy month in the school calendar, with summer coming on and so much to fit in before the end of term. Never more so than when you're one of the big ones who are now feverishly marking off the notches to the end of primary days. And the build up to Fun Day was what kicked off that crowded month for us all.

When the PTA first announced that the theme for this year was going to be "The Jungle" something in my head immediately said "Monkey Business". A story that only the monkeys were allowed to know. All about news and keeping secrets. And from that, a new song blossomed into existence. A bright and jolly tune in six sharps, to match those crazy monkeys swinging through the treetops in the yellow sunshine.

I suppose you could say the song was a kind of parting thank you to the school that had played such a large part in our lives for so many years. I may be wrong, but of all the songs I'd written for the children, "Monkey Business" seemed to be the one they enjoyed most of all. So there you are, Jamie Man, on the final video on my shelf. Singing your heart out with all your school friends on your final Fun Day. An enduring record of one of the highest and brightest moments of those closing days of primary school.

No, I don't know how you would have told this story. But I do know that you would have found a place for the joy and the smiling, as well as the sadnesses.

91. When the doorbell rings
Saturday 12 July 2003

Before I set out for the Spar, Mum asked if I wanted to hear about what had happened at Bruar the day before. I said she didn't have to tell me anything. It wasn't her fault. One unfortunate slip. Simply an accident. What was the point of forcing her to go over it all yet again? She told me a little more. I didn't ask any questions. Nothing either of us could say or do then was ever going to turn the clock back, was it, Jamie Man.

The police had warned Mum that reporters might turn up on the doorstep. Sure enough, the doorbell rang. There were two of them. Freelancers for the Sunday Papers. I told them to wait outside and shut the door again so that Mum and I could talk in private. What did she want to do? I would tell them to go away if that was what she'd rather? She shook her head. What was the point? They might as well get the story right.

Okay then. But if I wasn't going to put her through it all again for *my* benefit, she certainly wasn't going to have to relive the whole experience just for a couple of journalists. I would talk to them on my own. Mum didn't argue. She went back in to sit with Nicola and Kyle, while I went outside for my first experience of facing the press.

MONKEY BUSINESS
Carr-Bridge Primary School Fun Day 2003

There's something funny in the air
Folks are going ape to find what's up
It's a tropical mystery
What's this monkey business?
Is it bananas? Is it nuts?
Hold the front page! Stop the press!
This is exclusive. No ifs or buts
Truly monkey business!

> *People want to hear it*
> *And gorillas long to know*
> *Chimps are going crazy*
> *For our private, primate show*
> *We tell them all the same thing*
> *It's a monkey revelation*
> *Or to put it in a nutshell, see*
> *Our headlines aren't for sale*
> *You cannot buy our story*
> *If you haven't got a tail!*

We recommend you cats keep out
Curiosity is bad for health
We might smile, but our lips are sealed
Secret monkey business!
No point in trying espionage
Got no time for nosiness
This is a story that you can't have
Cos it's monkey business!

> *Hear no evil*
> *Oo, oo, oo!*
> *See no evil*
> *Ee, ee, ee!*
> *Most of all we tell no tales*
> *It's not your monkey business!*

92. People want to hear it
Saturday 12 July 2003

I really hate doing this, but…

It was tempting to inquire why he didn't go and get himself a different job then? In fact I told him I would speak to them in their car but I wasn't prepared to let them into the house. Nicola and Kyle had just lost their wee brother.

The reporter did the talking. The photographer mostly just sat and listened. It felt like the day following an operation in hospital. Everything moving in slow motion after the anaesthetic. Lights brighter. Edges sharper. Sounds louder and coarser. And the pain? Oh, yes, the pain is there. Deep and ever present. And yet, at the same time, the body is somehow cushioned by its own bruising and swelling. Muscles and joints have yet to recover the freedom of movement that will reveal one injured part moving in contact with another. That is the slower pain that will come only with time and reflection.

To be fair to them, they weren't particularly pushy. They didn't really need to be did they, Jamie Man. It was hardly going to be a test of their creative ingenuity to find the poignant tragedy in this particular story.

Tell them only what you want to say—that was what the police had advised. Okay then. Here goes, boys. What's my line? Bruar has happened. That was yesterday. End of story. I'm going to tell you about the good things. The special things. About the best and most wonderful final week that I could possibly have wished for with my youngest son. About the days of fun and make-believe. I'm going to tell you about the boy who lived…

93. Pictures of you
Monday 21 July 2003

At the end of term Leavers' Service, each of the P7's was presented with a class photograph as a reminder of your time at Carr-Bridge Primary School. We have it up on the wall in the lounge here now, alongside all the other school photos. I said then that it was one of the best class pictures I'd seen. Every one of you relaxed and happy. Not a single child caught at the wrong moment.

Unbeknown to me at the time, you'd had another card from the school as well:

A special memory of Jamie Gasking, Carr-Bridge Primary School,

Inside, there's a classroom snapshot of a much younger Jamie Man, captured in mid exclamation with the caption:

There's nothing like a little problem solving to brighten up my day.

That card was still in your school bag, buried down the bottom under your pencil case. It only came to light by chance—on the morning of your funeral of all days—when Kyle and I were on the hunt for some missing *Gameboy* stuff to keep Cousin Alan entertained. It was a complete surprise when Kyle pulled the card out of the bag. But perhaps it was a rather apt moment to come across that extra little message of goodwill from the school. A piece of light-hearted fun to send you on your way out into the world.

94. Freely given
Friday 16 July 2004

You know, Jamie Man, when I got in touch with the school photographers in Cornwall, to ask if I could use your picture in our book, they sent me a whole parcel of photographs at no cost whatsoever. And there was another full set for Mum too. It's amazing how kind people can be, even right down at the other end of the country! It was the same with the lady who made the map for the back cover—a stranger to us before, and yet still so eager to be involved in helping out.

In fact, in the preparation of *Hey, Mr Big!* not a single person or organisation has asked for anything at all in return for the use of their pictures or other material. What a wonderful thing to be able to tell you!

95. Every little counts
Thursday 31 July 2003

This morning Denise Robertson and I went to Aviemore to open the bank account for *The Jamie Fund*. Imagine that, Jamie Man—a special fund with your name on it!

Yes, in some respects it is a sad business. But I hope we will at least be able to achieve something that you can be proud of with this fund. Something that will truly make a difference.

Alice made the medals for the winners of the "Draw a picture to make us smile" competition for the children at our *Jamie Weekend* in January 2004.

At first sight, some donations might appear to stand out. It's tempting to focus on the generosity and significance of the bigger contributors. But then I recall the old parable of the widow's mite, which reminds us that it's not the size of the gift that counts. (This causes my thoughts to leap ahead to a day in March 2004 and the anonymous wee friend who left you a red toy car and fourteen pence beside your headstone).

Every donation, whether small or large, comes with its own story. From individuals whose lives have been touched by you in some way or another, Jamie Man. People who think of you now with fondness and who will carry a memory of you in their hearts for the rest of their days. I thank them, one and all.

So on reflection, there is only one other contribution to *The Jamie Fund* that I'd like to pick out here. Before we went to Aviemore today, I took the coins out of your piggy bank in the bedroom. They came to £3.88. And I paid that into the bank too when we opened the account this morning. It was what I thought you would have wanted me to do with the pocket money that you left behind. And I've promised to take your Piggy Bank to Anne in the Post Office, for anyone else who wants to add something there.

96. Sunday papers
Sunday 13 July 2003

Nicola went up to the Spar and bought a selection of Sunday papers to see what those journalists had come up with. And now she's been cutting out all the articles and pictures for her collection of Jamie stuff. I didn't read any of the stories at the time myself. But it was pretty clear that you were in all the newspapers that day. And I could tell too from Nicola's exclamations that the reporters had come up with a selection of different angles to sell to the various editors. It was no better than Saturday. Each paper with its own particular crop of errors and inaccuracies. Apparently we had a different family set up in every single one. What do you make of that then, Jamie Man?

97. Torn again
Saturday 12 July 2003

Nicola and Kyle wanted us all to stay together again on the Saturday night. Would I go to Mum's house in Inverness? Yet again I was torn. I wanted to be with you. And at the same time I wanted to be with them. Nicola and Kyle need me now, more than ever before. My head told me that you were in Dundee, far away and out of reach. My heart insisted that you were there at home in Carr-

Bridge. Still roaming through the woods outside the back gate. Still pacing up and down the stepping stones alongside the wall. Still laying Dad traps with your constructions across the patio and up the hall.

If I listened carefully, I was convinced I could still catch the scrunch of your feet approaching down the drive. I just wanted to escape from the world of journalists and impossible news. To open the back gate and walk free out into the woods, where the memories of you still clung so close. Like that tang of wood smoke on a dark winter's night when the stove is lit and the chimney is steaming into a clear and starry sky.

But it was not to be. It was Nicola and Kyle who mattered most at that moment. There would be other days for you and me to catch up on such things. It hurt so very much to open my hand and let you slip away like that. But I did what I had to do. I left Carr-Bridge that evening and went up to Inverness for the next two nights.

98. Making arrangements
Saturday 12 July 2003

However, before we could even begin to think about setting off for Inverness, there were still tasks that had to be attended to. Top of the list? Well, what do you do when someone dies? How do you arrange a funeral? What's the procedure with undertakers? We were starting completely from scratch. It was not something we'd ever considered, let alone researched, or practised.

We thought there *might* be an undertaker in Grantown. But then, *you'd* been taken down to Dundee. And by a funeral firm from Perth. It seemed there was going to have to be a post mortem too. Who to talk to first? The Police? The hospital? The undertakers down there? Or someone up here?

Mum rang the Police Station in Pitlochry. The post mortem would not be until Monday at the earliest. Evidently the fine, summer weather the previous day had brought people out en-masse and there'd been a whole crop of accidents and sudden deaths as a consequence. There was one, small crumb of comfort. At least the police were suggesting that no more than a superficial examination was likely to be required.

I tracked down the local undertaker, Johnny Ross, in *Yellow Pages* and rang his number in Grantown. I caught him out on the road somewhere and he promised to check up on everything. He'd call me back later. More waiting. When I was your age, Jamie Man, I remember a plaque in the house with the text, "They also serve who only stand and wait." There was certainly plenty of standing and waiting involved as we picked our way through family and funeral arrangements.

99. First visitors
Saturday 12 July 2003

Shortly after lunch on that first day, Sarah McWilliam appeared at the door with her Mum, Sharon. Sarah was a year younger but you'd been together in the combined P6-7 class all year. She'd brought us a wee bunch of flowers from their garden, along with a very special letter that she'd written when she heard the news about your accident. We put the flowers in the small crystal vase. And they sat on the hearth in front of all the other big, fancy bunches that appeared over the course of the next couple of weeks.

Sarah's letter was written in bright green ink and there was a picture of water and flowers that she'd drawn on the other side. I think you would have liked it, Jamie Man. I will certainly always remember that letter as one of the kindest and most thoughtful messages that we received. Yes, I did cry some more when I read it. But it also made me feel very proud to read what Sarah had to say. Well done, my Wee Man!

SARAH'S LETTER
Saturday 12 July 2003

I'M SORRY

Dear David and Pam Gasking

I am terribly sory to hear about Jamie he was such a nice lively happy boy. Nothing ever made him unhappy. He always made people laugh if they were sad. He will be missed a lot by lots of people and one of them is me. Jamie was such a good friend to me he was supportive to the people who didn't win at the talent concert. He had many friends who liked him dearly and who are going to really miss him. Jamie was always very proud of his Dad and his music he would always try the hardest when David wrote a new song. And he was really looking forward to coming up to the high school because he said that he would get to see Kyle his big brother every day. I will really miss Jamie, he was such a lively boy and very kind hearted. He tried very hard in every thing he did even the things he didn't like. Jamie was a fabulos boy with a great personality and I am very, very sorry.

Yours sincerely

Sarah McWilliam

---

100. The loss of a child
Saturday 12 July 2003

Mum and Nicola and Kyle took Corrie Dog out for a walk in the afternoon while we were waiting for Johnny Ross the undertaker to call back. I wasn't on my own for very long though. Almost at once there was another ring on the doorbell and there was Liz Bishop from the Slochd on the doorstep.

Liz had brought a copy of a poem called "Love is love's own reward". She said she'd had it for many years but she couldn't remember who the writer was. When I look again now, it is still the same two lines that jump out of the page for me:

> *He'll bring his love to gladden you and should his stay be brief*
> *You'll have a host of memories as solace for your grief.*

Liz and I sat in the lounge here and she told me how she and her husband Ian had lost their own youngest son in a car accident, seventeen years ago. Liz herself takes a very philosophical, very Swedish view of what happened. She says she feels grateful for the time that she had to share with her child. Ian finds it much harder to accept the loss. And so I think it was very brave of him when he called by a week later and the two of us sat on the front step, talking over how we each felt about the loss of a son.

By the time the others returned from their dog walk, I think I was beginning to realise that a tragedy that seemed at first sight to close so many doors could also at the same time cause some unexpected ones to open. Other people have walked this road before us. There are folk who come forward now to speak of things which previously they kept locked within themselves.

101. The word out on the street
Saturday 12 July 2003

> *Have you heard the news?*
> *Isn't it dreadful!*
> *The poor wee soul!*
> *I can't believe it's true!*
> *He always had such a cheery smile.*
> *I was only just talking to him two days ago.*
> *I remember when he was in Primary 3 and he...*

It's not really so hard to imagine some of the conversations in the village that first Saturday, Jamie Man. I've heard enough since to gain a pretty good idea.

Even in a quiet, out-of-the-way place like Carr-Bridge, we've had our share of tragedies and losses. And we've mourned the passing of some folk before their time. On the whole though, I guess for the vast majority of funerals these days there is at least some element of celebrating the end of a good innings. Year upon year of relative peace and security has taught us to expect certain rules and patterns to be observed in such things. It's quite straightforward really. Nothing difficult to understand. In a small Highland village, healthy children simply do not die. Once upon a time, maybe yes. In our grandparents' and great grandparents' time. Each family with its own group of little stones to be tended in the churchyard. But not now. Not in the 21st Century. It just doesn't happen anymore. Except, it just did. It happened to you, Jamie Man. You were the shocking exception to the statistics. The boy who didn't live. The headline story.

102. Pulling together
Saturday 12 July 2003

As we were driving out through the village late that Saturday afternoon, we passed a bunch of people talking in the road at the top of the school drive. There was a mother with a baby in a buggy. I think Foster McGowan may have been there too. Was it really only a day since he and I had exchanged casual greetings alongside the meat counter in Tesco's? Nicola pointed to the group as we drove past:

Look at those idiots, standing in the middle of the road!

Seeing them there, deep in conversation, I was reminded of the times back at New Year, and again at Easter, when the water supplies to the village ran out and we all had to go down to the car park to collect our bottled water. People were stopping to exchange news in the street then too. There was a common purpose. A feeling of…community.

I made no comment as we drove on up the road towards Inverness. But something told me I didn't need to hear what those folk were saying to know the story on their lips that afternoon. Carr-Bridge was pulling together again. Though this time it wasn't something that could be solved by a few complaints to Scottish Water, or by picking up a pack of bottles and missing a few baths. Oh, how many days I would go thirsty or dirty now, my Jamie Man, just for the chance to turn the clock back by a few, critical hours.

103. First foot
Saturday 12 July 2003

Nothing seems to make any sense anymore. How do I come to be washed up on the shore here in Inverness? It's the first time I've ever stepped inside this house. Now I'm getting a guided tour of the place where you came after I waved you off on the bus each Saturday morning. The room that you shared with Kyle. The bed where you slept that final night before you set out for Perth. Your collection of model ships on the shelves above. I'm surrounded by the evidence of a world that I'd heard about but never seen.

Yet now I'm the one climbing into your bed, Jamie Man. I'm the one creeping down under the Harry Potter quilt. And I'm the one falling asleep hugging your floppy polar bear tightly in my arms. Saturday passes into Sunday in a blur of unreality.

104. A day in Inverness
Sunday 13 July 2003

There are vague recollections of walking the dog. And of aimless shopping trips. Yet more time on the telephone. And in between, those incessant, subdued conversations about how you'd done this, and that, and the other. A few, rare smiles amidst a sea of countless tears. Holding on to one another as we reminisced and suffered together.

Nicola reminded us about the *Fast Food Rockers* and their silly song that you used as part of your *Fast Food Boys* routine. And I recalled how you'd chattered so excitedly after the Talent Show that this would be the very first CD you'd ever gone out to the shop and bought for yourself. You took it back to Mum's house and played it almost non-stop all weekend. Fifty three times in all, you told me so proudly when you came back home that Sunday night. It had driven Nicola up the wall. Now here she was wondering aloud whether we should play it again for you one more time…at the funeral!

But good sense prevailed later in the day, when Nicola came across your *Slug Story* that you made up on the train going down to visit Nan one time. The smiley slug that you drew in wax crayon on the cover was still perfectly clear, though the accompanying caption had faded so much that we couldn't read it any more. Now, so many years later, we found cause once again to smile, as Nicola read aloud the wee tale that you'd dictated for Mum to write down for you that day. Of course, there are other, more recent and more accomplished stories. But your *Slug Story* will always retain a special place in our hearts, as that quirky little scrap of imagination that said so much about a life of make-believe, where nothing was ever *quite* beyond the realms of possibility.

We can only speculate now about what else you might have come up with, if you'd been allowed those extra weeks, or months, or years that it would have taken to complete the longer but equally wacky *Kangaroo Adventure* that you were working on in your spare moments. All the time in your world was simply not enough for all the dreams...

A SLUG STORY
by Jamie Gasking

Slugs are slimy, shiny and black. Slugs can go underground. If you see a slug you will see that it can't walk, so it slides along, but it can't fly, and it is not bigger than a person.

I have looked at a slug and it is quite fat. A slug is quite small and it is quite good at playing the piano and guitar.

It cannot drink out of a bottle bigger than it, but it can drink out of a bottle smaller than it.

A slug likes to play with Action Men like Kyle's. Slug houses have cupboards, bathrooms, landings, lofts, stairs, a lounge and a kitchen, colour TV's and bedrooms with lights, sofa's and beds.

Slugs sometimes wear coats, trousers, jumpers, and they have not got vases but they do have slimy portraits of their ancestors. Some slugs have fires to warm their antennae. A slug called Nicola is in the slimy bed and she is the queen of the house. Kyle slug is the king of the house and Jamie slug is the servant.

Mummy slug is the maid of the house. Daddy slug is the washerperson and Nan slug is the train driver and Newcastle is the platform. But only one train stops at Newcastle and that is the Queen's train.

One day Mummy, Daddy, Nicola, Kyle, Jamie and Nan all went for a bike ride. Then a little old lady came along and took them on a train ride, where they all went to the buffet. On the train ride they went to Darlington and New York. When they got hungry they had more orange juice and doughnuts.

---

105. Cast adrift
Saturday 6 September 2003

You can put on a brave face, but that doesn't take away the hurt, Jamie Man. In the book I've just been reading, one of the characters says:

> *In peacetime, the child buries the father, but in time of war it is the father who buries the child.*

King Theoden has a somewhat similar line in the film of *The Two Towers*. There is no war here. But now there is no peace either. No one prepares you for this. You can't do a try out. One moment, you're just another obscure parent. The next, everyone's looking at you with strange and sad eyes in the street. There's no warning. It simply happens and you have to deal with it. While all the comfortable habits that saw you through from one day to the next are suddenly cast to the wind.

I have lost the light of one of my guiding stars. There are great yawning gaps in my timetable for the years ahead. Each one of those countless moments that I expected to share with you. I find myself drifting rudderless through a sea of silly objects that had a value and meaning only with you there beside me to share and treasure them. I am fortunate, I still have Kyle and Nicola. I am unfortunate, I no longer have you.

I search the heavens for some pointer to the new balance and purpose that I must find in my life, all the while looking back over my shoulder to the many tiny things we did together. So ordinary and inconsequential at the time. Never again to be recaptured.

106. There's going to be a Talent Show
Beginning of June 2003

You and Bryce cornered me after school to tell me there was going to be a Talent Show later in the month. Could I help with the music that you needed?

Er, yeah, sure. I don't see why not.

Now…? Tonight…?

Aa–ah. We–ell, I am kind of tied up with "Monkey business" just at this very moment, Jamie Man…Could it possibly wait until <u>after</u> Fun Day?

That's alright, Dad. Oh, but, by the way—can we do a search on the internet tonight, to find a Pizza Hut logo for my costume…?

My Mr Big was gearing up for the next big event…

107. So that's Fun Day over then…
Saturday 7 June 2003

Kyle was playing with Carrumba in Inverness so it was just you and me on Fun Day this year, Jamie Man, with "Monkey business" first up on the programme.

Just as for "Going for gold" last year, we had the keyboard set up in the staffroom, with the speakers outside. Which is fine for keeping everything dry—you just can't hear a word of the singing! I had to play the keyboard and rely on Mrs Banks conducting out the front to keep all you musical monkeys in time. But it sounded fine on the video afterwards.

Once the singing was all over, I breathed my usual sigh of relief and you went off to help Mrs Rennie on her "throw a sponge at the teacher" stall. I think you must have been a pretty good salesman there, because she ended up very, very wet, didn't she!

Later, when everything was over for the day, we helped stack up the chairs and shift the tables back into the various classrooms and into the nursery before we came home. It felt like the end of an era.

I was permitted a brief sit down after dinner. But then, before the keyboard had even cooled down from Fun Day, you had me setting it up again in the lounge to start work on that *Fast Food Boys* routine for the Talent Show. No rest for the wicked Dad!

108. Costumes and fancy dress
June 1998–June 2003

What an array of outfits there's been over the years, Jamie Man. I was just looking at the pictures I took of the three of you all dressed up in your space costumes for the Fun Day fancy dress back in 1998—truly one of the classic years. Nicola was the fierce, four-armed bog-monster from a galaxy far, far away. Kyle was a starship trooper with his helmet, visor, backpack and blaster ray. And you were the one-and-only R2D2, all rolled up in an enormous sheet of bubble-wrap and decorated with cut-outs and stickers. By the time you were topped off with a bike helmet covered in silver foil, all we could see of you was two eyes, two ears, one nose and the tips of your toes!

You always loved dressing up: shows, fancy dress, or just plain make-believe. Like the demon doctor outfit for the children's Halloween party at Lochanhully last year. There was the giant balloon-pump with a plastic tube for your monster syringe. And a headband with a shiny CD attached for the surgeon's reflector. You put on my old white lab coat and we walked up in the dark with the torch to meet Bryce the Vampire outside. Wooo, scary!

This time you were going to be a *Fast Food Boy*, with Bryce as your partner in crime once again. We pinched the logo off the Pizza Hut website and printed it out really large for you to colour in with your felt pens. There was one for your baseball cap and another even bigger one for the T-shirt. Meanwhile Bryce was the fast food chef with his long, white apron and a matching cap. What a professional partnership. You looked just the ticket!

I'm still amazed how those poor paper Pizza Huts survived all the endless comings and goings. You crammed your costume over and over again into the nylon stuff-sack that you got when you went to see Scotland play Italy at Murrayfield in March. And yet somehow it always came out looking fine. Just one more of life's little miracles.

109. Scotland's missing mascot
Saturday 6 September 2003

Scotland were playing Ireland in the Six Nations Rugby today. They lost the match 10–29. You went on the minibus to see Scotland play at least three times, didn't you, Jamie Man, including that big day in 2000 when Kyle and the rest of his class played in the children's game on the pitch at half time. Grandma and Grandad down in England sat and watched the entire match that Saturday, just for the chance of seeing Kyle playing rugby on television, or a glimpse of your face amongst the crowd. But no such luck. The TV cameras didn't pick you out. And they went off to catch up on news elsewhere during the half-time break.

Talking of luck, I'm not sure you ever saw Scotland lose a match when you were at Murrayfield, not least the time when they beat the mighty South Africa 21–6 last year. Hearing this latest result today, I can't help feeling it sounds like the Scottish rugby team has lost its lucky mascot…

I'LL NEVER FORGET THE 11TH OF NOVEMBER
Your P5 match report: Monday 13 November 2000

On the 11th of November my Mum, my brother and I went to school to get on a coach to go to Murrayfield. I was really nervous and excited. When we got to Perth we stopped at Caithness Glass. We played on the play stuff at the back of the building. Then we got on the coach again at ten past eleven but we didn't start off again until quarter past because my Mum was late getting on the bus. When we got to Murrayfield I was really excited. We all went into the stadium. As we sat down a pipe band started to play and the Olympic medallists paraded around the pitch. Then we sang the National Anthems. Lulu sang "Flower of Scotland" with us. At twenty past two Miss Mathieson took the team to play. After the match we went to McDonald's in Perth. We ate our meal on the bus. We got back to Carr-Bridge at quarter past eight. I was so exhausted I fell asleep in the car going home.

At the bottom of the page Miss Mathieson wondered, "What was the score?"

---

110. The *Fast Food Boys* go into action
Sunday 8 June 2003

You and Bryce really threw yourselves into the preparations for the Talent Show. I remember you trying to estimate how many hours you'd spent working out and practising your song and dance routine. It added up to some amazing number. Thirty, forty, was it? By the time I came on the scene, you already had most of your plans in place: costumes, words, tunes, programme, the lot. Dad was just there to help with musical arrangements.

So on that Saturday evening after Fun Day we set off, jotting down words, chords and melodies, and sorting out the accompaniment styles you wanted. By midday Sunday, we had four of the five tunes worked out. All we had to do then was to jump on the bikes and ride along to Bryce's house to get the details of the one that he was still working on.

That gave us the perfect excuse too to try out the road to Duthil. Somehow you'd always had the knack of finding friends further out from the village. But now you were getting older and a couple of miles of hills and bends to Bryce's house shouldn't be so much of a barrier to getting together in the holidays. You'd done your cycling proficiency test at school. I could ride along with you each way to begin with, just to see that you were okay with the traffic. Then after that you should be fine making the journey on your own.

111. Dropping in on the Wolf of Badenoch
Thursday 7 August 2003

It's been seriously hot and sunny again today, Jamie Man. The kind of day when your hay fever and asthma would have been bad. You'd probably have got very red in the face. Though I don't think that would have stopped you wanting to join in the adventure. Kyle and I have been for our longest ever bike ride together—all the way to Lochindorb.

I got the idea from that book *The Wolf* that I came across in the library on one of our Scout nights back in the spring. The story concerned Alexander Stewart, the Wolf of Badenoch. He wasn't very popular with the Bishop of Moray, especially after he rode up to Elgin with his men in 1390 and burned the town and the cathedral to the ground!

Lochindorb is beyond the hills on the road across Dava Moor from Duthil to Nairn and Forres. That's wild and bleak country—badlands, Jamie Man. I'd been thinking it could be just the kind of place that you and Kyle might enjoy exploring on the bikes in the summer holidays. The big question was whether it might still be a bit too far for you to manage? But then we didn't have to go all the way. We could always start out and see how far we got. And that's what Kyle and I decided we should do today.

It's mostly uphill from the Duthil turn off. And with the hot sun beating down on our backs, it seemed like we'd never reach the big scoop of the pass where the road goes over between the hills. Eventually though, just after midday, we panted into the lay-by at the top and stopped for a drink of water and a packet of crisps. While we were there, one of those big, foreign tourist coaches pulled in to let the passengers stretch their legs and snap a few pictures. Kyle and I reckoned we'd worked rather harder to earn our rest break!

Then it was decision time. Turn round and enjoy the long roll back to Duthil and Carr-Bridge? Or press on for Lochindorb down the other side, knowing that we'd have to climb back up again on the way home? I left it up to Kyle. He was determined to go on.

The road over Dava is all narrow bridges, snow gates, passing places, steep hills, bends and snow poles to show you where the road ought to be when it's covered by the drifts in the winter. After that, you turn off the main road and there's a long sweep round to the far side of the Loch. We parked the bikes in the heather and took our lunch down to the edge of the water. From there you can look across and see the island with the ruined castle that was once the lair of the Wolf of Badenoch, six hundred years ago.

We'd taken the local castles book with us and, sitting there on the side of the Loch, I read out the history of the dark fortress of Lochindorb. It said that even Edward I, king of England, the Hammer of the Scots, once came to stay in the castle there. I guess that's okay if you're an honoured guest, or the conqueror. But I don't think I'd have fancied being invited to the dungeons of Lochindorb, or to the infamous "water pit" where prisoners were left to shiver in three feet of icy-cold loch water. Brrrrrr, Jamie Man!

112. Fast work for the *Fast Food Boys*
Sunday 8–Monday 9 June 2003

You and Bryce had come up with a medley of five, short songs for the Talent Show routine. Three of them were your own compositions. Then there was Nicola's favourite, the "Fast Food Song" (the one you taught to the Cubs and Scouts at the barbeque at Loch an Eilein). And finally a grand helping of "Food Glorious Food" to finish up with.

After you'd gone to bed on the Sunday evening, I was up until 2.00am with the earphones, keyboard, pencil and paper, sorting out the required musical arrangements and links. And then Monday was the big "studio day"—playing each of the tunes over and over again until I had the whole lot recorded, fumble-free, on cassette. By the time you arrived home from school in the afternoon that day, I'd just finished the job with about ten minutes to spare. But would my efforts pass the all-important Jamie Man test…?

THOSE TALENT SHOW SONGS

1. *Shake it, shake it! Shake it, shake it!*

    Move it, move it! Move it, move it!

    Take the top off and spray the ice cream.

    Let's shake it! Let's move it! And top off the ice cream.

2. *Come to Pizza Hut but don't ask why.*

    We can turn your toppings into a tie.

    There is cheese and chives and tomato too.

    Come to Pizza Hut and we'll do it for you!

3. *A Pizza Hut. A Pizza Hut. Kentucky Fried Chicken and a Pizza Hut.*

    MacDonald's. MacDonald's. Kentucky Fried Chicken and a Pizza Hut.

    (From "The Fast Food Song")

4. *All I want is Burger King.*

    Chicken wings and an onion ring.

    I had an onion ring for my wedding ring.

And I ate it in the end.

5.   *Food glorious food!*
     (From Oliver!)

---

113. So will that do...?
Monday 9 June 2003

I switched on the cassette player. You listened closely. You pondered. You frowned. Then you grinned and said it would be fine. Relief!

Of course we still had to get the tunes stitched together to make up the final backing tape for the show. And timed against the crucial three minute target too. Out came your twin cassette deck and the stopwatch. There was endless double-checking to make sure we didn't get the tapes mixed up and record over the top of the precious originals! But at last we were there. A copy for you. Another one for Bryce. And that was it.

Phheeewww! At least I wasn't going to have to do all *that* again...! We–ell, not until the following week, anyway...when you came home to tell me that Bryce reckoned that two of the songs *really* needed to be just a *wee* bit faster...!!!

114. We're all ready for the big day now...aren't we?
Thursday 19 June 2003

So I'd *re-recorded* the two offending songs. And made up the *new* stitched up version on cassette for you and Bryce. Everything set now for the show on Monday...?

We–ell, there was that minor panic the Thursday before the big day. When you came home to report this time that Amanda the drama leader wasn't actually quite sure how they were going to be able to play your backing tape. The problem was, it seemed, that the marvellous, high-tech mixing console that they were planning to use for the show...couldn't actually cope with playing a humble cassette tape!

No worry. Don't panic. My Dad will sort it out.

He will?? Would that be before or after the nervous breakdown????

115. Roll up, roll up for the Talent Show…at last!
Monday 23 June 2003

The big day dawned at last. Midsummer's Eve. Grandad's birthday. And crunch time for the *Fast Food Boys*. We'd survived the frantic dash up to school on the Friday morning with the amplifier from your electric guitar. We'd conquered all the cables and plugs to get it connected up with the school's weird and wonderful cassette player. And most remarkable of all, after some twiddling and tweaking…we actually had backing music! It had been a struggle, but none of that mattered anymore. Finally, it was *SHOWTIME!*

And what an array of talent there was on offer: pogo stick performers, poy artists, musicians, singers, dancers, and last, but by no means least, Jamie and Bryce: *Fast Food Boys* extraordinaire. What a show! How could the judges possibly make up their minds?

116. Back to Duthil
Thursday 7 August 2003

You might have got hot and tired on the ride out to Lochindorb, Jamie Man. But I'm sure you would have revelled in the exciting return leg from the top of the pass just as much as Kyle did. He simply put his nose down on the handlebars and *whizzed* all the way back to the T-junction, with Dad tagging along rather more cautiously in his wake.

We were there in next to no time. And since we were out that way, it did seem silly not to make the small detour along to Bryce's house. He wasn't back from his Granny's yet though. His Mum and Dad are going down to fetch him home this weekend. It isn't going to be easy for him at the new school when the start of term comes around.

I found it tough myself, pedalling away from Duthil, remembering the previous occasion when I'd set off to cycle that same road home, the day after Fun Day. You were my companion on that occasion, with the preparations for the Talent Show uppermost in our minds. So you didn't win the competition. But it wasn't a waste of time, all that hard work. The pair of you gave it everything you had. And the *Fast Food Boys* served up one more large helping of fun and laughter for everyone to remember for a long while to come.

117. Something to hold on to
Sunday 17 August 2003

The children going back to school have been very much on my mind, Jamie Man. New classes, new teachers, a whole new school for your friends from P7 last year.

All summer, people have been telling me how they remember you so much for your smile and will miss seeing your cheery face when the term begins. This weekend all sorts of things have suddenly come together in a new song. A new song for a new start:

HOLD ON TO THE SMILES
For the pupils of Carr-Bridge Primary and Grantown Grammar Schools

Leaves grow and tears fall
Trees reach up to the sky
Sun warms and ice cools again
But while seasons lead on to the future
Love and friendship still remain for ever

> *Hold on to the smiles*
> *Hold on to the fun*
> *Hold on to the times of laughter*
> *Then sadness will fade*
> *With the passing of days*
> *But hope will stay*
> *Ever after*

Wind blows and rain falls
Mist drifts and flowers bloom
Birds fly and then they are gone
But while seasons lead on to the future
Love and friendship still remain for ever

> *Hold on to the smiles...etc*

---

118. Rachel's song for you
Monday 25 August 2003 & Friday 16 January 2004

I haven't been the only one with new music on the mind, Jamie Man. As I was coming back up the road from the Spar this afternoon I heard someone calling my name. It was Rachel from your class, just off the school bus, fresh from another exciting day in S1. She gave me an envelope with the words of the song that she's written for you.

YOUR SMILE
by Rachel Sermanni

Your smile looking straight at me
Your eyes are the stars
Your cheeks are the roses smelling sweet

　　And I will remember you
　　Yes, I will always think of you
　　Forever more

The sun shining straight on you
The love in your heart
I can see your kindness and your love

　　And I will remember you
　　Yes, I will always think of you
　　Forever more

And now you look down on me
With the sun and the stars
Oh, I will always look up to you
Coz

　　I will remember you
　　Yes, I will always think of you
　　Forever more
　　OOOOOOOOOOOOOhhhhhhhhhhh
　　Forever more

Rachel sang the song all on her own to a packed hall in the Carr-Bridge Hotel on our *Jamie Weekend*, just after we'd presented the Royal Humane Society certificate for bravery to Andrew Dale. Truly a singer-songwriter of the future.

119. Practising poy
Wednesday 9 July 2003

Originally when I set out scribbling down notes on all the things we did that first week of the holidays, I completely forgot about your home-made poy. It was writing a thank-you letter to Rachel that reminded me. She and Sarah Norton did their spectacular poy routine for the Talent Show. And they were so good, they not only won the dance section at Carr-Bridge on the Monday, but they also went on to win the overall final in Grantown later that week.

You'd made your poy at Mum's house at the weekend, with a hard rubber ball tied up in a plastic bag on the end of each string. You got them out on the Wednesday for a try-out on the patio while I was making dinner. Even now I see you out of the kitchen window there, swinging them round above your head and practising the various techniques. You were still getting the hang of it and there were a fair few tangles and fumbles as I recall. Eventually it all ended up with a bump on the head and you came in looking a bit sorry for yourself. We had to agree that Rachel and Sarah definitely made this poy business look a whole lot easier that it really was! But after a big hug, you were soon having a chuckle about the whole thing. There'd be plenty of opportunity for further practice over the holidays.

A THANK-YOU LETTER
Tuesday 26 August 2003

Dear Rachel

Thank you so much for the kind and thoughtful song that you wrote for Jamie. Your Mum told me about the dream you had of Jamie after you heard the news of what had happened and I think that you have painted the picture of how you felt so very, very clearly. I look forward to being able to hear the music too…

…I have the P7 class picture up on the wall in the house here, with you standing just beside Jamie, and when I think of Jamie and his music, the picture of you and Sarah and him playing together at Music Club so often comes to mind. I hope that

you will be able to carry the good memories of those happy times with you into the future and not feel too upset about the sad side of things.

I know that music is very special for you, as it was for Jamie, and I think it is a very wonderful gift that you have given to him in writing your song. I will treasure it for him....

Thank you once again for the special gift of your song.

David

120. Our grand picture show
Wednesday 9 July 2003

A night in the Youth Hostel. A trip to Glasgow. A visit to Landmark. Sorting out the shed. Going up in the loft. Digging in the garden. Exploring in the woods. Reading stories. Imagination at full throttle all week. But that didn't mean you'd forgotten…

> *Da—addd…Can we get the projector out and look at those slides tonight?*

Tomorrow you'd be off to Inverness for the weekend. What better way to tie up a perfect week together, than with a grand picture show? And you had it all worked out in your head, of course. I was allowed to put up the screen while you set up the projector. But after that, you took charge of the slides and Dad was instructed just to sit back and enjoy the show.

You wanted to start in Pitlochry, of course. We saw "The Flat"—the first home I ever owned, with its sunrise and sunset views up and down the Tummel valley. Then it was down to the river and the little house that we moved into when Nicola was born. Up to the dam and round the Loch to the lab where I worked. From winter snows to autumn colours.

But that was merely Part One. After a week of delving into all sorts of corners, and tossing around ideas for the future, my Master of Ceremonies had decided that now was the perfect time for a look at Carr-Bridge history too. And so, on your final night in the house, you launched into a running commentary on the progress of *Seann Bhruthach*—old slope—from derelict dry ski slope to home and garden. It was a story that encapsulated your entire life from pudgy toddler to eager eleven-year old. Flowers slowly emerged from the wasteland. Tiny bare sticks, no taller than you were when you started in P1, stretched themselves up into mighty trees that now reach high above our heads.

The grand *Seann Bhruthach* picture show: from ski slope to *Old Slope*.
1. By the original ski slope. 2. More stones than garden. 3. Cutting logs, big time.
4. The front lawn to be. 5. Seann Bhruthach. 6. Before the playhouse. 7. Kjersti
Dog looks for the lawn. 8. Grass at last! 9. The playhouse takes shape. 10. Chaos
by the back gate. 11. The playhouse. 12. Our sycamore tree in autumn. 13. The
back lawn to be. 14. The patio and back lawn. 15. Frost on your stones.

And as with so much else that week, our thoughts turned once again to speculation on things to come. A future, as it turned out, that was destined to be a mere forty or so more hours. If I could have known what those following two days were to bring, is there anything that I would have changed? All I can say, is that I'm at a loss to think of a better way that we might have chosen to spend our very last evening together, Jamie Man. Or any other part of that final, precious week when you led me back through a whirlwind of visits to every single place that had been at all special in the magic years I was given to share with you. My compliments to the Picture Show Manager. I could not have asked for more.

DAD'S SUMMER REPORT
Extract from a letter, Tuesday 30 July 1996

...After nearly three years since we had the house built, I have finally managed to sow grass seed and I have just given the lawn its first ever cut this weekend. Seann Bhruthach means "old slope" in Gaelic and the land was formerly the site of an old dry ski slope which had to be dug out before the house could be built. Consequently there has been a lot of clearing up to turn the ground into a garden. The house is about 260m above sea level and it was -25C here last Christmas. Despite this, most of the trees and plants seem to be coming along well. During the holidays I have been building a playhouse in the garden for the children. Jamie loves to be outside in the garden and he is not happy for me to sit inside when there is building work to be done!...

---

121. The never-finishing story
Monday 14 July 2003

When they interviewed Mrs Banks on television, she said she thought you must have known the first four Harry Potter books off by heart. She could always rely on you to keep her right on the stories. The newly-published *Harry Potter and the Order of the Phoenix* came up a lot in our conversations that first weekend in Inverness. You'd looked forward so eagerly to the next book in the series and now you were never going to hear how the story would end. Somehow it seemed symbolic of so many other sadnesses that waited in ambush around every corner in those first few, dreadful days.

Nicola had zipped through the entire book the first weekend it came out. But you and Kyle and I were taking things more slowly, going through the story together. Well, perhaps slowly isn't *quite* the right word. Dad was undoubtedly in even greater demand than usual for reading aloud once the new Harry had arrived. An hour or two in the evening. Another chapter before Kyle went out to catch the school bus in the morning. We may have had all the time in the world, but that didn't mean you wanted to hang about!

When I returned to Carr-Bridge after the weekend in Inverness, I checked where we'd got up to in the story. Our bookmark was at page 276. Your *Order of the Phoenix* would forever finish with the announcement of the appointment of the High Inquisitor. Uncertain times ahead for Hogwarts School of Witchcraft and Wizardry.

122. Snuffy the rabbit takes a "hand"
Sunday 13 July 2003

I'll tell you something to make you smile, Jamie Man. A ridiculous little story to round off this weekend of glum faces, sympathy cards and sad words.

I'd been sitting on the stairs here at Mum's house, talking on the phone to Skip the Scout Leader. He'd rung the moment he got back from his holiday. Well, of course that was never going to be a short call, or an easy one, was it. Cubs and Scouts had been such a big thing in your life. And naturally Skip was...shocked? devastated? All that kind of thing.

Finally we said goodbye and I made way for Nicola, who settled herself down for a phone session of her own. In the meantime, someone had let Snuffy the rabbit out for some exercise, so he was now wandering around the floor at our feet. You know how his cage is tucked away under the bend of the stairs in the hall there at Mum's house.

Well, sometime later, there was this sudden screech from Nicola. We all rushed out to see what the problem was...and there she was dangling a useless telephone. Snuffy the rabbit had chewed his way *right through the trailing wire!*

I'm sure you can imagine the scene, Jamie Man. It's late Sunday evening, with everything else that's been going on, and at a stroke—or should I say at a bite?—we're cut off from the world! Mobile phones aren't much help if people are trying to ring in on the landline and just getting the automatic answering service! Whatever next?

I guess if you'd read that little tale in a book, you'd probably say something like, "Oh yes, pull the other one!" But I hope it will have brought you a smile, my Wee Man.

123. The phone saga continues
Monday 14 July 2003

So now, thanks to Snuffy, Mum was heading out in search of a new phone! Before they went, Kyle fixed Dad up with the ladder and instructions for the loft hatch. Rumour had it that the old flat phone was still up there in a box somewhere. Of course, *you* would have known where to find it straightaway, Jamie Man, I'm sure. Even when you were tiny—if something went missing—under the bed or wherever—it was always:

Just ask Jamie. <u>He'll</u> know where it is.

Barely two days in the house and here I was shinning up a ladder and crawling around in the loft with a torch—talk about a busman's holiday! But—miracle of miracles—there was the old phone in the second box I tried. Problem solved!
Solved did I say? You wish! Plug it in. Dial *1–5–7–1…*

You have five messages…

First message, nothing special. Press the button for the next one…Oh, *gr–reat*! It's an old fashioned phone, isn't it! Doesn't know about modern BT exchange services does it! Won't go beyond message one, will it! What *now*? Try the neighbours?

Hello, I'm from next door. Do you have a spare telephone I could borrow?

Back to Mum's with a fancy cordless phone. At least this should solve the problem. I plug it in and start to dial…and the doorbell rings!

Oh, hi, Jan. Come in. Grab a seat. Don't mind me. I'm just going quietly crazy over phones. I have a nasty suspicion this one needs to be charged up.

Down on my knees once more…Doorbell, *again*! The man from next door:

I was just thinking you might get on better with this other phone…?

Oh, er, thanks.

Swap phones. Shut door.

Sorry about this, Jan. I will be with you in a moment, honest.

Back to work again…just as Mum and the others arrive home from the shops. Greetings all round. More confusion. I dial *1–5–7–1*. Finger in the ear trying to hear BT:

> *You have five messages…*

Success at *last*!
Five messages. All boring. Nothing important. Nothing urgent.

124. Great empty spaces
August–September 2003

The weekends seem strangely quiet these days without your phone calls, Jamie Man. So often, fifteen minutes after you arrived at Mum's house on a Saturday morning:

> *Da–ad…have you got…?*

or:

> *Did I leave my…?*

or:

> *When I get back on Sunday evening, can you remind me to…*

Or at any other odd moment as the fancy took you. A brief and breathless two or three minutes just to tell me what you'd been up to. Or that funny little voice waiting for me on the answer machine. All reminding me how great it is to be eleven years old…

The hardest times to fill though, are not those long, weekend days, when Kyle is away in Inverness and I'm here in the house on my own. The worst empty spaces are the spare ten minutes, or quarter of an hour, here and there in the evenings after school. When Kyle is in the bath, or content doing his homework without any interference from me. That's when *you* were always there to fill the gap, my Jamie Man. I never learned to be the parent of an "only" child. I never anticipated it was skill I would ever require.

Evenings were a matter of organising my time for the two of you. Sometimes all of us together, like reading Harry Potter. Sometimes with one of you on your own, while the other was busy elsewhere. And of course, it wasn't uncommon to find myself tugged in two directions at once. Funny, I was never any good at juggling. You'd think after all those years of practice I ought to have been a natural.

Once upon a time, it seemed like there wasn't enough Dad to go around. Now, when I wave Kyle off for an evening with his friends, I'm not always sure what to do with the spare stock that's left over on the shelf.

125. Whatever next?
Monday 14 July 2003

After the media frenzy of the weekend, I was starting to wonder what we might find when we came back to Carr-Bridge. Reporters camped outside the house? Messages on the answerphone? Heaps of flowers on the doorstep? I simply had no idea *what* to expect anymore. I called Mrs Banks to ask if she could pop down to the house and check out the situation. She rang back a short while later. The house was fine. No problems there. However…there were TV cameras filming down at the school…!

Mr Whyte had mentioned over the weekend that the teachers were proposing to open a Book of Condolences for people who wanted to write a message. A kind thought. The sort of rallying-around thing that happens at such times. We just didn't imagine…

When Mrs Banks got down there, she was just in time to be interviewed by Grampian Television. And then as she was leaving, she saw the BBC film crew arriving! I know you would have found the whole thing hard to believe, Jamie Man. Mrs Banks reckoned it had worked out for the best, though. With the media all focusing on the school, it did at least seem to have diverted attention away from the house. So we could think about setting off back to Carr-Bridge undisturbed…We–ell, almost.

Ring, ring. Ring, ring…

The *Inverness Courier* this time. Looking for a last minute interview for tomorrow's edition. This is a job for Dad—*again*. Needless to say, it wasn't very early in the day when we finally passed the Primary School and drove back down towards the house.

E-MAIL, 8.58 PM
Tuesday 15 July 2003

Life is like a wild sea, throwing me where it decides, with very little regard for the course that I would pick, or the people that I would rather be talking to. The telephone rings, and rings again. People come to the door, well-meaning but exhausting...

...The post mortem was finally completed this afternoon. Thankfully in the circumstances only a superficial examination was required. We've not heard the official results yet but basically we've already been told by the doctor that Jamie died from a single blow to the head as he fell, that's all. Otherwise he was uninjured.

The undertaker is coming here to talk to us at 10.30am tomorrow. And my parents will be arriving tomorrow evening. The prospect of time alone to walk in the woods with my little boy still seems rather far in the distance.

Kyle is away for two nights with his best friend from school, which will be good for him, I think.

They opened a Book of Condolences at the school yesterday for people to sign and I'm told that there were reports about it on the TV last night. A friend has recorded the TV stuff on video for me and is collecting the newspaper reports too, so that I can see it all when I'm ready.

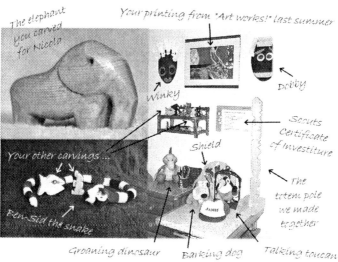

The elephant you carved for Nicola

Your printing from "Art works!" last summer

Winky

Dobby

Scouts Certificate of Investiture

Your other carvings...

Shield

The totem pole we made together

Ben~Sid the snake

Groaning dinosaur   Barking dog   Talking toucan

126. Just as you left it
Tuesday 15 July 2003

Apart from making space in your room for Mum and Nicola, we've returned to a house that remains essentially just as you would remember it from when you and I set out for the bus on Thursday. This morning we've gone from room to room, following your trail. So many priceless stories locked up in the tiniest of objects. Nicola and Kyle have gathered all the different instruments together on your bed as a reminder of your music. There's the chanter that was to lead you on to the bagpipes at the Grammar School, the recorders, the whistles, the classical guitar, the electric guitar—all so unnaturally quiet.

I led the two of them round the garden with their cameras, describing all the things that you were up to last week. They took pictures of your bird table in the playhouse. The road across the patio and along the path to your final check-point at the back gate. Our excavations behind the house. The ski slope where you climbed mountains and dug valleys. Your arrangements and rearrangements on the stick pile. So much to remember. So many pieces of the jigsaw to retrieve and preserve. How could we possibly ever hope to capture every one of those fleeting images in a few, small pictures?

127. A long and distinguished line of pets
1989–2002

There was a wee cross of willow sticks at the end of the vegetable-patch-to-be, beside the back gate. Still marking the spot where we buried the two guinea pigs last year. That was a sad time. Merlin was so lonely when Randi died that he too pined away just eight days later, on the first day of the summer holidays. The very last of a long and distinguished line of pets.

There was famous Frankie the goldfish, who survived a leap out of the tank and lying unnoticed on the carpet behind the sofa for ages. Sixpence the hamster, who would scurry around the floor and then stand begging to come up on a lap for a cuddle. Sparkles the hamster, who nibbled through Nicola's brand new sweatshirt in the night and thus provided Dad with a new gardening jumper...

Then of course you had your very special mouse, Giggles. Yasmin Harrower's brother Ben was very impressed by your new pet. He reckoned Giggles would make a really excellent stud mouse, with his highly distinctive markings. Unfortunately Giggles didn't seem particularly interested in the girls when Ben brought a couple round to visit. But you still loved going back to Ben's to see all his different mouse crosses.

128. Giggles Super Mouse
1998–2000

Looking back now through your school work, there's no doubt who was the hero of the moment in P3 and P4. Everything revolved around Giggles Super Mouse. One time in P3, you were asked about the best dream you'd ever had. And you drew a picture of Giggles playing the piano! On another worksheet that year, you wrote:

I like being myself…*because I have got a mouse.*

You drew a time line of the big events in your life. It had just three points:

1991—*I was born.*

1993—*I came here. (You didn't remember the two houses before this one)*

1998—*I got Giggles.*

And what would you do if you were a millionaire? You would buy further add-ons for the maze of runs and tubes in the cage that Giggles had inherited from Sixpence the hamster.

Mice don't live for very long and losing Giggles was one of the saddest lessons of your life. On your "Me and my feelings" sheet at school in P5 you wrote:

I feel happy when…*I play with my Dad*

I feel sad when…*my pet died*

Jamie and Giggles, a pair of super heroes.

129. "What makes you angry?"
2000–2001

When the guinea pigs disagreed with one another they would click their teeth. And if they got *properly* mad, they would rear up on their haunches and yawn really wide to display their fangs, trying to look as tall and fierce as possible. You and Kyle and Nicola didn't *always* agree with one another either. None of you were angels. It would be a very unusual house where brothers and sisters got on well with each other *all* the time. You would squabble and fight at times. In P5 you had a worksheet where you had to circle the things that turned you into what we used to call "Grumpy Man". You picked out these two:

Someone spoils my game

I'm very tired and hungry

I think that was actually quite an honest assessment, Jamie Man. Good for you!

130. Ben and the stick insects
1999–2002

Ben Harrower was definitely one of your heroes with all his different pet projects. In the drawer in your bedroom I found the article I cut out of the *Strathy* for you about Ben's rare lizard breeding. His Mum, Caroline, tells me that Ben's latest animal enterprise is a pair of Harris hawks. Who knows, maybe there'll be the patter of tiny claws someday soon!

Our stick insects came from Ben Harrower. Just half a dozen to start with. But by spring, it wasn't a question of six, or even sixteen. I think we eventually lost count at about fifty or sixty! We were finding runaways in the most *unlikely* places. Remember the one you spotted walking upside down across the bathroom ceiling? After that we started donating the extras to the pet shop in Inverness! Crazy creatures—but fun to watch, eh, Jamie Man!

131. Kjersti dog
15 March 1983–17 November 1999

I first held Kjersti Dog in my hand when she was just one week old. She was six or seven weeks old when she came to live with me in the flat in Pitlochry that you saw on the slides. I have a photo of her from around that time. It's hard to believe she was ever so tiny—snubby nose and little short legs. She was mainly black Labrador but with a dash of collie thrown in. And she didn't cost me a penny. What a great bargain she turned out to be!

Kjersti Dog used to come jogging with me at lunchtimes in Pitlochry and I'm sure keeping fit helped her to live so long. The tourists always thought it was highly amusing watching the wee puppy scampering up through the Pass of Killiecrankie to Soldier's Leap, or round Loch Faskally and through the woods. It was the day before your eighth birthday when Kjersti Dog died. She had slowed up towards the end and she couldn't see or hear very well by then. But nobody lives for ever do they, Jamie Man. We have to be prepared to say goodbye when the time comes, even when we're sad to see our friends go. Kyle says that he'd like us to have another dog and I have to admit, a new puppy would be nice…

132. A new generation of pet lovers
June 2003

All the indoor guinea pig gear went for Nicola to sell when she was doing her fund raising for Scottish Youth Theatre. That left the shabby old outdoor cage. Just before the end of term I finally got round to putting an advert in the

Strathy—going free to a good home. I was *amazed* how many calls we got. The folk who eventually took the cage planned to add a floor and use it for keeping ferrets. I wonder whether ferrets like guinea pig pong? What d'you reckon, Jamie Man? The perfect perfume? Or a permanent whiff of lunch to drive them crazy?

No sooner had I waved the cage off up the drive, than there was a telephone call from Mrs Bootle, your old learning support teacher. Her wee ones had just been given a guinea pig and now they were in the market for the whole kit. If only we'd known that a bit sooner!

133. Shredded Paper Supplies Ltd
Wednesday 9 July 2003

We don't usually need to throw much away in this house. Once upon a time of course, there was always a wee man who wanted me to save the empty boxes and containers for all his weird and wonderful projects. It's a sad business these days, tearing up the cereal packets for the compost heap or to burn on the stove, knowing that there's no one queuing up to turn them into road signs, or a puppet theatre, or whatever.

Our guinea pigs lived in homes decked out with cardboard, newspaper, and shredded paper. It was always a funny business, seeing the new heap getting tossed about after a cage clean out, wasn't it, Jamie Man.

By the time you came back from Glasgow on Monday evening, I was well into shredding paper for the Bootle's new guinea pig, Petal. You joined in and by the Wednesday we had a good, bulging sackful. We dropped by their house on the way back from the Spar that morning to pick up a bin bag to fill up for them. And we took them one of the guinea pig books from our bookshelf with lots of pictures for the two wee ones to enjoy.

It was such an ordinary visit. Nothing remarkable at all. David and Alice, were zooming back and forth between the two front rooms while you and I stood exchanging guinea pig stories with Mrs Bootle in their big hallway there.

What are Nicola and Kyle up to this week?

What have we got planned for the holidays?

Yes, it was all so very, very…ordinary.

134. An order for glycerine
Wednesday 9 July 2003

While I was filling up the bag of shredded paper for Petal, you disappeared off into the office to do a bit more on your latest project on the computer. When I looked in, you were deeply engrossed in the whys and wherefores of smoke machines. Much too busy to stop just then. So I popped back up the street with the sack of paper while you were finishing off there.

The smoke machine question all began with a request some weeks earlier:

> *Da…add, can you get me a bottle of glycerine when you go to Tesco's so we can make some smoke?*

At the time I presumed you must have found some instructions on one of your pack of science experiment cards. It was only later that I realised it was all based on a simple one-liner in your *Special Effects* book, saying how artificial smoke can be generated using glycerine. We had a look on the internet and sure enough that was indeed quite true…*as far as it went.* Unfortunately what the book did not take the trouble to point out, was that the process generally calls for high temperatures and a fairly sophisticated piece of hardware!

Ho hum. How best to match up eleven-year old enthusiasm with 21st Century reality, without too much disappointment? Hence the discussions with Grandad on the phone to set him up for some smoke experiments when they came in the summer.

135. That smoke machine project
Thursday 21 August 2003

I was sorting through some disks in the office while Kyle was out at his Carrumba drumming practice tonight, and I came across the one that you must have been using for your project on the computer that Wednesday. There was the first chapter, complete with all the pictures of smoke machines that I'd helped you download from the internet. You'd typed the heading for chapter two as well. But then the rest of that page was blank. Work in progress…

Grandad is just having his new computer installed and he'd said he would be setting up his e-mail account this evening. So I thought I would send him your project as one of his first messages. I knew he'd be sad you didn't get the chance to finish it, or to have a discussion about smoke machines when he and Grandma came in the summer. But I was sure that he'd want to see what you'd written so far. Clever Grandad managed to read the attachment *and* to send me a reply telling me that he would "treasure it greatly".

136. In between
Wednesday 16 July 2003

In the two days I've been back in Carr-Bridge I seem to have done little else but talk on the telephone, deal with callers at the door, and generally troubleshoot whatever comes up. Waiting for the results of a post mortem and trying to fix up arrangements for visitors and a funeral. Kyle is well out of it over in Cromdale with Richard and his family. There was a *Strathy* interview on the phone yesterday—another hour and a half. It was pretty clear what was going to be the big story in the newspaper today.

Nicola and Mum have gone back up to Inverness now to meet Nan off the train this evening. I went up to the Spar with them after lunch to pick up the paper before they left. Sure enough, there was the Book of Condolences at the top of the front page and my interview on page two.

When Mum and Nicola drove off up the road it was the first time I had been on my own in four days. And suddenly I didn't know where to go, or what to do. Grandma and Grandad were arriving this evening—they might even see Nan on the train. Mrs Banks had promised to come and pick me up in time for some shopping in Tesco's before going to meet them at the station. But all that was still another three or four hours away. Once again the world was all bright lights and hard edges. There were people coming and going round about. Talking. Noises. Cars passing up and down the road. Tourists—every single one of them.

I crossed over and headed for the woods. Better that than the lonely walk back up a street full of strangers. The river was low, as it has been all year. There were youngsters up on the Old Bridge amusing themselves—and the tourists—by leaping off into the pool of water below. Rocky and so very shallow…No one took any notice as I drifted on by, looking the other way.

Oh, for a glimpse of a familiar face.

Before I'd reached the woods, a car drew up alongside me. It was Caroline Harrower, Yasmin and Ben's Mum. I think we must have talked for about an hour or more. She too remembered our meeting at the checkouts in Tesco's on Friday. She said that they'd passed me on the road afterwards as well, when I was cycling up out of Aviemore with the shopping. I feel sure that she and Yasmin must have been the nearest friends from the village at the moment you fell…

When Yasmin heard the news, she'd told her Mum it must be a mistake. It couldn't be you. It would have to be someone else. You weren't the type to have an accident like that. You were too sensible and careful. Sigh...If only. Unfortunately such things don't always stop to check whether they have the right person or not, do they, Jamie Man.

137. Many meetings
Wednesday 16 July 2003

That chance encounter with Caroline became just one of many such conversations. Yet it seems somehow fitting that she of all people should have been the first. I came to realise in the days that followed that even the simplest trip to the shop for milk, or to collect the paper, called for a good hour or more longer than usual, just to allow for all the chats and hugs from friends—in the street, in the woods, or wherever.

On one occasion I found myself standing outside the Spar talking to Mr Malcolm from next door for about half an hour, all the while cuddling Mrs Malcolm to comfort her because she was so upset. But that's okay. It's just the way things had to be, Jamie Man. I think there were a lot of people who needed to find a friend to hold on to. And each time I came across someone new, that was their *first* chance to talk about their sadness.

No, of course it wasn't quite the same for me. Your name was on everyone's lips and I shared your sad story...I don't know how many times. Perhaps Ian the postman summed it up best several months later, on the day that was to be your 12th birthday:

He's a lad who will never be forgotten in this village.

Such was the goodwill of this year.

138. The *Oldies* on Cairngorm
Monday 14 April 2003

Grandma and Great Aunty Iris came up to see you performing in the Gang Show, so they were here with us that Sunday when I took the photos of you wearing the kilt. The next pictures on the film were from the Monday, when we took them for a ride up Cairngorm Mountain on the new funicular railway. The weather was fine but rather windy and we'd been making sure that the *Oldies* always had an arm to hang on to.

While we were browsing round the shop, I happened to mention that we'd need to check the bus times for going back. Next minute I glance out of the window and what do I see? Yes, there's Aunty Iris wandering out across the car park on her own to look for someone to ask! And before I can stop her, we have Grandma setting off in pursuit! Of course, the inevitable happened, didn't it…Two old ladies blown right off their feet by a sudden *whoooosh* of wind rushing down between the two buildings! If I hadn't been so worried, it could have been quite funny—like a scene out of some comedy show. Senior citizens or not, they both got a good old telling off for not doing what they were told that day, eh, Jamie Man!

139. It's one thing after another
Wednesday 16 July 2003

Even after the long talk with Caroline, there's still plenty of time for a shower and something to eat before going out. Maybe even a quiet sit down…

Ring, ring. Ring, ring.

It's Great Aunty Iris on the telephone. She's still upset by the news of your accident and worried that she won't be able to come to the funeral. I reassure her as best I can for half an hour and then go into the kitchen to put the kettle on. While I'm waiting for that to boil, I suddenly remember I've promised to ring Mr Whyte with an update on the funeral arrangements. It's his answerphone, of course. I wait for the beep and then…

Ding, dong.

I abandon the kettle and the teabags and go along the hall with the cordless phone in my hand. The final words of the message for Mr Whyte are on my lips as I open the front door. I click off the phone, make my apologies and look up into the face of the latest visitor. But *who* exactly is it?

140. A mystery visitor on the doorstep
Wednesday 16 July 2003

She wasn't a stranger. I was certain I did know her. But at that precise moment, I had no idea who this newcomer might be. She was holding a bunch of flowers in her hand and for an instant I thought that might be my salvation. She'll hand over the flowers and I'll be able to read the card…Unfortunately, I couldn't see any sign of a card. And anyway, it looked like she wasn't planning to pass the flowers over straight away. Foiled again!

We talked on for about ten minutes. She wasn't just a casual acquaintance. Clearly, she knew you and Kyle and Nicola in more than a passing way. But who on earth was she? My mind was a complete blank. Eventually, she shifted the flowers round and I saw that there *was* a card underneath in her other hand. At least I'd be able to solve the riddle...after she'd gone. We carried on and then all at once she paused and looked at me:

You don't remember who I am, do you?

How embarrassing! I had to confess that she was quite right. I gave her a quick précis of the afternoon since I'd waved goodbye to Mum and Nicola outside the Spar. I think I said how I was finding it hard to hold everything in my head all at once. Trying to keep track of what I'd said, and to whom. And feeling sure that some people must be hearing the same things over and over again. She was very understanding.

So who was this mystery stranger with the flowers, who knew you all so well? It was Mrs Scarfe, Kyle's maths teacher. She'd taught Nicola in the past. And she'd seen you on the introductory days at the Grammar School too. Nicola and her son Timmy used to play together when we were living down in Kincraig while this house was being built.

The trouble was of course, that I'd never met Mrs Scarfe on the doorstep here before. It had always been somewhere else. And as I told her, I just hadn't been able to place her when she wasn't wearing a Parents' Evening table, and a School Report!

141. Wee George
Wednesday 16 July 2003

I'm not sure I ever did get round to that cup of tea. I do know that by the time I'd said goodbye to Mrs Scarfe and hunted out a pot to put her flowers in, there wasn't much left of my quiet, few hours. A hasty shower. Something cold on a plate and I could *probably* still be ready for Mrs Banks by quarter to seven. Five minutes to fix dinner. Another five to eat it. Still time for a cup of coffee even. Sink down in the chair...

Ding, dong...

This time it was wee George, your friend from the playpark—five years old?—with his Mum and Dad. Come to bring me another one of those extra special cards, with his own crayoned flowers on the front and the message from the heart inside:

> *To Jamie's family*
>
> *I will always remember Jamie and miss him very much.*
>
> *Love, George*

Wee George. His voice so familiar from behind the high fence along that side of the garden. But now he was so quiet as his Mum and Dad talked a while. I wonder if he was remembering times like when "big Jamie" showed him how to keep himself going on the swings? That certainly came back to my mind later this summer, when I was out weeding the drive and overhearing "big George" passing on that self-same wisdom to one of the latest crop of up-and-coming wee ones, over the fence in the playpark there.

142. An appointment to keep
Wednesday 16 July 2003

I waved goodbye to George and his parents and came back inside. For a whole minute at least. Long enough to gulp down the remains of the cold coffee, grab up my wallet and set off trotting up the drive for the rendezvous with Mrs Banks. She'd been waiting in the car at the top for about two minutes. All things considered, I reckoned that was well within the limits of the time game for that particular day. Don't you agree, Jamie Man?

I pushed a trolley round Tesco's feeling once again like I'd just emerged from the operating theatre. Dull pain, bright lights, no sense. Mrs Banks guided me gently along, with suggestions of food for a visiting family. Tins of this, packets of that. What did it matter? All I could think of, was that *this* was the place where I'd been, five days before.

The train was close to time and Grandma and Grandad's journey had passed without event. It was scarcely a joyful reunion though. Muted greetings were more the order of the day. It was probably just as well we had Mrs Banks there to sort everyone out and make sure the shopping ended up where it should. With the rest of us blundering round in a nightmare, almost anything was possible.

143. Dad the video criminal
Monday 14 July & Wednesday 1 October 2003

Life carries on in its relentless time warps. Today I've finally got round to watching the TV reports that everyone else saw on the day of the Book of Condolences at the school. I suppose that means your old Dad ought to be arrested and clapped in jail now, Jamie Man. Mrs Banks recorded the news on BBC and Grampian TV that night. And strictly speaking, I'm not *really* supposed to watch things like that, since we don't have a TV licence. It's hardly worth it for the signal we get with all the tall trees round about. In the circumstances though, perhaps they'll be willing to forgive my crime, just this once.

That video tape has been up on the shelf in my bedroom for nearly three months, waiting for the right time. Last week Mum and I had a meeting with the Procurator Fiscal, to hear about his findings. And I suppose that has set me off thinking about many things that I put aside for later, back in July.

You were the headline story on *North Tonight* on Grampian. They began with Fergus from P6 signing the Book of Condolences. Then there was an interview with Mrs Offord as the head mistress. Mr Whyte, as the minister. And then finally Mrs Banks, as a teacher and family friend. All of them were very kind in what they had to say about you.

I'd like to be able to report that some of the other stories on the news that night were happy ones, to make up for the sadness of our loss. But it wasn't the case, Jamie Man. It seemed to be non-stop bad news from beginning to end. Accidents on Loch Lomond and the Clyde. Bad and cruel people sent to prison. Is there *no* good news in the world?

The weather forecast for the 14th of July spoke of unbroken sunshine. It brought back images of endless warm, sunny weather that failed to keep you in the shelter of the House of Bruar...

144. A rhubarb card
Monday 14 July 2003

The television camera zoomed in on the card from Mr and Mrs Banks. You could see your name at the top but I wonder what people might have made of it, if they'd been close enough to read all the words in Helen and David's very individual message. Mrs Banks confided to me after the funeral that she'd been sorely tempted to send you a wreath of rhubarb. You would have smiled at that, Jamie Man. All those times we wandered up through the woods to their house with a wee gift from behind the ski slope.

JAMIE
a card from Helen and David Banks

You had only just turned into a butterfly
We shall never know where you would have flown
and what achievements you would have realised.
But in your short life, you gave pleasure to so many.
I shall miss the cheery smile and greetings,
the helpful ways and the eagerness to please.
I shall miss you sitting beside me with your array
of instruments at Music Club and the teasing and
giggling when I made a mistake.
I shall miss your expert knowledge of Harry Potter,
and your polite correction when I made a mistake
With an account from one of his books.
I shall miss your visits to the house with the rhubarb
from your garden, which you knew David loved.
It is hard to take in that you are gone,
yet you will always remain in our hearts.

145. Harry Potter on the move
Friday 25 July 2003

Uncle Bob and Co set off for home this morning. Nicola, Kyle and I thought it might be nice for Cousin Alan to have something special of yours to take with him to remember you by. We decided on your set of cassettes for the second Harry Potter book, *The Chamber of Secrets*. A fun story to keep him entertained on the long journey back to Berkhamsted in the car. So something good for Uncle Bob and Aunty Pam too!

That was the only one of the Harry Potter books we didn't have on CD. I never got the chance to tell you this, Jamie Man, but there was a special offer on in July and I'd been planning to buy that last book on CD as a surprise, to complete our set. I've decided I'm going to go ahead and order it anyway. How could we not think of you each time we listen again to those stories that you enjoyed so much?

146. Fitting everyone in
Thursday 17–Saturday 19 July 2003

It's quite a business organising where to put everyone as they arrive for a funeral, Jamie Man. Grandma and Grandad are okay in the house here with us. They're in your bedroom. But then it was back to to-ing and fro-ing on the telephone again. I was worried that everywhere would be booked up—second week of the school holidays and the hottest, driest summer for several years. But in the end it's all worked out fine. Mrs Cormack at the Crannich next door has a free chalet that Uncle Bob and Co can use. Better still, she also has room for Aunty Iris to stay with her up in the Guest House.

How about that then, Jamie Man? We can go and fetch Aunty Iris each morning after she's had her breakfast. And then deliver her back just in time for her night-time cocoa, or whatever. And Alan will be able to pop down the garden from the chalet anytime he fancies. Out one gate and in the other and there he is at our back door. I won't say it's perfect—because *you're* not here to enjoy having Cousin Alan next door for the week. But, in the circumstances, I guess it's better than I could have dared to hope.

147. Seeking my Wee Man
Thursday 17 July 2003

I woke up this morning hearing music. Had I been dreaming it? Or did it just come to me as I surfaced from sleep? I've no idea. All I can say is that it was there, going round and round in my head as I got out of bed. A sequence of three chords repeating over and over again in different ways. All I knew, was that this fragment was linked to three words:

My Wee Man.

The music had a sad, solemn feel. A blend of browns and purples suggesting many flats, more minor than major, moving from one discord to the next. Different voices would take up the key phrase in turn, the mood shifting from light to dark, triumphant to mournful, high to low, according to the changing harmonies and the character of the individual instruments. Whether it would ever reach such an advanced stage of arrangement and development, well that remained to be seen.

It was the Grandparents' first morning and I half expected to find Grandma up and about—she's never slept well. But all remained quiet in the house. I went through to the office and sat down at the keyboard with the earphones, scrap paper and pencil, just as I'd done those nights when I was working out the music for your *Fast Food Boys* routine.

The first and third chords were straightforward, B-flat and F-minor, no problem there. It took rather longer to settle on the one in-between: A-flat augmented. A very "henchman" type of chord, if you recall your *Piper* tunes, Jamie Man. By the time Grandma appeared, I had the first couple of lines of melody worked out and a handful of further chords, sliding around from one key to another, without ever quite settling on any one of them. There wasn't much likelihood of taking the music any further that day, or for some while to come. But at least those back-of-the-envelope jottings would be sufficient to know that I wasn't going to lose the idea…And that was what really mattered just then.

148. "My Wee Man" returns
Friday 27–Saturday 28 November 1998 & Monday 1 December 2003

The past few days have been a time for music and reflection, Jamie Man. On this final weekend of November five years ago, a matter of days after your seventh birthday, we stepped out on stage for *The Piper*: the culmination of two and a half year's work. Now on our five-year anniversary, my thoughts have returned over and over again to my Wee Man, up there in lights—*Mr Big*.

There was no Music Club this Friday. Kyle was away in Inverness as usual. I have been alone here in every sense of the word. Much of the weekend has been devoted to a couple of recorder quartet arrangements that I'd promised for Mrs Banks. Both of them were tunes that you would have recognised straightaway, Jamie Man: "My child is the future" from *The Piper* and "Building bridges" from our *Bridge to the Future* millennium celebrations.

This morning I returned to that music that emerged in the chaos of funeral arrangements, condolences and visitors back in July. "My Wee Man" is finally complete, or at least for keyboard anyway. Where do such things come from? I have no idea. But I do know that today the second section took shape in very similar fashion to the first.

There are times when I will find myself agonising over repeated developments and alterations of a musical idea. But not on this occasion. What you hear now is almost exactly what I first put down on paper. I feel no obligation to make excuses for the haunting discords, or to justify myself for writing it. It's a very private piece of music, between you and me, Jamie Man. It doesn't matter whether anyone else will ever want to listen to it, or to like it. On this weekend of all weekends, it seemed the appropriate thing to have been working on, at a time when my wee Mr Big and *The Piper* have both been so very much at the forefront of my thoughts. And that is all that matters.

149. Sad Fwog and Dog
Saturday 19 July 2003

During that first weekend in Inverness something got us on to talking about cartoons. I think it was remembering when you sprained your ankle at Christmas and had to go round on crutches for a couple of weeks. I'd drawn you a get-well card with the Dog stilt-walking on *his* crutches. You still had that card up on the shelf beside your bed. It's funny how the Dog never got a name, even though he turned up in so many guises over the years. Fwoggie the tree frog had a name and he was a new arrival this year. He first appeared on my good-luck card for Nicola's exams in May. And then he was joined by his girlfriend, Fwogette, who turned out to wish Nicola well at Scottish Youth Theatre.

I happened to remark that one thing I'd never done was to combine any of the different characters in a drawing. That thought stuck in my mind afterwards. How would Fwoggie and the Dog be feeling now? Wouldn't *they* be sad too, at a time like this? Wouldn't *they* want to be together...? In the early hours of Saturday morning, with everyone else in bed, I sat in the office and started to sketch out a possible answer to that question. Fwoggie and the Dog together. It was okay, for a first try. But there was still something missing. What that was came to me the next day, during the morning service at the church. While I was looking up into the sunlight and shadows of the roof...

150. The Primary School Leavers' Service
Wednesday 2 July 2003

The Leavers' Service on the final Wednesday of term is always a big event in the school calendar. Last year the children were doing a repeat of my Fun Day song, "Going for gold". So I was on the keyboard again and just as much on the edge of my seat as everyone else. This year, however, I was off-duty and could just settle back and savour the occasion—the end of primary school, both for you and for the whole family.

Mr Whyte welcomed us all and then handed over to the first group of P7's who did a poem about friends. You were in the next group, with a shared reading based on the familiar theme from Paul's letter to the Corinthians. Messages of friendship and love to carry with you to the Grammar School. Then of course there was music too. In my mind's eye you're still there now, sitting amongst your classmates playing your big tenor recorder with Mrs Banks conducting.

THE FRIENDS POEM FROM THE LEAVERS' SERVICE
(Author unknown)

Friends are kind, friends are fun
Friends will talk and listen too
Friends can help, friends will smile
You like them and they like you
Friends will share, friends will care
Friends take turns along the way
Friends say sorry, friends forgive
Friends don't sulk and run away
Friends are good, friends are great
Friends can laugh and joke with you
Friends are true, friends are cool
Friends enjoy the things they do
I like friends, don't you?

One of the songs that we all sang together that day, "Silver trumpet", spoke about getting ready to go to heaven. I guess it's inevitable that you see things in a different light when you go back and look again at the Order of Service. It's the same with the collection of awards and reminders that you brought home with you that afternoon.

At the end of the Leavers' Service there remains one further tradition which makes this closing act of the summer term in Carr-Bridge so very memorable. Like all the years before, your class formed up outside the door and as the rest of us left the church, we passed along the line shaking hands with each child in turn. And thus in your final act of farewell to Carr-Bridge Primary School, Jamie Man, you received the congratulations and best wishes of every single person who attended the service that day. I'm sure I can't have been the only one whose thoughts have strayed back to the significance of that simple ceremony, as we faced up to the news that was to follow a mere nine days later.

There's nothing like a little problem solving to brighten up my day.

Carr-bridge Primary School
for outstanding recorder playing
2003

Jamie Gasking

Well done, you have been a pleasure to teach and have made a valuable contribution to the music in the school and the community.

Signed H.D. Bawher

Ron Macdonald Award 2003

Presented to
Jamie Gasking
For
His positive attitude and helpfulness.

P7!
2003

The
Fast
Food
Boys

JAMIE   BRYCE

Saying goodbye to Primary School

151. Looking at things in a different way
2000–2001

In P5 you learned about the Buddhists' *Eight-fold path to enlightenment*:

1. *Being kind*
2. *Living wisely*
3. *Awareness of others*
4. *Telling the truth*
5. *Relaxing and meditating*
6. *Understanding suffering*
7. *Thinking unselfishly*
8. *Not causing harm*

You heard the story of Kiaragotami who sought help for her dead child. The Buddha advised her to go and look for a house where no one had died and to ask there for mustard seed. Kiaragotami visited one place after another but she failed to find a house where no one had died. You wrote that she had had to see that people do die every day and to accept that her child too was dead. Then you had some questions to think about:

Have you lost anything you loved?...*My mouse.*

How have you learned to live with it?...*I accepted he had died.*

And you made up your own eight rules for a good life:

1. *Don't steal*
2. *Don't lie*
3. *Try to keep peace between you and other people*
4. *Try to relax*
5. *Brush your teeth at least twice a day*
6. *Don't bother your school teacher*
7. *Don't drop litter*
8. *Laugh five times a day.*

Miss Mathieson wrote underneath that these were "great rules".

152. Natural choices
Thursday 17 July 2003

Mr Whyte was there with us at the Leavers' Service. He was the first to arrive on the doorstep on the day of your accident. And with those final days of primary school still so fresh in all our minds, it seemed the obvious thing to ask Mr Whyte if he would lead the funeral service for us here in the church in Carr-Bridge.

I'd never given any particular thought to burial *vs.* cremation for a child of mine. Why should I? What reason was there to suppose that each of you could not look forward to a long and fulfilled life ahead? But now, when I found myself forced to stare into the shadow of death? For you, for us, and—so very importantly as it seemed at the time—for the classmates and friends who'd grown up alongside you, Jamie Man, once again there seemed only to be the one possible choice. You should be laid to rest in the cemetery here in Carr-Bridge, surrounded by the woods that you loved so much. In a place where anyone who is missing you now can go and spend some quiet moments in your company.

FAITH, HOPE AND LOVE
Wednesday 2 July 2003
(You read the opening lines, Jamie Man, and Bryce read the closing ones)

[Jamie] Jesus said to His disciples, "I am giving you a new commandment: that you love one another. As I have loved you, so you must love one another. If you have love for one another, then everyone will know that you are my disciples."

So then, love is much more than a word we <u>Say</u>, love is what we <u>Are</u> to each other.

St Paul said, "Love is patient and kind

Love is not jealous or conceited or proud.

Love is not irritable or rude.

Love does not keep reminding us of what we have done wrong.

Love is not happy with lies but is happy only with the truth.

Love never gives up, and its faith, hope and patience never fail.

[Bryce] Love lasts for ever.

We have Faith, Hope and Love, and the greatest of these is Love."

---

153. According to J.K. Rowling
Thursday 17 July 2003

Mr Whyte was in and out of the house here throughout that week. Listening. Supporting. Being introduced to the family as they arrived. Grandma and Grandad and Aunty Iris. Uncle Bob, Aunty Pam and Cousin Alan. Nan and Aunty Alyson.

Conversation turned to many topics. One night I remember we sat up late talking about Harry Potter and the way in which J.K. Rowling has latched on to some of the most fundamental human needs, longings and values. The struggle between good and evil. Self-sacrifice for what is "right". The unique power of a mother's (or a father's!) love. The loyalty of the secret keeper. And of course, we shouldn't underestimate the attraction of all that freedom to roam and rule-breaking to spice up the thrills for any child reader!

Mr Whyte came up with a couple of quotations from Harry Potter, both of which ended up on the printed Order of Service for your funeral:

> *To have been loved so deeply, even though the person who loved us is gone, will give us some protection for ever.*

> *After all, to the well-organised mind, death is but the next great adventure.*

My response to Mr Whyte was that, where adventures and well-organised minds were concerned, you must be experiencing one helluva mystery story just now, Jamie Man, the way your thoughts were always leaping ahead to the next new project!

154. Making arrangements
Friday 18 July 2003

Realistically, no one expects the job of organising a funeral to be great fun. There's no doubt that you do have to tread very carefully, with everybody hurting so much already. It's so important to try to make sure that everyone is as "comfortable" as possible with whatever is planned. Easy said—not always so simple to bring off in practice. I certainly don't regard myself as an expert. The best advice

I can come up with, is to keep in mind that you don't have to deal with *everything* on the one day. There'll always be things that you can come back to in the quieter moments afterwards.

There's a great deal of symbolism involved in a funeral. I suppose each of us seeks our own comfort and significance in different aspects of what's going on. I talked a lot about this with Grandad, and with Mr Whyte too. It seemed to us that there are some very fundamental traditions—rites of passage you might say—things that are common across societies and cultures the world over. Like the communal laying to rest. Formal paying of respects. Shared mourning. Recounting the deeds of the departed. But then we find these are overlaid with a whole variety of other "conventional rituals" that people perhaps feel obliged to observe, simply because that's "the done thing". Hmmm. Once again, easy said. Not so easy to separate the two in practice, Jamie Man.

E-MAIL, 8.01AM
Saturday 19 July 2003

I sleep for about five hours a night, and yet each day is still too short to deal with everything and everyone.

I know that you will say that I need more rest than that, but in fact those quiet few hours when everyone else has gone off to bed are very helpful, and when I do finally turn out the light I sleep, deeply and without dreams.

The same is true with food, I eat something, a little less perhaps but something, at around the usual times, and that way I am best able to keep things running smoothly for Jamie and for everyone else who is looking in.

The funeral is now set for Monday at 1.30pm. I know I do not need to ask where your thoughts will be at that time…

---

155. Climbing the mountain
Sunday 20 July 2003

Uncle Bob, Aunty Pam, Cousin Alan and Great Aunty Iris arrived this afternoon. Nan and Aunty Alyson came down from Inverness with Mum. All of a sudden the house is very busy with all the new arrivals. This week has been like climbing a mountain. Another step uphill each day from one base camp to the next. No pause for rest quite long enough to escape from the ever-present ache. Nonetheless we've made it to the weekend and a determined effort now should put us within reach of our goal tomorrow.

156. Time with you
Sunday 20 July 2003

Mum, Kyle, Nicola and I walked on ahead up to the church this evening, leaving the rest of the family to follow on. It was my second visit of the day, after the morning service with Grandma and Grandad. Last weekend we were in Inverness and we've been out of public circulation for most of the time since. So this morning at the church was something of a "first contact" situation and I was rather grateful for the practice run. The way things have worked out, with the funeral on a Monday afternoon, we have at least had the chance to work up in stages towards that final climb.

It was good to see Mr Whyte there, waiting for us at the door. Not just as the minister but a familiar face too. A friend who'd known you well. And someone who'd been involved in recent events right from the very first afternoon. He led us inside to where you were waiting for us at the front of the church. We gathered round: Mum, Nicola, Kyle, and I with you in the middle, still so very much at the heart of all our lives.

There'd been more than a week to imagine this moment. I think a part of me had anticipated—feared—something dreadful and shocking. But that wasn't the way it was at all. You were…beautiful, Jamie Man. Unmarked, but for the one small dressing on your forehead. Everything about you spoke to me of peace, your face relaxed as if in sleep.

157. Nicola and Kyle's messages
Sunday 20 July 2003

While Grandma and Grandad, Nan and the others were with you, Jamie Man, Nicola and Kyle went off to sit together over on one side. Both of them had written a letter for you to take with you. And now in this quiet moment, they exchanged letters, so that each could share what the other had said. Thinking back to that scene now, the two of them sitting there quietly together, it seems like one of those moments when time has slowed up almost to a halt.

158. Zulu Bear
Saturday 19 July 2003

Mum chose Zulu Bear—who she made for you all those years ago—to go along with you on that final journey. Each night that week she cuddled him in bed with her. On the Saturday, however, she had to leave him here in Carr-Bridge for Johnny Ross to collect, along with the clothes that she'd picked out for you to wear. So Mum asked if I would look after Zulu for you that night. I thought about it a lot. Yes, I could've taken him to bed with me. But in the end it seemed the right thing to ask Grandma if she would keep Zulu company for his final night. She said yes at once, of course. I think it meant a great deal to her. And I'm quite sure no one else could possibly have done the job better. Except you, Jamie Man.

159. So very young
Sunday 20 July 2003

Mum had chosen the Scout uniform from the Gang Show for you, with the special blue sweatshirt, and the red necker that you were wearing in the kilt photos. I can't really explain this, but it seemed to me as if you looked so very grown-up lying there in your smart outfit, and yet so very young at one and the same time. My Mr Big. My Wee Man.

160. With flowers
Saturday 19 July & Saturday 1 November 2003

I guess if the choice of family flowers had been up to me, you might have ended up with a wreath of giant docks or dandelions from the ski slope, Jamie Man, to go with that bouquet of rhubarb from Mrs Banks. Anyway, to be on the safe side, we left all the arrangements with the florist for Mum and Nan to sort out and I think they did the job just fine.

Many people find comfort in flowers at a time like this. The Primary School have given a special memorial holder for the graveside. And since the funeral Mum has been bringing new flowers to keep that stocked up each week. Now that winter's beginning to close in, however, she's switched over to the silk flowers that she and Nicola brought back for you when they went to Spain in the summer. Real flowers wouldn't stand up so well to the frost, or to the cold winds at this time of year, Jamie Man, would they.

161. I will go there and back again
Wednesday 13 February 2004

The weather has turned mild again for a while. The snow of two days ago has melted into memory. That's not to say that winter's over yet by any means. No doubt we still have further snow and ice, wind and hail to come before the spring. But today I've taken my walk through the cemetery and seen the first signs of the snowdrops there.

I've passed that way most days this winter. On occasions in sunshine. At other times thrusting the first set of tracks through the drifts of snow. I try always to go in by one gate and out by another. A visit to see you should lie on the road to somewhere, not at a dead end. Sometimes a wave and a hello is all we need. On other occasions it is necessary to linger. I have learned that the most painful time to leave is when the frost is hardening on the ground and night is falling. No child should be abandoned to the dark at a time like that. I turn and walk away with the heaviest and most reluctant of steps. So often I hear in my mind the words of the song at the breaking of the fellowship in the first film of *The Lord of the Rings*:

> *When the cold of winter comes…*

> *…I will go there and back again.*

162. The bond that holds us together
Monday 18 August 2003

This *Scrapbook* of ours has led us into many uncharted regions of the soul, my Jamie Man. We've drifted into waters that I never anticipated I would ever be called upon to explore. How often does a child turn and look up into eyes of a parent to ask:

> *If you could have just one wish, what would it be…?*

I'm quite certain that Grandma and Grandad must remember occasions just like that with wee Dad. And with Uncle Bob. And Nan, with wee Mum too, no doubt.

How best to respond? Lightly? Selflessly? Optimistically?…How many us, I wonder, would feel it necessary to "waste" that single, precious wish on something as self-evident as "your safety"? Is that not part of the very fabric of the parent and child relationship?

But do we always succeed in communicating the depth of the bond that holds us together? Or the strength of the feelings that move us most? Do our actions always reveal the power of our attachment—our love—our emotional responses—beyond all doubt? Think of some of those times, Jamie Man, when you've been caught up in something *really* good and thrilling. Like when you were up on stage in the finale of the Gang Show. Then just imagine, if you could open a little window and say, hey Mum, Dad, Nicola, Kyle...this is how it *feels*! This is how wonderful it really was!

If I could say to Nicola, this is what it was like for me when you were born and the midwife declared, "It's a wee girl!" Or to Kyle, as I watch him now growing up and doing so well, "This is how proud I feel of my big son."

You and I, Jamie Man. We have our *Scrapbook* to help us share some of those unique moments that might otherwise have been lost entirely. Perhaps this touches too on the way that I feel towards Andrew Dale. And why I believe so very strongly that his efforts for you should not go unrecognised. You were my son and I could not be with you when you needed me most. Andrew Dale was there in my place on that day in July.

163. Parent and child
Sunday 20 July 2003

After we said goodbye to you at the church tonight, Nicola wanted to walk for a while before we went back to the house. At the bottom of the church drive we came upon Uncle Bob, who seemed to have had the same thought. The three of us drifted along to the Old Bridge and round up Station Road into the woods. Almost a dress rehearsal for the route we'll be following with you tomorrow. We stood beneath the tall pines on the path overlooking the cemetery. No one suggested going in but Nicola pointed to somewhere up in the top corner. I couldn't see that far but, as it turned out, she was quite right. That was indeed to be your resting place.

Uncle Bob didn't say much, but I know he was feeling very deeply for you tonight, Jamie Man. He and Aunty Pam only have the one child, Cousin Alan. I think we can imagine some of the dreadful thoughts that will be going through their minds this week while they are here with us. They don't call it every parent's worst nightmare for nothing. And yet, there is no alternative to allowing our children the freedom to venture out into the world and to roam...fearing for them, yes. But trusting that they will be as safe as they can be.

164. "Little Brown Island"
Sunday 20 July 2003

The family drifted off in ones and twos until finally I stood for the last time with each of my three children. Nicola was on your left, I was on your right and Kyle was at your head. You were quiet but otherwise still so much a part of our thoughts and our conversation. A few minutes later Cousin Alan reappeared and came to join us at Kyle's side. There'd be some concern about how well he would cope at just ten years old. Now here he was back of his own choice, a perfectly relaxed and natural addition to the group. And good company too for Kyle when he was ready to leave.

Nicola and I remained, leaning on the edge of the coffin, across from one another. And in the stillness and closeness of that moment she asked me a question.

Dad, do you know that tune, "Little Brown Island"?

Ye–es.

I was playing that this morning, on my big whistle that Jamie always wanted to borrow when he came to Inverness.

A shiver ran down my spine at her words. I was stunned.

What time was that, Nicola?

She frowned.

I'm not sure. Maybe around 12 o'clock?

Then I told her a story from my visit to the church that morning. Mr Banks was on the door and just after the service began he slipped into the empty seat beside me. Mrs Banks was at the organ and when it came to the offering, she started to play a familiar tune. I leaned across and whispered to Mr Banks that I couldn't remember what it was called, but I felt sure that you would have approved of her choice. He murmured back.

It's "Little Brown Island".

And now I'd learned that at the same time as Mrs Banks was playing that one tune from amongst all our Music Club repertoire, 25 miles away in Inverness Nicola had felt moved to pick up the whistle and play the very same piece of music. Each of them thinking of you in an eerie and yet strangely comforting conjunction. I repeated the story for Mr Whyte when he came over to join us a few minutes later. Wherever we choose to place our faith in this life, there is no doubt that events do sometimes conspire to move in surprising and mysterious ways. Whether through coincidence or purpose, it's hard to imagine a more deeply symbolic moment for a story such as that to reveal itself.

E-MAIL, 11.51PM
Sunday 20 July 2003

Tears and sadness at the church, of course, tonight. But I think that most of us came away feeling better for the chance to have seen Jamie and said our last good-byes. Nicola and Kyle were wonderful: upset and hesitant to begin with but by the end there was just the three of us there with Jamie and both of them seemed suddenly so much more grown up and stronger for the experience...

...At the very end, I had a few minutes all alone with my Wee Man, and that was very special, a moment to carry with me through the days ahead. As always it was "Good night, sleep well, I'll see you in the morning."

And just like my Wee Man, I came away with an air of peace.

Tomorrow still looms large, but we will get through.

---

165. Starting the final climb
Monday 21 July 2003

I have no recollection whatsoever of how the morning began. Perhaps I woke up around 6.00am like most days at that time? Did I just stare into space? Or possibly the first four or five hours of the day simply never happened? As far as I'm concerned, Monday started somewhere closer to midday, with a white shirt and a black tie and a hunt for the missing *Gameboy* stuff that unexpectedly turned up your special memory card from the school instead. After that, it was just the chaos of getting a dozen people fed in time for a black car at one fifteen.

Is this what they call surreal? I rather suspect it might be. Sufficiently surreal anyway, for it to seem perfectly reasonable to find myself sitting in the office and eating my lunch while attempting running repairs on Cousin Alan's sun glasses. Snipping off a strip from the roll of Duck Tape that you bought me for my birthday (and which of course mostly got used for your fixit jobs). Amongst all the decidedly un-normal comings and goings, it was a job that brought me back closer to you, Jamie Man:

Something breaks? Dad'll fix it!

Or as your henchmen in *The Piper* might have put it,

Sorting out the business, according to plan.

Half an hour later I was in another world entirely. Travelling up the street in muffled slow motion. Hearing little but the sound of your voice in my head as you reminded me of all our many conversations about people who go by car, when they could perfectly easily walk the distance. Forgive me, Jamie Man. Sometimes you just have to do "the done thing". And make plans because you don't know what the press might do…

As we took our seats in the church, the place seemed half empty…until they opened the other doors and started to let some of the people come through and fill up from the back hall. The remainder would follow the service over the speaker system. Half empty? There wasn't room to fit in everyone who wanted to be with you that day, Jamie Man!

166. On this day of all days
Friday 27 February 2004

Grandad's sent me the notebook that he was carrying with him that week. It makes strange reading, following the familiar events through different eyes. There are no great surprises but I did find one reminder to fill in a gap in that missing space first thing in the morning on the day of the funeral.

Uncle Bob and Aunty Pam had arrived the previous afternoon. So this would be Cousin Alan's first chance to come round and visit us on a new day. And what a day, of course. Grandma and I were in the kitchen at the time. She was at the sink, washing up, I think. All of a sudden she let out a scream and pointed out of the window, moaning "Jamie, Jamie," over and over again.

I looked out and saw Cousin Alan over the wall in the end of the Crannich garden, smiling and waving to us. Standing on the path beyond the long grass, it must have seemed for a moment to Grandma as if he was floating. And in that brief instant as she glanced out, her eyes told her that it was *you* she saw out there, Jamie Man, smiling and waving to her in just the way that she would have expected you to. Poor Grandma. She was so upset. But it wasn't Alan's fault. How was he to know?

Be careful what you wish for, it might come true? But that was exactly what we *did* want to come true, Jamie Man. On this day of all days, every one of us so desperately wished that we could look out of the window and see you there, making your way round to the back door, just like normal.

167. The funeral service
Monday 21 July 2003

So we embarked on the final stages of our long and difficult climb. Once more we gathered to sing "There is no one else like you" and "One more step along the world I go", just as we had done nineteen days earlier at the Leavers' Service. Once again too, we heard the "Friends" poem read aloud, shared this time between Mrs Offord, your teacher for P6 and P7, and Stephen Macdonald, Skip the Scout Leader, coming forward to read with his ankle still in plaster.

It was a child's service. Your service, Jamie Man. Mr Whyte offered a few, simple words, telling us that it was natural to feel sad, but it was okay too to smile when we remembered the good times with you. He said that you had touched the lives of so many people that a part of you would always stay with us in spirit, even when we could no longer see you there alongside us from day to day. Our memories of you would live on.

Then at the heart of the service, Kyle and Richard with the poem that Richard had written for you. Followed by Nicola with your *Slug Story*. And just as I know you would have wished, amidst all the tears and the sadness, there were the smiles and chuckles at your account of Queen Nicola and a train that went over the ocean to New York.

JAMIE GASKING'S POEM
by Richard David McKendrick

Black of hair
Big of smile
Everlasting heart
One who we'll miss
But always on the list
Of people close to our heart

Gone too early
For all to see
The end is such a shame
It'll be
The hardest thing
Not seeing you
Day by day

---

168. Setting out on the journey
Wednesday 2 July & Monday 21 July 2003

Two very special services in close succession. The one echoing the other in its message of love and friendship. Two services, much alike, but each pointing to a very different destination. One road leading towards the Grammar School and the start of a whole new chapter. The other to the conclusion of a life story. No line of smiles and handshakes for us maybe on this occasion, but you're not setting out on this journey alone by any means, Jamie Man. You're going on your way in the company of friends.

169. Here and now
Monday 21 July 2003

We emerge from the church to a scatter of rain. Johnny Ross offers an umbrella but Kyle and I shake our heads. We will take whatever comes this day.

Time edges forward at half pace. I'm walking out in front with Kyle and Richard. We're passing the Primary School. Folk on either side of the street stand in silence to observe the progress of a slow, dark car with its tragically small burden. Vehicles up ahead pull aside to allow the scene to flow over and past them. And all the time I'm thinking how proud you would have been to be heralded on your way by Mr Barnes, your chanter teacher, who's interrupted his holiday just to be here to play the pipes for you.

It's Grandma, coming along behind in the second car, who looks round as they swing into Station Road and sees the lines of people following on foot, stretching back to the church. Those brief tears of rain have come to nothing and the sun is shining from a clear sky once more. We walk on. Cousin Alan is catching us up. I give him the nod and he slips in to make our number five for the remainder of the way—Richard on the left, then Kyle, myself, and Alan, with you in the lead. How, I wonder, will the three of *them* look back on this moment in years to come? Or the friends behind? Seeing you safely on your journey.

170. Honour guard
Monday 21 July 2003

Johnny Ross's folk lift you out of the car and we follow the short distance to the very spot that Nicola was pointing out last night. And the people come. And they come—forming up in a great arc of faces stretching out around the next aisle. The scene comes back to me now as fleeting snapshots. The remainder of the film is lost somewhere on the cutting room floor. I see Mr Whyte there speaking a few words. The honour guard forming up. A *Who's Who* of the Cubs and Scouts in the Highlands. Skip's there—stubbornly refusing to allow something as trivial as a broken ankle to prevent him from playing his part in this final tribute to a member of his small Scout pack.

Three Scout uniforms along either side. I'm standing at your feet. Kyle is at your head. We take up the cords and together we lower you to a place of final rest. And in that quietest of moments, Mr Barnes lays aside the pipes and takes up the chanter for the haunting strains of "Highland Cathedral". There are tears in his playing and tears on my cheeks as I recall the countless times I've listened to you practising that selfsame tune.

Where is *that* chanter now? Back lying on the communion table at the front of the church, alongside your folded green and yellow Aviemore Scout necker. Just as they had both lain throughout the funeral service. Still and silent.

171. What now?
Monday 21 July 2003

The ground was strewn with pine cones. Aunty Alyson complained that a falling cone had landed on her head! I wasn't looking for explanations that day. But in my first turning away from a new graveside, I did take up one of those cones and pop it in amongst all the fancy flowers. My gift to you, Jamie Man. In lieu of those missing docks and dandelions?

I see now that this was one of the few unplanned spots in all the arrangements of the day. Up to that point, everything had been organised down to the last detail. The cars. The Order of Service. The slow procession to the cemetery. Mr Barnes with the pipes and the chanter. Who would hold which of the cords. Words and a prayer from Mr Whyte. And in due course everyone would be making their way down to the Carr-Bridge Hotel. But what was supposed to happen right *now*? Who, what, where, how?

172. Queuing up
Monday 21 July 2003

I still don't know. *Is* there a proper way to leave the cemetery, when everything there has run its course? The cars were all set to go. I spoke to one of the drivers to make sure that Skip would have a ride down to the hotel with his broken ankle. I turned back and there was James from your class, with his Mum, Susan. James was upset and so I just gave the two of them a hug. When I looked up, it was to find a queue of people waiting their turn. An echo of the Leavers' Service perhaps?

Certainly there was something different to share with each one of them. A few special words. A precious recollection. Sad smiles. Some tears. The cars were beginning to move off and people were gradually following in their pairs and threes and fours. It was soon clear that I was destined to be amongst the last to arrive at the Carr-Bridge Hotel that afternoon.

Mr Barnes had slipped way to pick up the pieces of his holiday. Andrew Dale and his wife Pamela had also been there and I didn't even know. So many people who felt the need to be with you on that day of all days, Jamie Man. So many thank-you's still left to say.

Finally it came to the Cub and Scout leaders who had held back till last. We stood in a ring with linked hands as we talked of you and I thanked them for the part that they had played that day, and over the years. The source of so much joy in your life, Jamie Man. So many good times to look back on. So much to be supremely grateful for. Not least the companionship now of Chil, Arkela and all the rest as we made our way down the road to the Carr-Bridge Hotel…with Skip resolutely hobbling all the way on his broken ankle.

173. The case of the falling pine cones
Thursday 31 July 2003

The explanation for all those pine cones on the ground at the cemetery only became clear about ten days later. I happened to meet Lynne from the Landmark shop as she was walking her dog through the cemetery together with her mother. We stood and talked for a while and then all at once Lynne's Mum remarked on the birds that were roosting in the tops of the pine trees round about. Scottish Crossbills, she said. They were the culprits who were responsible for throwing down all the pine cones. And hence for Aunty Alyson's cone on the head on the day of the funeral. One more mystery solved!

174. A late reading of the *Glenmore Times*
Monday 22 September 2003

Remember your animation theatre that I was telling Nick Park about in the letter? You started with a cut-down cardboard box and you were slowly building it up with strips of newspaper and wallpaper paste. One more thing that I had to tidy out of the way in a rush with all the extra people coming and going in the house. I put the theatre itself inside the giant cardboard fort in your bedroom to keep it safe. But then there were the big sheets of glossy paper that I'd given you to put down on the kitchen floor where you were working. They just got bundled up quickly and pushed to one side. Until today, when I was setting up to repaint the wood burning stove and needed something to catch the drips. As I was spreading the sheets out on the hearth, a picture caught my eye:

That looks like a pine marten…

Sure enough that's exactly what it was. When I looked more closely, I found that the pages came from an old conservation newsletter called the *Glenmore Times*. We were interested in pine martens because we reckoned there were some living in your favourite *Sesame Street* woods, just along from where the developers want to put all the new houses. So I took a few moments to see what the paper had to say about them. When I'd finished reading, I glanced down at the article beneath and the word *crossbill* jumped out of the page at me. Would you believe it! *The Scottish Crossbill.* The very same birds that I'd just learned had been roosting in the trees overlooking the cemetery.

CROSSBILLS
from the <u>Glenmore Times</u>, Forest Enterprise, 1998

The Scottish Crossbill is the only bird unique to Scotland. Scientists accepted that it is a separate "endemic" species in the 1980's. Before that, it was thought that all the crossbills which regularly bred in Britain were common crossbills—a species with a huge world range which spans most of the boreal forest zone from Scandinavia to the Pacific and across North America.

Subtle differences, including chunkier bills and deeper voices, set Scottish crossbills apart from their continental cousins. But a distinctive badge also unites them. All crossbills have amazing beaks, with mandibles over-lapped to help them tweak seeds from cones.

Grappling with pine cones is the crossbill's most frequent task. It can sometimes tackle cones in spruces, firs and larch trees, but its deep, strong beak is custom made to prise the pine cones apart and extract their big, food-rich seeds.

The downside of this close association is that when cone crops are poor in fragmented forest portions crossbill numbers may crash. But as more and more native forest areas, like Glenmore, are expanded, and if possible linked, these special Highlanders should be better able to find food and thrive.

So there, Jamie Man! You have some very important neighbours hanging out in your trees. And you have good neighbours too in the Highland Council and the Woodland Trust, who own the land on that side of the cemetery. They encourage people to walk in their woods and they're doing everything they can to make sure things stay just right for birds like the crossbills. In the circumstances, I reckon we can put up with the occasional pine cone on the head, don't you?

175. When the funeral is over
Monday 21 July 2003

What do you do with the rest of the day when the funeral is over? The hall at the Carr-Bridge Hotel had been full of people. Each with their own particular bittersweet memories of you. There were folk here from every facet of your life, past and present, including those parts where my role as Dad was little more than to make sure that you arrived at the door on time, fed and watered, and with all the appropriate gear in hand.

At eleven years old you were launching out into all sorts of new directions. Growing independent. It made me proud to meet all these different people who spoke so warmly of the contributions that you had made. It might have been the sad business of a funeral that had brought us together, but I took comfort from the fact that you had given so many folk good reason to remember you—not for the unhappy manner of your death, but for the way in which you had lived your life to the full, and in doing so had enriched theirs.

Eventually though, the time comes when everyone has to say goodbye. The conversation dies away and the hall grows quiet and empty. What then? What do you do with the rest of the day when the funeral is over? Do you?—can you?—ever go home?

E-MAIL, 1.21AM
Tuesday 22 July 2003

Quarter past one in the morning and the day has been…something special.

Physically I do feel rather steamrollered just at the moment, but emotionally the general peace of mind of last night when we went to the church to see Jamie, and of the funeral this afternoon, still persists.

Even through the tears of the service, and of the procession…I found myself looking at that coffin and seeing something more than simply the closing of a door. There must be hope for something better…

…I am so glad that we were able to spend time with Jamie together last night, Nicola, Kyle and I together, chatting quite naturally with one another and with him. I see him there still in his special Scout Gang Show sweatshirt and neck scarf, Zulu the bear at his side and with the letters that Kyle and Nicola had each written to tell their wee brother how special he was to them. That was the abiding image that carried me through the day…

…When I spoke to one of the teachers afterwards, she seemed to be finding it hard not to feel bitter about the unfairness of how things had turned out for Jamie. And for some reason I found myself talking of it in terms of bottles, and of Harry Potter.

Dumbledore points out to Harry that, although he does have certain features in common with Lord Voldemort, it is ultimately the decisions that he makes that distinguish him from his enemy. The bottle of life comes in all shapes and sizes, and none of us knows for sure what lies ahead. Jamie may have been dealt a much smaller bottle than any of us anticipated, but I think that the reactions of folk today clearly demonstrated that he managed to take the eleven years of his bottle and fill them right to the top.

And he was fortunate too to be able to have lived out his entire life in a place as special as Carr-Bridge, in the company of so many very special people.

So, all in all, the day went well. Many tears. Many hugs. But with a hope of further sunshine on the horizon.

---

176. Journey's end
Thursday 14 February 2004

At the outset, all I sought to do with this *Scrapbook* of ours was to collect some words each day so that I would not forget. Since then I've dipped into the "box" and gradually pieced the story together for us, Jamie Man, block by block. Like building the drystone wall, I've tried to look for just the right size and shape to fit each new space, chipping off a little here and there to get the best fit I can.

Much of the early work was done in silence. Or occasionally to a background of classical or church music. Since Christmas though, I've been listening to the music for the three *Lord of the Rings* films. I start in the morning with *The Fellowship of the Ring* and when I reach the end of *The Return of the King* I go back to film one again. I don't know why. I've never worked quite like that before. But when you follow these words on the page, Jamie Man, don't be surprised if you do catch the odd whisper of hobbits and wizards and elves and men and orcs echoing faintly in the background. Then you'll know you can rest easy, like Frodo and the elves as they sail away into the west:

You have come to journey's end

Sleep now

177. Happy Birthday to you
Tuesday 18 November 2003

It was early September before I had the opportunity to go back and complete the Fwog and Dog picture. Two months later I printed it out as my birthday card for you:

To my Jamie Man, with love from Dad.

Other people may look if they wish, Jamie Man. But I drew it for you.

178. Waking up to pain
Tuesday 22 July 2003

In the quiet hours late at night, when everyone else is asleep, there is the opportunity for reflection. Tears that flow then may prove to be healing and joyful, rather than simply hot and full of pain. By contrast, it is at the moment of waking perhaps, that we are at our most vulnerable...

The first news of violent death strikes like the slash of a knife, wounding and numbing at one and the same time. Rest and sunrise bring fresh bleeding. For one, brief, waking instant, there is hope. The self-delusion of disbelief. Then memory. This is no mere nightmare to be shrugged off with the arrival of daylight.

My son is dead. You, my Jamie Man.

For a period, time stands still, while all around pointless and meaningless life grinds on. Later, there comes a second and equally-inescapable day, when I wake up to the realisation of a further, deeper hurt that also can never truly be healed.

Yesterday we laid my son to rest in a box in the ground. You, my Jamie Man.

I surfaced this morning with words on my lips. Did I fashion them in my dreams? Or did *you* perhaps bring them to me as you passed this way in the night? I cannot tell.

Once again, everyone else was asleep as I went through to the office to write down those lines. There was little or no editing. I merely recorded the words that I found in my head. A repeating refrain for a lost star. A picture of my thoughts as we laid you to rest.

ONE OF MY STARS
Tuesday 22 July 2003

One of my stars is fallen
But his footsteps still light the sky
One of my smiles is sleeping
But his story still fills the days
One of my tunes is silent
But his music can never fade

One of my loves is missing
Till the next time the piper plays

---

179. First morning, first visit
Tuesday 22 July 2003

Grandma was up and about by the time the new poem was safely down on paper and I suggested a walk. We gathered some flowers from the garden and made our way slowly up through the woods for our first visit to your grave. It was all so very different from the scene the afternoon before. The ground was flat now, the bouquets carefully spread out to mask the joins in the grass. I left my poem there for you, under the small bunch of purple flowers from beside our front door.

Eight o'clock in the morning. A month after midsummer, with the sun already well above the trees. It struck me then that, in this quiet corner of the cemetery, you would have sunshine all through your day. Rising at your head and going down at your feet. From now on the progress of the sun, and the cycle of the seasons would be the new way markers on your road. And your legacy would be measured in the memories that last. Not in the goods that fade and pass away.

I returned to visit again later in the day with Uncle Bob. By then the sun stood high and bright in a clear, blue sky. Peaceful...for a while, at least. As we stood there talking, we were suddenly interrupted by a thunder of noise up ahead. Next moment, with the familiar, ear-splitting roar, an RAF jet came screaming in low towards us before shooting away across the treetops behind. It's not that uncommon, especially on a bright summer's day. But you know, for all their low-flying exercises and training flights, that remains the one and only occasion when I have ever seen one of the jets actually pass over the cemetery while I've been there. This one flew from your head to your toes as if it was all part of some greater plan. Not everyone earns their very own, personal, military fly past, Jamie Man. Only the most special people. Like you.

180. Hey, Mr Fund Raiser!
Saturday 3 May 2003

Nicola was really upset when Scottish Youth Theatre wouldn't let her go back after the funeral. After all the effort that you'd put in to help her get the money to go in the first place, Jamie Man. Mum was organising all sorts of fund raising up in Inverness and you were determined to do your bit for your big sister.

Time to switch into "Jamie Salesman Mode" once again, like for the Scouts at Aviemore Primary in December. You and I were on Christmas tree duty that day. You were out the front in your Scout uniform, dragging in the punters. And Dad was assigned to shoving the trees around—fresh, sticky pine resin everywhere! You were in your element. Folk needed a very good excuse not to cough up for one of your trees that day. You even managed to sell one to Dr Irvine, and she's someone who's got her head screwed on!

Now in May there was to be a car boot sale for Nicola and her big SYT effort. You recalled the "Pay a pound and pick a square" game that had worked so well for the Scouts at Christmas. Could I help you sort out something similar?

We began with a hunt in the loft for a suitable sheet of paper for your grid of squares—the back of a big poster or something like that would do. In the end we settled on some old year planners.

Hey, why not trim off the bits you don't need and use the calendar itself?

"Pay a pound and pick a day"? That would certainly give a new twist to the idea. Or even "Pay a pound and pick two days"! There were plenty of squares to choose from after all. And people always have their own favourite dates in the year: birthdays, anniversaries, holidays, etc. It looked like you could be onto a winner. Mind your backs! Here comes Mr Fund Raiser!

While you were busy with your grand game scheme, Dad was sent to scour the house for suitable objects to sell. As far as you were concerned, anything that wasn't actually nailed down would be fine. I spent the best part of that weekend up and down to the loft while you were away at Mum's. By the time you and Kyle came back on Sunday evening I had the stack of potential merchandise piled high in the porch waiting for your approval. So, would that do? Hmmm…Sly grins.

Ye–eahh, not too bad…for a Dad.

You threw yourself into that Car Boot Sale, just like everything else you did. Mum reported afterwards that our Mr Fund Raiser had been most effective, with few people being allowed to escape without buying something from your boot and signing themselves up for some special days.

181. Two boys
Wednesday 23 July 2003

This unforeseen trip to Scotland is a big adventure for Cousin Alan. And most of the time that seems okay for Kyle. But every now and then, I sense that he is struggling to match up the novelty of this non-stop cousin with the sadness of the week. It's not Alan's fault that there are moments when the very novelty of his presence cannot help but underline the fact that *you* are missing from the scene. It's going to take both Kyle and Nicola some time before it feels right to be happy again. Or to have fun. Or to be out and about with friends thinking of other things. They will not forget you, Jamie Man. But they will have to move on. Carrying you with them in their hearts.

This morning Kyle went across to Landmark with Alan and Co. I took over after lunch so that Uncle Bob could drive the *Oldies* in to Aviemore to see the doctor. Grandma and Aunty Iris had packed in such a hurry to come away that we weren't sure they had all the tablets they would need till they get home again. It was my first visit back to Landmark since that Tuesday morning when you and I climbed the tower to investigate the progress on the new car park. So many echoes. Dad moving at half speed.

Not so for the two of them. No sooner had we got back from Landmark, than Kyle and Alan immediately announced that they wanted to go off on an expedition in the woods. I nodded:

> *Right, okay. How's this then? Explorer's tea. Rucksack, flask of soup, bread rolls, hot dogs, crisps, cartons of juice, fruit…?*

They reckoned that sounded just fine and I set about the preparations. There was no point trying to build a fence around them. And what purpose would it serve to remind anyone that those were precisely the same sort of supplies that I'd fixed for *you*, Jamie Man? Like the day when Jamie Boult came over and the two of you went out to build your big den in the woods? (And you fetched me to help you shift branches in the rain). Or when Bryce was round with his broken arm in a sling and you galloped off exploring together for the afternoon? What's left of life must go on.

So I stood on the back doorstep and waved as my two eager explorers set off with their rucksack of supplies. Picking their way round the posts and planks of your road that still lay out across the patio. Over the stepping stones and past your wooden road block to the back gate. Out into the woods for a few hours of unsupervised high adventure…while I came back into the house, closed the door behind me and burst into tears. Overwhelmed by the *right* scene, played out by the *wrong* pair of boys.

182. Jolly Catherine to the rescue
Wednesday 23 July 2003

Kyle and Alan were off in the woods. Uncle Bob and the others were still away in Aviemore. The house suddenly seemed so desperately quiet and empty. Too much silence to expect to find comfort indoors. Better to be occupied elsewhere. It was Wednesday afternoon and so I set out for the shop to see what the *Strathy* had to say about the funeral. On the whole, probably another one of those jobs that was best faced alone.

Catherine Jones was there in the Spar. Jolly Catherine, or Happy Catherine as you and I always described her. Never short of a smile. She inquired how things were going and I began to tell her about Kyle and Alan off on their expedition. I hadn't got very far before I was crying all over again, right in the middle of the shop. Catherine gathered me up in her arms and gave me a big hug. And anyone who wanted to get by just had to wait. I guess people do sort of expect that kind of thing, Jamie Man. But, well, you know. It isn't easy…

183. A quiet moment
Wednesday 23 July 2003

I drifted up towards the cemetery. Once again, sitting up there on the grass with you seemed like the proper place to pause and take a first look at the paper. I've just read that article through again. It talks about some of the same things that we have in our *Scrapbook* here, Jamie Man. But I think the headline says all that's required just now:

Schoolboy Jamie laid to rest.

And I sat with you, sharing the peace of that rest for a few, quiet moments.

184. A bright idea
Wednesday 23 July 2003

I've found a new use for your big cooler bottle with the pouring tap, Jamie Man. You always loved your ice cold water from the fridge, dashing in from school on a hot day. What was I going to do with it now? Then just as I was going out this afternoon I had a brainwave. And I was right. Your bottle makes the perfect container for carrying water up to the cemetery for the flowers when the rain butt up there hasn't seen a drop for weeks. Dad's cool solution, eh!

There was another small event with flowers yesterday. When I got back from the visit to the Registrar there was a card in the postbox saying that a delivery had been left "in the shed". They meant the playhouse, of course. When I unbolted the door, I found a large bunch of flowers from the ladies in the shop at Landmark. The strange thing was though, that without knowing it the delivery driver had left the bouquet on the wee table that you were varnishing the morning before you caught the bus for Inverness...

185. Ski slope stories
Tuesday 22 July 2003

I didn't take in much detail round about when we were up at the cemetery on the day of the funeral. Since then, however, several more things have begun to piece themselves together. Sometimes in surprising ways.

That first morning when I went back with Grandma, I noticed the name on the headstone to the right. It was Ramie Taylor, the JCB driver, who died in August last year. He was the man who excavated the ski slope for us, and who shovelled up the heap of soil that we kept back for making the garden. Yes, "the ski slope" that you played on, dug on, sledged on, and acted out your stories on all your life. So if you're ever at a loose end now, you'll always be able to exchange digging ski slope stories with a fellow expert!

Then just further up, at the top of the path, there's the grave of Karl Fuchs himself, the man who originally created the artificial ski slope at the bottom of the hotel gardens. At one time the Fuch's owned the Crannich Guest House next door as well, which would have given more space for the skiers to run out at the bottom. Nowadays they'd go crashing straight into my drystone wall!

And talking of the Crannich, just behind you, there's the headstone for Mrs Cormack's husband, Forsyth, who used to run the Guest House with her. In fact, the more you look around your corner of the cemetery, the more you find the familiar names from our end of the village: Struan, Crannich, Braeval, Woodside and Rose Cottages. Quite a little club, eh!

That heap of earth that Ramie Taylor left for us started out right up in the corner of the garden. One of my first tasks after we moved in was to climb up on top with the spade and dig us a way out to the back gate. Over the years, you saw your ski slope shrink and creep back behind the house as the wasteland gradually gave way to garden. You always loved joining in with the work. It's sad to think you won't be there to chop back the new crop of weeds for me come the summer. Or to enjoy the results when all the hard work is finally completed.

Few people are fortunate enough to experience such life-long pleasure from something as simple and straightforward as a pile of earth. I find it so apt that the last photograph I took of you should have been just after we'd finished digging. You were looking forward so much to continuing the excavation of the mysterious stone tank over the summer holidays. It's good to think that *Seann Bhruthach*—the old slope—was still able to turn up a new source of fascination for you, right up to our very last full day together, my Jamie Man.

186. Corrie Dog has her say (or should that be her woof?) *Friday 25 July 2003*

There's another funny little story that links the funeral and the garden in a rather unexpected fashion, Jamie Man. I think it's a tale that would have made you chuckle. It all starts that afternoon at the Carr-Bridge Hotel, after most of the people had gone home.

There was still food left over, so Mrs Banks fixed up with the hotel staff for them to pack a big "doggie bag" for us to bring home. Then we wouldn't need to worry about dinner for a house full of relatives that night. The next day she dropped by again with further cakes and biscuits from an event in Aviemore. So people here ate sandwiches, and sausage rolls and so on. And then toasted sandwiches the next day. And the day after…Eventually what was left just had to go out. I said to Grandma that it was a shame to waste them, but at least they could go on the compost heap. What I failed to explain clearly enough, however, was that it would all need to be put out there *in a bag*, till I could go and dig it in later.

It was only on the Friday morning that I realised Grandma must have taken me at my word. She'd gone out and simply tipped the whole lot on the top of the compost heap. No matter. I'd just have to pop out and cover them up. The strange thing was though, that when I *did* get a moment to go out there, there wasn't a sandwich to be seen!

It took me a while to work out the explanation for those amazing disappearing sandwiches. Mum had come over to pick up Nicola on Friday afternoon. And as usual she had Corrie Dog with her. And I did remember seeing Corrie snuffling around by the compost heap…

Well, you'll have guessed it already, Jamie Man. That's right, Corrie Dog had managed to squirm her way in past the wooden pallet at the front and got herself up onto the heap. Where she'd then proceeded to "woof down" the best part of two carrier bags' worth of rather old and dog-eared sandwiches from the Carr-Bridge Hotel! I won't say there was no harm done, because I wasn't at Mum's house later that day to see whether Corrie Dog was moaning about a fat tummy. On the other hand though, I guess we can truthfully report that none of the sandwiches did actually go to waste in the end. No wonder Corrie Dog seemed to have such a smug, contented smile on her face when she climbed (heavily?) back into the car with Nicola that Friday afternoon…!

187. Cutting the grass
Sunday 27 July 2003

I finally got round to cutting the grass today, Jamie Man. Once upon a time, in a galaxy far, far away, jobs like that, and the weeding, and painting the playhouse, and all the rest, were going to be finished before Grandma and Grandad arrived. But of course things didn't quite work out that way. So the grass was a *lot* longer than usual. And just to complicate matters, the wire of the mower kept getting tangled up amongst all your posts and planks on the patio. Yes, I know it would have made more sense to clear that stuff away before I started work on the lawn. But hey, there hasn't been a great deal of sense about anything round here over the past few weeks, has there.

It's a scene that you would find so familiar, Jamie Man. I'm over here pushing the lawn mower. Grandma's busy going round dead-heading the flowers. Taking her mind off things. And all the while there's this non-stop conversation going on with you in my head. Just like Grandma, you were never more content than when we were both out here working in the garden together. I might be doing the grass like today, when you came home from school. Or some weeding, or using the chainsaw, or chopping logs. But whatever it was, you'd be inside just long enough to drop your bag and get changed. And then it would be straight back out again to join in, or to get started on one or other of your own projects. Perhaps with the secateurs, like Grandma this afternoon. Or some new building and landscaping. Or maybe the next chapter of make-believe…

It's hard not to imagine that any moment I will hear that same old scrunch of your footsteps on the stones, coming down the drive towards the front gate. Or that if I glance across towards the back gate, I won't see you over there, striding up and down on the stepping stones in the middle of the latest story. Yes, it is hard going, in one sense. And yet these will be the memories to fall back on when I begin to get through this first, dark barrier of your going away. Like in the woods, the garden will always be one of those places where I will come closest of all to you, my busy, digging, shifting, story-telling Wee Man.

188. Finding our way in a new world
Tuesday 29 July 2003

This morning was set to be Grandma and Grandad and Aunty Iris's final visit to the cemetery before they go home tomorrow. Setting out up the road there was the same old question hanging in the air—who would we meet along the way this time? These days it's as if all the familiar faces and old acquaintances have suddenly become transformed into new characters. The world outside the house is divided between those I've spoken to in the last eighteen days, and the rest who are still to be introduced. And I'm beginning to realise that the past is not always the best guide for the future, Jamie Man.

Each one of us grows up from different roots, in different soil. Our individual responses to things like death and loss and grief are inevitably conditioned by what life has taught us along the way. I'm sure it is true to say that there's been a great deal more holding hands and hugging going on around Carr-Bridge in the past few weeks. But not everyone is comfortable with that kind of thing. Some people find it easier to express their feelings in other ways—like cards and flowers, or practical help. For others, the only possible response to tragedy may be to shy away from it completely. Keep a safe distance. Act as if nothing whatsoever has happened. It's safer to talk about the weather.

I see now too, that there are some individuals who are so overwhelmed with the weight of their own sorrows, that they need comfort and understanding from *us*. We shouldn't by any means assume that suffering is a one way street.

And of course *everyone* knows about "not wishing to intrude…"

It's like one of those abrupt changes of scene when you were up on stage, Jamie Man. The loss of you has thrown the whole world into a new light. And now all the actors are struggling to sort out who they are with their new roles and their new lines to speak. For now, we just have to accept that each fresh encounter in the woods, in the shop, or on the street is another venture into uncharted territory for all concerned. We're all beginners here. And it's not an easy business.

Today's encounter at the cemetery was with Margaret the dinner lady. She remembered standing at the bus stop with us that Thursday. Travelling on the same bus with you to Inverness. The cheery smile you gave as you waved goodbye and got off at the stop before her. What more permanent feature in the life of a child, than the school dinner lady who has seen you grow from a wee P1 to a big P7 leaver? It's painful for Margaret too. We are not the only ones who have been hurt this summer, Jamie Man.

189. Evening primrose time
Tuesday 29 July 2003

The weather has turned cooler and cloudier today. Such a change from the past weeks. Not at all like that day you set off for Perth, or the frantic period of time that followed it. So many of the flowers in the garden that would normally emerge slowly and last for weeks have shot out this year, only to wither away to seed in a matter of days.

But guess what I saw when I looked out of the kitchen window tonight? Over in front of the rowan tree, three or four tall, new, yellow flowers. I couldn't believe my eyes. After all my futile attempts to grow them from seed, we finally had our first evening primrose flowering in the garden! Those seedlings that Denise Robertson's husband Bob gave us from his garden last summer had suddenly sprung into bloom. On the night before Grandma and Grandad and Aunty Iris go home. So much better for them to be able to see the flowers themselves, than just to hear about them on the telephone.

190. A salute to Wallace & Gromit
Tuesday 29 July 2003

We've been watching the Wallace & Gromit video that Grandad brought with him in the suitcase. It's the one we sent him for Christmas last year—*Cracking Contraptions*. You were looking forward to seeing it when they came and it was sad to think that our biggest Wallace & Gromit fan wasn't there to chuckle along with us. But I'm glad I told Grandad to keep it on his list to bring with him all the same.

You remember how we downloaded *The Soccamatic* clip from the internet when the video first came out? I know you would have loved the rest of Wallace's ten wacky inventions too—like *The Bully Proof Vest*, *The Christmas Cardomatic* and *The Snowmanotron*. I'm certain it would have given you all sorts of ideas. I'm not sure it won't have got Grandad's brain going either. We'll have to keep a close eye on him, eh!

There was a behind-the-scenes visit to the Aardman studios on the tape too, with Nick Park and the rest of the crew talking about all the fun they have working with Wallace & Gromit. It was just your sort of thing—bringing to life all the ideas in the *Cracking Animations* book that I bought you that Christmas, was it...two years ago?

After everyone else had gone to bed, I wrote my letter to Nick Park to say thank you for all the fun that Aardman had brought you over the years. Perhaps it was a silly idea. I'm sure they must get thousands of letters every day and I doubted it would even reach him. Nevertheless, it seemed an important thing to do at that particular moment.

I wonder, do most people meet story characters who touch their imagination in a special and enduring way, like Wallace & Gromit did for you? Or is it perhaps just the lucky few?

191. Everyone goes home
Wednesday 30 July 2003

Grandma and Grandad and Aunty Iris caught the train home this morning and Bob Robertson came to give them a lift to the station. So when we got back here afterwards, I was able to show him the success with his evening primroses. He says the flowers should seed themselves now. So in years to come there'll be evening primroses in July–August time to remind us of you. And of all the kind people who've done so much to help.

Bob was keen to see our archaeological dig too. In fact, we were standing and talking about it for so long in the end that Denise had to ring up to find out where he'd got to. Oh dear, wicked Dad!

192. Alone
Wednesday 30 July 2003

Writing is a solitary occupation. Practically every single word in this *Scrapbook* of ours will have been written while I've been alone in the house. Or when everyone else is asleep. A long time ago, when you were still very small, Jamie Man, someone asked you what you wanted to do when you grew up. That was before you ever met Wallace & Gromit or dreamed of animation. I've never forgotten the answer you gave:

   I'm going to dig the garden, like my Dad.

You pictured your future then in terms of what you saw. What did it matter to you what went on once you were tucked up fast asleep in bed? Ten years working from home. Giving people advice over the telephone. Faxes and e-mails composed and sent late at night. Then the novels and scripts. I've got used to *working* alone. But *being* alone…? That's quite a different matter.

The visitors are all away now. Kyle is on Skye with Richard and his family. Nicola and Mum are flying out to Spain tomorrow. It's just you and me once more, Jamie Man.

Maybe Kyle will want us to go away somewhere when he gets back. I'll have to wait and see. He might prefer just to potter around quietly at home together. We're still feeling our way here. We have all sorts of old routines to relearn. And new ones to build.

In the meantime, I have empty hours to fill for the first time in more than two weeks. The Grandparents say goodbye with reluctance. They express regret that they have to leave me on my own. The reality is, there are so many jobs that I can't even begin to think of doing while anyone else is around. And there's no running away from it all. Sooner or later, I have to set about gathering up what's left of the old life.

There was actually some rain for a short while when the *Oldies* were setting out for the train this morning. But it's brightened up again since and I've had all the bed clothes drying nicely out on the whirly this afternoon. That all sounds very domestic and efficient—apart from the tears that were streaming down my face all the time while I was stripping the beds for the washer. The beds in your room.

Focus on the good things. The sky this afternoon cleared to patches of the brightest blue, with clouds that made me of think of splashes of wallpaper paste, like the glue you were using in the kitchen to fix the strips of newspaper on your little animation theatre.

Cracking weather, Gromit!

193. Why "Highland Cathedral"?
Wednesday 30 July 2003

I was explaining to Grandma and Grandad about when we first learned to play "Highland Cathedral" at Music Club. And how Mrs Banks said it was, "As used in the film *Four weddings and a funeral*." That's why I picked *Four weddings* as the first video off the shelf after everyone had gone home. To remind myself where the music appears in the story. There's not an awful lot of it in fact, but you can still pick it out quite clearly as the guests are leaving the church at the end of the Scottish wedding.

I can stand in the kitchen these days and still hear you practising that tune on the chanter in your bedroom. Just as clearly as I hear Mr Barnes playing it for you at the cemetery. I think that Mrs Banks is wary about suggesting that we should play "Highland Cathedral" at Music Club now. But as far as I'm concerned it brings back only the very best of memories. It makes me think of you, Jamie Man.

194. Matthew's tribute to Gareth
Wednesday 30 July 2003

Watching *Four weddings and a funeral* again reminded me once more of the poem that the character Matthew reads at the funeral of his friend Gareth. It's called "Song IX", by W.H. Auden. I think it speaks of loss in a very universal way, Jamie Man. And the struggle that we face trying to fill the gap:

> …*He was my North, my South, my East and West*
> *My working week and my Sunday rest*
> *My noon, my midnight, my talk, my song*
> *I thought that love would last forever: I was wrong…*

195. Looking down into the past
Monday 11 August 2003

Bob Powell from the Highland Folk Museum has been to look at our hole in the garden this afternoon. Once upon a time I would have anticipated so much more progress by this stage of the holidays. As it is, I've scraped away a little more of the earth to make the pattern of the stones underneath easier to see. But otherwise, it still looks very much the same as when you and I finished work out there that Wednesday lunchtime. I suppose some people might ask, why bother at all? Well…what price a promise, Jamie Man? I said I would finish it for you, didn't I.

I told Mr Powell about the old stone septic tank that Ramie Taylor had uncovered when he was excavating the bottom end of the ski slope. And I pointed out that corner of the lounge that's now sitting on the seven cubic metres of concrete that the Building Inspector insisted on to fill up the hole! And then over there the two biggest slabs in the patio, which once made up the lid of the tank. Not forgetting the countless stones that got salvaged and reused in building the drystone wall. Waste not, want not, eh!

Mrs Cormack next door reckons there's at least one further tank over the wall in the bottom of the Crannich garden too. You pointed out the top of an old vent pipe to me over there earlier this year, when we were looking for your lost tennis ball in the long grass. So, what did our expert visitor from the museum think about it all?

On the whole, he seemed to agree with our analysis, Jamie Man. It looks as if we have another tank like before. Just further back and a little lower down in the ground. And with railway sleepers for the lid this time, rather than the stone slabs. According to Mr Powell, the main railway line came through the valley here in 1863. So by the end of that century, the first of the original wooden sleepers would have been coming up for replacement. Hence all the different structures from about 1900 onwards—garages, sheds, tanks, footbridges, etc—all built with second-hand railway sleepers. He says we should try to get the timbers out now and then just carry on digging down to see what turns up. Oh, and keep taking the photos to record the progress along the way. Like that first one with you…

196. An act of kindness
Saturday 2 August 2003

After breakfast today I found myself humming the song "You'll never walk alone". A few minutes later the postman arrived, bringing me an unexpected parcel.

When we were looking through the photographs before the funeral, we'd come across the pictures I took of you and Kyle with your presents from Grandma and Grandad last Christmas. You with your low-D tenor whistle and Kyle with the new crash cymbal for his drum kit. I'd done the ordering over the internet and this visit in the summer was going to be Grandad's first chance to see the famous whistle he'd heard so much about.

Your whistle was made by a man called Tony Dixon, who has a workshop down in Devon. The one-piece instrument that I ordered was actually out of stock at the time. But Mr Dixon simply sent the more-expensive, two-piece whistle at no extra charge, so you wouldn't be disappointed for Christmas. That meant that it was tuneable and also that it could be swapped between the whistle head and a flute head. When I explained all this to Grandad, he said he'd like to buy the extra flute head for me, so that I could have it to play at Music Club.

This morning I opened my unexpected parcel to find the new flute head, with a note inside from Tony Dixon saying that there would be no charge, yet again! I fitted it onto your whistle and tried it out. Perfect! And the first tune that I played…?

> When you walk through a storm
> Hold your head up high
> And don't be afraid of the dark…
> …and you'll never walk alone [from Carousel]

New
Year
2003

&

your
first
tune

Making music, with the theme you composed for your
Kangaroo Adventure.

E-MAIL TO TONY DIXON
Saturday 2 August 2003

Dear Tony

Amidst all the heartache of the last three weeks, the kindness and generosity of friends both near and far has been a constant source of comfort and wonder. And your unexpected little parcel arriving in the post this morning was just one further reminder that there very definitely IS such a thing as society, and community, and all those other concepts that rise above mere self interest…

…My older son, Kyle returned today from a few days away on Skye with the family of a school friend. After two weeks of visitors, etc this was the first time that the two of us had had the chance to be truly alone together in the house, where previously we were always three. After a bit of a rest he said that he would like to take a walk up to the cemetery. As we were leaving, he asked if we could take the flute/ whistle up with us to show Jamie and to tell him of your kindness. And so we stood together at the graveside; I played the same "Highland Cathedral" that Jamie's chanter teacher had performed on the day of the funeral…and then the two of us sat together on the grass for a while and talked about some of those questions to which none of us can ever truly hope to know the answer until our own time comes.

…For that short period of time on a breezy and sunny Highland evening your generous gift brought me a truly privileged moment of closeness and understanding in the company of both my sons.

…each time one or other of us takes out the whistle or the flute to play, we will think of Jamie and be reminded of your generosity.

We are in your debt.

With thanks.

David

197. A father and son story
Friday 1 August 2003

The second video that I've been watching is an Italian film called *Life is beautiful*. It's about a Jewish man during the war and the lengths he went to in order to convince his young son that life in a slave labour camp was all part of a big fun game. I think it's one of the most poignant father and son films ever made. Greater love hath no man...

After Doctor Calder had called me with the news from Bruar, it was Mr Whyte who sat with me through those very first, dark hours when there was still so much confusion and disbelief. I'm afraid that Mr Whyte had to put up with a lot of very unhappy talk that day. Thoughts about how I'd not been there with you and things like that. It felt like I'd failed you, Jamie Man, at the time when you needed me most. Do I think that it should have been me and not you? What parent wouldn't?

LOVE THAT TAKES A LIFETIME
from <u>Out of the silent planet</u> by C.S. Lewis, the man who gave you <u>Narnia</u>

"This love...takes his whole life. When he is young he has to look for his mate; and then he has to court her; then he begets young; then he rears them; then he remembers all this, and boils it inside him and makes it into poems and wisdom..."

"A pleasure is full grown only when it is remembered. You are speaking...as if the pleasure were one thing and the memory another. It is all one thing....What you call remembering is the last part of the pleasure,...When you and I met, the meeting was over very shortly, it was nothing. Now it is growing into something as we remember it. But still we know very little about it. What it will be when I remember it as I lie down to die, what it makes in me all my days till then—that is the real meeting. The other is only the beginning of it."

---

198. Making a start
Thursday 31 July 2003

I've been out in the garden today, gathering up all the planks and posts that you used when you were building your road to the back gate. There's no way to hold on to what is already lost. Nevertheless, each piece of wood that I move out of place seems like another tear in the fabric of everything that we once had, Jamie Man. The best I could manage for now was to prop it all up against the wall of the house to dry out in the sunshine.

After lunch I tried to make a start on sorting out some of the stuff in your bedroom that I'd had to push to one side before. I ended up sobbing when I came across the folder of English work you had from the two days you spent at the Grammar School in June:

Jamie Gasking, 1X/1A.

Your handwriting. Your new class. Your future.

I thought of the *Smoke Machines* project and your *Slug Story*. Of the three, wacky chapters of the *Kangaroo adventure* that you'd completed so far, with your notes on the rest of the plot to come. The first sketches for a map of the garden that you'd been planning to complete in the holidays—inspired by the orienteering sessions with the Scouts. So many dreams that you would be missing out on. All those many things you'd looked forward to for so long. What happens to all that fun when it isn't being used? Does it have somewhere else to go? Or does it simply melt away into nothing?

Well, for all my tears, I have made a start. The rest will have to wait for another day. And many more after that, I'm sure. Tomorrow I'm going into Inverness to investigate masons and headstones. That's yet another thing that's never going to be easy. But it's probably better to get the ball rolling just now, while everyone else is away.

199. Was that you, Jamie Man?
Thursday 31 July 2003

I suspect that many things will never quite go back to the way they were before. The world has moved on and I don't think I've kept pace. After the continual comings and goings of the past couple of weeks, it's so very quiet in the house now. But from one moment to the next I can't make up my mind whether that spells peaceful, or something else. Aloneness, or loneliness? I see now that there is a difference. Much of the time it seems easier to be outside in the garden, or off in the woods somewhere. Out in the places where you still seem so close, without walls pressing in on me from all sides.

There was quite a breeze this afternoon but the weather stayed fine and I decided it really was time to do something about painting the playhouse. Who could have imagined that I still wouldn't have that job completed by the end of July, when it was only hours away? In the event, it's still not finished even now—because the tin of wood preservative ran out! I've done the whole of the sunny side and I thought there was going to be enough for the front door as well. Then all at once while I was painting round the window from the inside, the wind suddenly whipped up. *WHOOSH!*—in one door and out through the other. I had the pot of preservative standing in a plastic tub on the floor "to catch the drips". Huh! I think you can probably picture the rest of the scene!

I did manage to rescue some of it from the paper on the floor, but not enough to finish the door any more. Very funny, I'm sure, Jamie Man! I think *you* need to have a strong word with whoever up there's been messing around with the wind controls today! Or perhaps it was one of *your* little jokes? Just to remind your old Dad that you're still game for a laugh. Anyway, the door looks a bit weird now, with a pale, unpainted strip right across the bottom. Oh, and there's this funny, dark-chestnut patch on the floor inside as well, would you believe.

200. Hey, Mr Big!
Saturday 1 May 2004

Our scrapbook has been complete for several weeks, Jamie Man. I have it sitting on the desk here beside me now. 320 pages, 120,000 words of the most difficult piece of writing that I've ever undertaken. Grandad has a copy too and he's working his way through that now. *The Jamie Scrapbook* is our big record, with all the everyday little details and facts that we wouldn't want to lose hold of in the years to come.

Now I'm into the next stage. Picking out the parts for the book that we can publish. Finding the story for all the people looking in. Some of them will be old friends. Others may only come to know you through words on the page. I've been thinking that *Hey, Mr Big!* might be your kind of title. What do you reckon?

All the money from the book will go to *The Jamie Fund*, so I do hope that folk will want to buy it and make things happen for your friends.

The past few days have been full of questions about self-publishing and how to pay for it all. I went to bed last night with my thoughts in a whirl…

…and you came to me in my dreams. I was in a panic about going off on a journey somewhere. I think I was supposed to be catching a train. It was due to leave at midnight but I never got as far as the station. The last thing I remember is that you were suddenly standing there at my side with two questions:

> *Can I help you with your book, even if I haven't managed to finish mine?*
>
> *Will there be a part for me in your story?*

You've been helping me already, Jamie Man. All the way through. I couldn't have made it this far otherwise. After all, what kind of story would this be…without my Mr Big?

201. The Loch an Eilein connection
Thursday 31 July 2003

There was one further present from Grandma and Grandad before they left for home yesterday. A small picture from Alice and Jeff's shop. I didn't notice the tiny writing in the corner at first. But now that I've looked again more closely, I find it strange that Grandma and Grandad should have happened upon that *particular* scene. I told them about it on the phone after they got home. The picture shows a view across Loch An Eilein, towards the ruined castle on the island, with the Cairngorms in the distance. It's the same view that you must have seen when you went on your Scout camp in June. If you look very closely at the photograph that Frances took for the newspaper that evening, you can even make out the fuzzy shape of the island in the background.

A ruin on an island? Hm, I wonder what the *Land of Castles* has to say about that?—I thought so. The book describes Loch an Eilein as a sister castle to the one that Kyle and I cycled out to see at Lochindorb. It says that some people reckon that Loch an Eilein was another stronghold of the Wolf of Badenoch. It certainly has all the right credentials, lurking out there amidst the dark, cold waters of the Loch. Cool castle, eh, Jamie Man!

202. The bus that got away
Friday 1 August 2003

Can it really be three weeks already since you set out that day? For everyone else anyway, Jamie Man. As far as I'm concerned, it's still just the first week of the holidays. I walked up the road in slow motion this morning. Another "first" to be confronted. Standing at the bus stop where I said my last goodbye to you. Catching the bus to Inverness, just as you did that day. That smile and that wave as the bus drew away…

I was on my way to investigate stone masons. Someone was chatting breezily about the weather. The Aviemore bus came and went. Just one other person waiting for Inverness. And waiting. Eventually he went off saying he was going for the train instead. It was perfectly clear—the bus wasn't coming. But I couldn't move. I was cold and empty. Rooted to the spot. Taking the train demanded a decision and my brain had developed lock jaw. In the end I simply burst into tears. On my own. Right there at the bus shelter.

Somehow I managed to stumble back up the road and round to Denise Robertson's house. Mairi Robertson (of Monty the Dog fame) was there too. She and Denise were just about to go out swimming together. I got a hug from each of them and then after they'd gone I stayed and talked to Bob (of evening primrose fame) for the rest of the morning.

So much for my planning. I was imagining myself having to go through the same process all over again tomorrow. But then after lunch Denise said she had to go to Inverness and I could get a lift with her. So I did visit the stone masons after all. I even got a new lot of wood preservative as well. It's not the same type as before but the man in the shop insists they're all the same inside the tin. He'd better be right, Jamie Man!

When I got home, I'd only been back in the house for about five minutes when Kyle rang to tell me that Richard and his family are thinking of coming back early from Skye. He says it's been raining non-stop all week over there. Rain? What's that? All we've had here has been empty blue skies and sunshine, sunshine, sunshine.

But if Kyle could be coming home tomorrow, then I guess it is just as well that I got the stone masons over and done with today. At least now I think I've decided which one to go to for your headstone. And that's a small step forward. I'm still not absolutely convinced that Denise didn't make up an excuse to go to Inverness this afternoon, just for me. But I'm not sure either that I was in any state to argue about it at the time.

203. An unwelcome letter
Thursday 7 August 2003

Just before we set off on the bikes to ride to Lochindorb this morning, I found a letter in the postbox. Hand-delivered in an expensive, white envelope. Two copies. One for *The Owner*. The other for *The Occupier*. One of those "Oh-God-what-have-I-done-now?" letters. It turned out to be from the people who want to build all the new houses in the woods. We thought we'd seen the worst of their plans already. You stood up and said what you thought about them at the meeting in the Village Hall last year. What did they want *now*?

I imagine there were plenty of angry people around this end of the village when they saw those new plans today. But I don't suppose anyone else sat down and cried about it. Kyle came and gave me a hug. I try not to cry like that when he's around. I don't want to get him upset. But this time I couldn't help it. I knew just how unhappy you would've been to see the even bigger scheme that they're suggesting now. They say they want to bring the new road in from much further outside the village. And to pay for that, they're suggesting extra houses right across the entrance to *Sesame Street*.

We always thought that part of the woods was safe because it was marked for conservation and amenity in the Local Plan. I need to look at the maps more closely. Maybe they won't get it all their own way. Perhaps there's still hope for the pine martens and all the other animals that like the shelter of the trees along your favourite walk.

PINE MARTENS
from the <u>Glenmore Times</u>, Forest Enterprise, 1998

Pine martens like to have tree cover in their home base. This may be because the trees help them to move around without attracting attention and also shelter a bigger range of other creatures (both on the ground and in the branches) which martens eat. Marten territories are smaller where there are more trees. In an open Highland area with only scattered trees, a male's territory can be as large as 20 square kilometres—nearly five times as big as a male's patch in good woodland. Although native pines and other conifer forests suit them fine, it seems that broadleaved woodland, where trees are more closely packed, is their favourite hang-out.

---

204. *Sesame Street*—just the place for pine marten
Thursday 7 August 2003

There's a whole mixture of sizes and shapes of trees on the wet ground around the ditch at *Sesame Street*. And right in the middle of the wood there, where I spotted the pine marten that time, the ground has been so waterlogged in the past few years that several of the trees have just lost their grip and tipped right over. That's made a very dense, jumbled area that looks just perfect for animals like the martens. For now, it's still quite remote from the village. But that would all change if there were houses right up to the edge of the wood. And what about the animals that like to move between the trees and the marsh? How will they do that, if they're cut off by houses and gardens and a road?

Why is it called *Sesame Street*? Well, that's simple, isn't it, Jamie Man. When I was first exploring the woods out there I discovered a fancy *Big Bird* fairground balloon caught on the ground beside the ditch. So I came home and invited you and Kyle and Nicola to come with me on a visit…to *Sesame Street*.

That was many years ago. The *Sesame Street* balloon is old and flat now. But it's still there, if you know where to look. Just like *The Robin Hood Bridge* and *The Bow & Arrow Tree* and *The Picnic Track* and *The Uphill Stream* and all those other unforgettable places that always meant so much to you.

205. Mum & Nicola return from Spain
Friday 8 August 2003

Mum and Nicola flew back to Manchester from Spain today and now they're on their way home by train. By the time they get to Inverness, the entire journey will have taken about nineteen hours. Oof! It's been around 30C in Aviemore again today, and even warmer down in England. So Mum and Nicola are going to be very hot and tired, even if they're on time. Not at all the kind of trip for you, eh, Jamie Man. Some like it hot, but not you, or me!

Nicola's coming here tomorrow to tell us all about the holiday. Meantime Kyle's gone over to Richard's for the night. After he went, I popped out to finish staining the rest of the playhouse. Huh! I should be so lucky! Despite all those confident assurances from the man at B&Q, that new tin of wood preservative is *nothing* like the old stuff. The colour's different and it's so weak it looks as if it's going to need a second coat, or more.

Before Kyle left this afternoon, he wanted us to take some more flowers up to the cemetery for you. Usually at this time in August, there would be plenty to choose from in the garden. But this year everything's drying out and going to seed so quickly. So this time we've taken some of the ones from the bouquets that people have been bringing to the house. A little brightness for Mum and Nicola when they come to see you tomorrow.

While they've been away, Kyle and I have made a collection of pebbles to spell out your initials, "*JG*", on the grass of the grave. Rocks and stones will always make me think of you, Jamie Man. Come next year, when the headstone is all sorted out, I think I'd like to build you a little walled garden. There's plenty of stone to choose from here. All the leftovers from building the drystone wall. Or maybe some pieces from the old tank. And you can have some of our own, home-made compost too. Remember all that sieving and wheel barrowing to make the new lawns, eh? Another reminder of the good times.

This evening after I came in from painting the playhouse, I've been listening to *Harry Potter and the Chamber of Secrets*. It may be the new set of CD's now, but it's still the same old story that you enjoyed over and over again on the cassettes that we gave to Cousin Alan. I close my eyes and you're still sitting there in the chair, listening along with me, enthralled by every single word of the story...as always.

206. Local plans...
Sunday 10 August 2003

I thought I should try and write a letter to the Planning Department about the new housing plans, Jamie Man. No doubt there'll be plenty of objections. But no one else can tell the people on the Council how sad *you* would have been about this latest scheme.

Before lunch today, I went out to *Sesame Street* with the map and the new plans to pace out the whole thing, just like you and I did before the meeting in the Village Hall last year. Seeing it on the ground, it's actually worse than I imagined. To make room for the extra houses, they'd want to cut down *all* the tall pine trees at the back of the horses' field on the way to *Sesame Street*. And they'd be going right out into the wet ground on that corner of the marsh as well. No, Jamie Man. You wouldn't have liked this at all. But we mustn't forget it's only an *application* at this stage. It still depends what the Planning Committee decide. And they have to listen to all sides before they make up their minds.

I came back over the marsh to the other end of the picnic track, where you and I went exploring on that hot Wednesday afternoon, between digging at lunch time and our grand slide show in the evening. It's strange how, even after all these years of outings in the woods together, we still conspired to find you somewhere new for that final walk of ours. I like the thought that you spent your very last afternoon in the woods pioneering into unknown territory. Just what the Swallows and Amazons would have chosen. And following those same, secret trails again today, I found my way back to a log that you had hunted out for me that day. I put it under my arm and carried it home with me. One more, inconsequential piece of fuel for the stove, transformed into a rare treasure...simply by your touch.

207. ...and brain scans
Sunday 10 August 2003

I came very close to you again this afternoon, Jamie Man, when I was hunting out the Local Plan to check the boundaries for the new housing scheme. At the bottom of one of the boxes on top of the wardrobe, I suddenly came across the printouts from when you went to the hospital for the brain scans.

Benign Rolandic Nightime Epilepsy. That was the fancy name they gave it. You never had many fits—half a dozen perhaps. Always while you were asleep—four in the morning, or thereabouts. The doctors said that it was just a childhood thing that you would grow out of by the time you were ten or twelve years old. It must have been a year or eighteen months since you last had a fit. It shouldn't be any trouble to you in later life…

I'd put those big computer pictures of your brainwaves away at the bottom of the box there to keep them flat. I'd thought that they would make an interesting souvenir for you when you were older. It was sad, coming across them unexpectedly like that. In a way though, seeing all those weird and wiggly lines marked out on the paper, it made me feel like I was looking inside your head. Squeezing myself into the tight space in amongst all those non-stop stories and adventures. I wonder which of the lines on the chart would have lit up for walks to *Sesame Street*, or for saying goodbye at the bus stop, like we did a month ago today…?

208. Sky watching
Thursday 28 August 2003

There's been much talk of planet Mars on the news this week. Apparently it's especially close to the earth just now and we should be able to see it brighter than normal in the night sky. It puts me in mind of Harry Potter and his encounters with the centaurs in the Forbidden Forest—"Mars is bright tonight."

All this talk of celestial bodies takes me back to our grand, nocturnal expedition to observe the eclipse of the moon earlier this year. Some people even managed to catch a glimpse of the event too. There were pictures in the newspaper to prove it. But we weren't quite so fortunate. I wrote up the account of our unsuccessful adventures in a song, *The Scotch Missed Blues*, and the *Strathy* printed it in their *Foolscap* column the following week.

That all seems like a lifetime away now—which of course it is, I suppose—but amongst all the irony and sadness of that fact, I am glad of the memory of such a unique moment of madness with my two big sons. In years to come I hope I'll be able to remind Kyle of the events of 31 May 2003 and see a small smile creep back across his face.

THE SCOTCH MISSED BLUES
Saturday 31 May 2003

You remember on May the thirty first
In the year two thousand and three?
When I woke you up at three a.m.
Just to see what we could see?

      But then, weren't you always saying
      That you knew your Dad was crazy?
      Mister doctor man he tell me
      It's hopeless for yours truly
      When he diagnose your ol' Pappy
      Got them dreadful, one-and-only, eclipse-of-the-sun blues

What's the point of nocturnal wandering
Through the woods at quarter past three?
Creeping past a bunch of sleepy cows
Doing field astronomy?

      Well, that big star man was saying
      There was something special coming
      Optimistically predicting
      A ring of fire sun rising
      And you know how they're awful catching
      Them ol' mentally disturbing, eclipse-of-the-sun blues

On the Grantown back road past Auchterblair
Looking east towards Mullochard
We watched mist that went, and then came back
But the sun was...kind of hard

      So we might have missed this party
      But we know sidereally
      On July the twenty third, see?
      Two thousand and ninety three—ee
      That's the next time they guarantee—ee
      An event to bring those looney, eclipse-of-the-sun blues

209. Holding hands with the best of times
Friday 29 August 2003

When I reflect on the best of times with any companion, it seems to me that it is often looking at something together: a sunrise, a sunset, the sky, the stars, the sea, nature, scenery, animals. Or engaged in some shared activity: reading, listening, playing music, watching a film, digging in the garden, spring cleaning, making something. Or simply being side by side: walking in the woods, sitting on a wall swinging legs in time with one another, or on the rocks dangling feet in the water—holding hands maybe.

You were always a great one for holding hands, Jamie Man, right to the very end. I remember when you were small. I would come home from a day out with arm and fingers feeling quite worn out, simply from all that holding on. And now? Now I still feel you holding on tight. So tight, that it can often bring tears to my eyes...

A LETTER FROM EOGHANN'S MUM
Sunday 20 July 2003

Dear Pam and David

In time you may wish to ask the school to protect the tree that Jamie planted in the grounds when he was in P2.

I visited it the other evening—I remembered where he and Eoghann and Bryce had planted their trees—it is in the stand of (now big, strong) Aspen at the back of the school—now within the Nursery School enclosure. Oddly it is only Jamie's tree that still has his name tag attached. It's in the middle of the stand. So you will know exactly which tree he planted.

I know it is a small thing, but I felt I should just mention it to you.

Sheila

210. Look at that big tree now!
Spring 1998 & Friday 25 July 2003

Grandad and I walked down to the school this evening to take a look at your tree. Things have certainly changed a great deal since that spring when the PTA organised for every child in the school to plant a tree. You were six years old then. It must have been just around the time when we were starting to recruit some of the actors and singers for *The Piper* later that year. I went in to school to help on the Monday when you all came out class by class to plant your trees and tie on the name labels that you'd prepared. You wrote "Jamie P2" in wobbly, just-learning-your-letters handwriting.

I have vivid recollections too of spending most of that Sunday down there with the mattock and the iron bar, levering out rocks and so on, as one of Sheila's gang of willing hands. Our job was to prepare all the holes, ready for the big planting the next day. You were thrilled with all the digging and tool work. And afterwards you came up and down the street with me, as we trolleyed some of the biggest rocks back here to use when I was building the wall. I remember how determined you were that we should get that really *BIG* boulder out—the one by the corner of the drive. We never did manage it. In the end it was decided just to raise it up so it would stick up above the ground and make a special feature. You can go down to the school and still see that rock there to this very day—the Mr Big Boulder, you might say.

Nicola was in her final year of primary school when the three of you planted your trees. Just like you now, coming up to the end of P7. I could always remember which was her tree, even though it lost its label long ago. It's the last of the tall aspens on the right hand side of the path, as you go down past the nature area.

Kyle and the rest of the P4's planted their trees in the big groups up near the mounds and the football pitch. I was telling Grandad how I remembered thinking at the time, poor Jamie and his friends had to be content with a secluded, shady spot round the back where no one would ever notice.

What a difference five years have made! Look at those three big, strong trees nowadays! And since they've added the nursery onto the back of the school, your tree stands in pride of place with Eoghann's and Bryce's in the centre of the grassy play area that they've fenced off for the wee ones. The PTA are talking of putting a bench round the bottom of your tree, so that the nursery children will have somewhere special to sit. When I think back to what Gregor's Mum was saying about how you looked after her wee boy when he was unhappy going into nursery, I see now that there couldn't have been a better place for your tree, Jamie Man. Or a more appropriate way for the children to remember you in years to come.

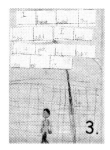

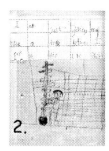

My tree: Illustrated by Jamie. Written by Jamie. Spring 1998.

1. I am just going out to plant my tree.

2. I am just giving my tree a drink before I put it into the soil.

3. I have planted my tree and I have just put my name tag on it.

Tree planting then and now: every picture book tells a story

211. With you
Sunday 11 July 2004

Early this morning I went down to the school. On the way my thoughts were of all those years of holding your hand. And how it had grown to be such an automatic habit for you to walk on the inside, away from the traffic, safe from harm.

I laid my hand on your tree and I thought once again of that day, just yesterday, when I watched you press the earth in around its roots and mark it forever with your name. Then I took the scissors from my bag to cut away the old, fraying string and I retied your fading label with a new piece of string for the years to come.

There was a broken branch on Nicola's tree. I cut it off with the secateurs and in the quiet of the morning I carried it with me up to the cemetery as a gift for you on this, our first anniversary. Did I do right, my Jamie Man?

212. The world moves on
Sunday 25 April 2004

This year's P7's (your P6's) will be the very last of the tree planting generation. Tiny trees and tiny children growing up together. And now in a few months time it'll be their turn to move on to the Grammar School. This weekend I've been writing a new song for Mr Whyte to use at the Leavers' Service 2004. My present to him and to all your P6 friends.

THE TREES GROW TALL
For the Leavers' Service, Wednesday 30 June 2004

The trees that we plant are our present
To those who will follow this way
A gift of goodwill for the future
The message of hope from today
We listen to past generations
In the stories we learn
Each day we are gaining the wisdom
That we should pass on in our turn

A new chapter starts
When the child is small
Then the world moves on
And the trees grow tall

As the sun shines down
And the raindrops fall
So the world moves on
And the trees grow tall

The magic of growth and renewal's
At risk if we fail to reflect
The earth is a sensitive treasure
It's something we need to protect
It needn't be hard or expensive
If we all share the cost
From youngest to oldest amongst us
The stories must never be lost

A new chapter starts, etc

---

213. Speaking for you
Thursday 21 August 2003

My letter to the Planning Department is printed and sent. Can I truly put myself inside your head and do justice to the words that you would have said? No, of course not. The best I can hope for is a fragmented picture, a broken mirror. All too often as adults, we speak only from the cold, financial logic and self-interest of the head, discounting the deeper values of the heart. But perhaps, like the messages from your friends, we are more likely to find an open and honest window on the world through the eyes of a child.

GROWN-UPS LOVE FIGURES
from The Little Prince by Antoine de Saint-Exupéry

"Grown-ups love figures. When you tell them that you have made a new friend, they never ask any questions about essential matters. They never say to you, 'What does his voice sound like? What games does he love best? Does he collect butterflies?' Instead they demand: 'How old is he? How many brothers has he? How much does he weigh? How much money does his father make?' Only from these figures do they think they have learned anything about him."

---

214. Waking slowly
Sunday 21 September 2003

I didn't set the alarm last night. Consequently I woke up slowly, drifting in and out of sleep, half dreaming, half wondering what time it was. There haven't been many dreams that I remember these past couple of months. But that's okay. Better to dive down deeply into oblivion and then leap out in a single bound on the other side, than to be thrashing around all night.

Today I emerged from the extra hours of sleep dreaming of you for only the second time, Jamie Man. I was out searching for you in the woods. You were on your way back from somewhere and you needed me to guide you home. I was whistling over and over again as I went along, in the way that I always used to do for Kjersti Dog. I was sure that you would recognise the sound and know that it was me. But only if I was close enough for you to hear.

I was growing anxious. I desperately wished for a proper whistle—like the ones referees have—so that the sound would carry further. But my name's not Harry Potter. And this wasn't the Room of Requirement.

I thought I heard a call. Was it you? Was that "Dad" you were shouting? Was it happiness that we'd found one another? Or a cry for help because you were in trouble? I couldn't tell. It seemed to be coming from across the open space and away into the trees beyond. But it was just too far off for me to be sure. I carried on, whistling and walking. Pausing to listen. Trying to decide if it truly was you, on your way home…

…once again I wondered what the time was. Just after eight o'clock, I guessed. I reached out for my glasses and blinked at the numbers on the clock radio: *08:02.*

The trees were gone. The sound of your voice had faded. My feeble whistle had not been strong enough to carry you home. And though the sun was shining in between the curtains, I struggled to find any good reason to climb out of bed to face the new day.

TO THE PLANNING DEPARTMENT
Thursday 21 August 2003

…This is not an easy letter for me to write and it may be that some people might consider what I have to say as being more emotional than objective. If that is so, I make no apologies…

…I was as surprised as anyone…when Jamie, at just 11 years old, stood up and addressed that hall full of adults to express his concern that if so many houses were built out in the woods, no one would be able to go out walking there anymore. It was something that mattered very much to him. His words were clear, simple and child-like but I feel sure that they expressed the deep-held views of many if not all of those who gave him such a respectful hearing in the hall that night…

…we recognised…the desirability of having a steady supply of a few, new properties each year that would be within the reach of young people growing up in the village, as well as folk coming in who were going to live and work here and who would help to strengthen and maintain the community.

I fear, however, that what we are being offered in this scheme is a desperate attempt to squeeze as much profit as possible out of a booming property market, with little or no regard for safeguarding the character of the existing community, or of its surrounding environment.

I think if Jamie were here, he would be saying that there were greedy men at work who did not care about the future of Carr-Bridge in the way that he did.

---

215. Another meeting, another hurdle
Thursday 28 August 2003

Kyle and I were going up to the Hall this evening for the public meeting to discuss the new housing plans. No escape from the memories of the previous time, when you stood up and said your piece.

On the way, we took a detour down to the Primary School to look at the trees. We still can't decide exactly which is the one that Kyle planted. The front of the field there catches the wind and weather and the name labels are all long since gone. But maybe that's the way it should be. Perhaps, like dog owners, children also grow up like their trees? Nicola is a big star out the front. You offer a quiet place for the wee ones to sit. And Kyle is one of the games-playing gang, rushing here, there and everywhere.

As we made our way into the meeting, I couldn't help remembering that this would be the first Scouts evening after the summer as well. There would be a sad gap at the Village Hall *and* at the Scout Hut tonight.

When we'd set out from the house, I'd said to Kyle that it looked like it might be a fine, clear sky for spotting planet Mars after the meeting. So of course, no sooner had we come out of the Hall at the end than—almost unheard of this summer—the rain started to fall, hammering down in big, heavy, stormy drop-lets.

"Let's run!" shouted Kyle. And so we did. He may be able to leave me stand-ing on the bike these days. But I reckon I still have the edge on him when it comes to a sprint. Though, as I was forever telling the pair of you, it won't be very long now before it's poor wee Dad who's puffing to keep up. So we might not have succeeded in seeing Mars but we did nonetheless manage to round off our evening in memorable fashion—running back down the road side by side and getting very wet together!

216. A fwog hug for Grandma
Friday 29 August 2003

Grandma will be 75 years old on Monday—catching up with Grandad all over again. Kyle drew a card for her last night after the meeting at the Hall. He took a lot of trouble over it, which meant that bedtime was rather delayed. He didn't object. Well I suppose some things are worth losing a bit of sleep over, aren't they.

It was hard to know what sort of card to go for this year. Trying to decide how to hit just the right degree of light-hearted comfort for Grandma, when a big part of her is feeling so very sad and not like celebrating at all. In the end I decided you can't go wrong with a hug. I've sent this Fwoggie to some of my friends as well, which I suppose makes it a sort of "group hug". I'm sure Grandma won't mind. And you can have a big one for yourself too, Jamie Man.

217. Mars is bright…at last
Wednesday 11 September 2003

We've had so many cloudy nights recently that I was beginning to suspect that catching a glimpse of Mars from the house here was doomed to turn out rather like our famous eclipse back in May: fine in theory. The trouble is, we need the clear sky at just the right time to get a good line of sight between the tree tops. But then last night it all finally fell into place—completely by chance, of course! I was coming through from the office at about half past midnight and the moon was so bright in the kitchen that I didn't bother to turn on the light. Then when I glanced out of the window, there was the Red Planet shining so clearly between the trees. You know that patch of open sky above the Crannich garden where you and I have so often picked out the pattern of Orion the Hunter on a cloudless, starry night? Well, Mars was certainly bright this night, Jamie Man. Did you manage to see it too? I do hope so.

218. A long wait for home-made chips
2002–2003

I've been promising myself a vegetable patch for all of ten years now. 2003 was *definitely* going to be the year of the home-grown potato. So much for my crystal ball.

It all started with that tree stump, didn't it, Jamie Man. No problem when it was buried under a ski slope. But now if we wanted to grow vegetables, I was going to have to dig down and get the roots out. It shouldn't be too difficult…Ha, ha, di, ha!

So what did I find? An enormous "S" bend and multiple roots going down several feet deeper than I ever expected, plus a 7 or 8 inch trunk that had to be cut out with the chainsaw! It was all I could do to carry it down to the stick pile. I took a photo to send to Grandma and Grandad. A picture is worth a thousand words and many hours of sweat!

My guess was that it must have got bent over when they were laying the outlet pipe for the old septic tank. And then after the poor seedling had spent years and years turning itself back upright again, it was rewarded by being chopped down to make room for a dry ski slope! That might have been the end of the story. Except that when Dad went on digging, he found to his surprise that the ground was starting to trickle away *downwards*. And he was hitting something hard. Something wooden? Something…very mysterious!

219. Grantown show
Thursday 14 August 2003

The village samba drumming band, Carrumba, were booked to lead the procession for the Grantown Show today. It was peculiar for everyone, gathering by the War Memorial ready to take over from the pipe band. The group were all so used to seeing you around whenever Kyle was playing. Sharon McWilliam was there. She said they'd been away on holiday at the time of your funeral. But they'd stopped at Bruar on the way so that Sarah could leave some flowers there for you.

It was a tough gig for the band, marching all the way from the Square to the showground in the hot sun. Particularly for the ones like Kyle who had the big drums banging against their legs all the time. No wonder he was so tired and bruised afterwards!

The field was packed with people out to enjoy the show and the fine weather. Yet again I had that overwhelming feeling of moving through the crowd at half the speed of everyone else. There were horses and cows and sheep and bulls being put through their paces in the showring. Even water buffalo, would you believe, Jamie Man! And all the usual sideshows as well, of course—including several stalls selling giant cuddly toys. One after another Winnie the Pooh looking down at me...

On the way home, we stopped off at the *Strathy* office on the High Street to pick up the photos of you and Kyle that I'd ordered. Your Scout picture from Loch an Eilein. And the one that Frances took of Carrumba for their *Big Music Day* fund raiser back in May. Enlargements to add to our collection on the wall. Each of you doing your own thing with your friends in 2003.

220. Judith at the Show
Thursday 14 August 2003

I bumped into Judith—Countryside Ranger and friend from Music Club—at the Show today. The latest chance first meeting. It gave me the opportunity to ask her about that unusual bird of prey that was flying over the cemetery a few days back. I've often seen buzzards above the trees there. But this bird didn't have the same cat-like cry. And it didn't fly in the same way either. The wings were narrow, with dark tips, and the flight was jerky, almost as if it was stalling. Judith reckoned it sounded like a male hen harrier, Jamie Man. A rather more rare visitor come to see you.

The last time I saw Judith was when she came round to the house to deliver the case for your electric guitar. That all started back at the Carrumba *Big Music Day*. I'd told Judith how disappointed you were when you were outbid for the fancy guitar case in the musical instrument auction and she said she had a spare case. It was a wooden one that a friend had made but it didn't fit her bass guitar and you were welcome to have it. You were overjoyed when you came home from school that day to find the case waiting for you there. That would certainly keep your guitar safe from harm. All you had to do now, was to make sure that you didn't damage anyone else with it, it was so hard and strong!

I was digging in the garden when Judith turned up with the case. It was around the time when I'd just started to uncover the first of the wooden sleepers. So when I saw her at the Show again today, I was able to give her a progress report and tell her about all the fun you'd had helping clear away the earth ready for Mr Powell's visit from the Museum.

As things worked out, you never got the chance to take your guitar case to show everyone at Music Club, did you, Jamie Man. Now it's gone to a new home with Nicola in Inverness. And I'm sure she will be aware of your presence with her each time she's out making music with *her* friends.

221. Gus comes to *Sesame Street*
Tuesday 10 September 2003

Gus Jones from the Conservation Group came round today for a guided tour of *Sesame Street*. He had this amazing piece of satellite technology with him. Just press a few keys and there's an instant record of the grid reference for anything of interest. I could imagine your fingers itching to get hold of it. Like a smoke machine…?

We took the usual route: out the back gate, over the Snakey Bridge, across the ditch by the stepping stones, and then over the fence to the big pine trees that they're saying they want to cut down to make room for all the extra new houses. Gus reckons that belt of mature trees is a very important landscape feature as you come into the village from the south. They definitely got a mention on his satellite gizmo.

We went right through *Sesame Street* and back round in a wide sweep across the marsh. Gus was very impressed by the giant, gnarled Scots pines hidden in amongst the newer trees beyond the ditch. He said they could be 150–200 years old. We always called them the *Treebeards* because they look so much like ancient Ents lurking in the deep Forest of Fangorn.

But Gus was finding a lot more than just trees, Jamie Man. There was rare stuff like Lady's Tresses and narrow-headed ants. Plus all the different birds that he spotted darting amongst the trees. I can't remember them all now, but he's obviously got much better eyesight than I have! And we talked as well about juniper and capercaille and red squirrel and pine marten and owl and badger and hedgehog and…all the rest. So much to fire your imagination, Jamie Man. I'm sure you must have been there with us, listening in to every word.

222. The chimney sweep comes
Thursday 14 August 2003

We had to rush back home after the Grantown Show because the chimney sweep was booked to come this evening. I threw together a super-fast pizza for Kyle and it was just ready to come out of the oven…when the man turned up three quarters of an hour early…!

I'd warned him on the phone that it was a high roof but he'd insisted that that wouldn't be a problem. Now he stood and gazed up at the chimney and I really thought he was going to say his ladders weren't long enough to reach. In the end he decided to give it a go. But I had to stand on the bottom of the ladder. With dinner busy drying out in the oven all the while…

There was one thing on the plus side though. This new man also did odd jobs, so I was able to get him to fix the outside tap while he was here. Do you remember how the pipe blew up last winter after that cold spell? Minus 18C that time, wasn't it? I was so *convinced* that I'd drained the tap down at the end of the autumn. So much for *my* memory. Anyway, it was certainly spectacular when the thaw set in and a high power jet of water suddenly went shooting across the patio and right out over the wall into the garden of the Crannich next door, eh, Jamie Man. That certainly made you laugh!

Well, we can sleep a little easier now, anyway. There's already been at least four separate, small fires in the woods roundabout in the last few weeks. And with everything so tinder dry on the ground underneath the trees, it's some comfort to know that we can have the hosepipe connected up and ready once again. Just in case...

223. New wheels on the trolley
Easter 2004

I remember something else that went off like a rocket. The tyre on the trolley that time when we were fetching rocks for Anne Mitchell's garden. Silly old Dad put on one too many. Half way home, *bang*! Just like a rifle! Everyone in the street simply froze...

A collection of scrap Dexion framework that was being thrown out from the lab in Pitlochry years ago. A couple of old bike wheels. It's a real home-made, Mechano-type construction that trolley but it made all the difference when I was shifting the rocks for building the wall. I still hadn't got round to fixing the shredded tyre but that didn't bother you when you were out trundling fence posts and all the rest around the garden. Yes, you and that trolley...

I had such wonderful plans to use the trolley for shifting the earth from the big excavations. Who'd have thought I'd have the whole tank dug out and taken apart stone by stone before I've finally managed to sort out the big tyre question. Ah, but you would have loved the solution in the end, Jamie Man. Solid mountain bike tyres with no inner tubes to blow up this time! And you would have laughed too to see the acrobatics it required to persuade those tyres to go onto the rims as well! But I wouldn't have minded. I don't think it's only the trolley that's been needing new wheels fitted in these scrapbook months, Jamie Man. Or finding it so quiet without your laughter just around the corner.

224. A book and the holidays both come to an end
Monday 18 August 2003

Kyle and I finished reading *Harry Potter and the Order of Phoenix* yesterday, Jamie Man. We reckoned it seemed quite a dark book. Harry is angry for so much of the time. He ends up feeling really bitter towards the world and dwelling a lot on the meaning of life and death. Hmm...I wonder whether we might have felt differently about the story if you'd been there with us to hear how it all turned out...?

The end of the book yesterday. And now the end of the school holidays today. As I'm typing this, the wind is rustling in the aspen trees outside the office window. The sun is coming and going, shining on the broad leaves of the big sycamore tree above the playhouse. And I'm just waiting for Kyle to come back from Inverness after his weekend away at Mum's. It feels rather like the beach waiting for the tide to come back in.

What is it now, five and a half weeks? People nod and say hello in the street. They talk about the weather and their holidays. How Chelsea beat Liverpool in the Premiership yesterday. Whether England or South Africa is more keen to lose the latest test match in the cricket. Tomorrow morning Kyle will have to walk up the drive to catch the school bus all on his own. I can't forget either the last thing that Bryce said to you before he went off to his Granny's for the summer:

Don't forget to save a seat for me on the bus.

Now he too will have to face tomorrow at the new school, travelling alone.

225. Making the most of the last day
Monday 18 August 2003

Our big plan for the final day of the holidays went without a hitch, Jamie Man. First of all we rode up to Ian Bishop's at the Slochd so that we could leave the bikes there with him to be serviced. And then we walked home along the forest tracks. When Kyle and I were up that way in the summer, we came back round past Jamie Boult's house, your den-building friend. You'll remember the place well, of course, from all those times you were up there to play. You even cycled once or twice, I think, didn't you. His Dad's the game keeper and they're right out in the wilds. No noisy neighbours there, eh, Jamie Man!

Coming back this time though, Kyle and I stuck to General Wade's military road and came over the Sluggan Bridge. You were there at the bridge with all the other cyclists from school the day when the new Sustrans cycle route was officially opened, weren't you. Sluggan Bridge is like the Old Bridge here in the village, only bigger.

It's amazing all the different things Kyle and I found to talk about on our walk home. When we got back there was still a bit of physics to be sorted out. Unfortunately a lot of the summer homework has had to be squeezed into this last week of the holidays. But then when that was done, and dinner was over, we were free to devote the rest of the evening to some serious board gaming. You know, Jamie Man, I got the biggest earning film ever in *Let's buy Hollywood*—over $20 million!—and he *still* managed to beat me!!! But I did get my own back in *The Game of Life*, just for once.

The latest Harry Potter is a hard act to follow. We decided to start book two of *The Earthsea Trilogy*. Remember how we all read book one together? About the young mage Ged who couldn't escape from the dark creature that was pursuing him, until he accepted that he must stop running and turn to face up to the evil thing that he'd let into the world? I suppose there's a lesson there that could be applied to many things in this life, Jamie Man. Sooner or later, we all have to face up to the consequences of our actions and choices.

I was doing some searching on the internet after Kyle went to bed and my very last act of the summer holidays this year was to send that e-mail to The Royal Humane Society, asking if I could nominate Andrew Dale for an award in recognition of his courage.

226. School starts again
Tuesday 19 August 2003

Even at the best of times, it can take a few days to get back in the groove for school. Kyle managed to drag himself out of bed and we found all the right bits of uniform. Breakfast. And then it was out the gate and up the drive for the school bus. It's hard to know how Kyle was feeling inside but I came back indoors and cried all the way through filling up the washing machine. We haven't had the washer on so much recently. There's been a lot of shorts and T-shirts weather, of course. But inevitably, there are fewer clothes to wash now as well…

There's been less housework done around the place too. Though I don't think I can honestly claim that that's because there's been any less dirt! There's always something needing to be cleaned. But it can wait. There are other things that only pass by the once and cannot be recalled if we fail to seize our chances when they're offered. Every single minute in the life of a child is a never-to-be-repeated opportunity. Buy now—while stocks last.

Grandad rang for his usual Tuesday chat while I was still hanging out the washing. Then no sooner had I put the phone down from that than Mr Whyte turned up to let me know that the Primary School have arranged a Remembrance Assembly for tomorrow morning. They're going to invite all the P7's from last year to be there too.

It was getting on for five o'clock before the school bus got back into Carr-Bridge this afternoon. I waited, watching the clock. Pondering that the only time the bus had ever been as late as that before was back in 1999, when it ran off the road and Nicola ended up in hospital. Telling myself not to fear the worst. Not on the first day of term.

227. Word perfect?
Thursday 28 August 2003

Yesterday I broke my "Word Perfect" coffee mug. I caught it with my elbow and watched it go skidding away off the worksurface. So what? It's just a mug. I would smash every mug, plate or whatever in the house for one more day with you, Jamie Man. But as I gathered up the fragments, it seemed like another sharp-edged symbol of everything else that's been lost and broken in this desert of a summer.

It was just a mug. But it was an eleven-year old mug. It came with the software for my first work computer. I launched my consultancy business on a Monday and you were born exactly one week later, on 18 November 1991. Come together. Gone together.

228. The end of the library books
Thursday 28 August 2003

I'm finally coming to the end of the last of the books that I was collecting from the library when you were at Bruar, Jamie Man. It's called *The half brother* by Lars Saabye Christensen. A prize winner in Norway—that was all I knew about it when I asked Helen if she could get the book for me. Reading it now, it feels like the story belongs to some other lifetime. But this morning when I got to page 693, I came across a couple of sentences that really touched the spot. See what you think, Wee Man:

> *This is my only comfort today. That sorrow does not have retrospective effect. That the sorrow of today cannot erase all of yesterday's colours.*

229. Finishing the story
Tuesday 19 August 2003

This first day back at school has been on my mind all summer. Almost from the first of those telephone calls on Friday 11 July. How would the children cope when they all came back together again for the start of a new term? Mere speculation. Until all of a sudden that day is here. Kyle has gone to school. Your classmates in P7 are now fully-fledged secondary school pupils. Carr-Bridge Primary School has its new generation of wee ones. The rest of your class from last year are now the big ones. Everyone has moved on. Good or bad. Sink or swim. Like that other day back in July, it's out of my hands.

Nevertheless a voice within me cries out to mark this day in some way. With something beyond the ordinary. Thus I find myself sitting down to complete the final four chapters of *Swallowdale*, the book that you and I didn't quite manage to finish together.

I know there are people these days who would say that the *Swallows and Amazons* stories are slow and old fashioned. But then others insist that youngsters still love them because they hark back to a time when children were allowed to run free without adults worrying about their safety every minute of the day. All I can say, is that you were looking forward to reading the rest of the series just as keenly as I did at your age, Jamie Man. Perhaps you were old fashioned, if that means you could take pleasure in the thought of sailing adventures in a world without television, or computers, or cars, or mobile phones.

I think of my conversation on the telephone with Skip that first weekend. And it does seem to me that there is something about the simple camaraderie of so many of the books that you loved—like *Swallows and Amazons*, *Harry Potter*, the *Jennings* series—that has much in common with all that is best in the Cubs and the Scouts, where you were made to feel so very much at home. Anyway, that's how I filled up my spare time today, Jamie Man, reading to the end of *Swallowdale*. But it is sad to start a book with such a good companion and then to have to finish it alone. And not to have you there to chatter about all your favourite bits, standing at the bus stop waiting to go to the next Scouts night.

230. The super-duper log transporter
Wednesday 9 July 2003

I always used to reckon that having you around the house was like living with the tide. First the bedroom filled up, then the hall, then the lounge. And when it reached the stage where it was difficult for the rest of us to move, then it was time to declare high tide. Of course, with the fine weather that first week of the holidays, there was expansion into the garden to think about as well. But you still found time for the creation of one last indoor obstacle. The super-duper log transporter. Surely one of the classics. At least on a par with the junk-box computer. Or the build-it-yourself recording studio.

Your inspiration on this occasion came at the end of chapter 30 of *Swallowdale*, where Titty gets a ride home with the woodsmen after Roger has hurt his ankle. And then you saw some of the old wheels when we were up in the loft of course…

Dreaming of crocodiles, cranes and log transporters, with Grandma.

I pointed out all the various components to everyone when they were here for the funeral and I described how you'd fastened it all together to make your very own log transporter like the one in the story. There were bits of bamboo cane and a broomstick and the old hoover tube, with the bicycle outriders at one end and the toy train wheels at the other. And all fixed together with masses of string and elastic bands.

I really ought to have measured that super-duper log transporter. It just seemed to grow longer and longer every time I looked. I reckon it must have been five or six feet along the hall in the end. And then round about that, you set up your entire stock of cardboard hazard warning signs that you'd been cutting out and colouring in over the past few months.

Your felt pens stand idle in the pot these days. No one asks me to save the empty cereal boxes for making road signs anymore. And it seems such a long, long time since the tide last came back in. Is it any wonder that we miss you so much?

231. In our mind's eye
Saturday 17 July 2004

Should I regret it when I come across a gap in the picture collection? How could I have failed to record each and every one of those unique, make-believe creations? Why no cute snap of The Jolly Postman? Or a video of your *Fast Food Boys* routine? Only one solitary newspaper cutting of Mr Big...?

Isn't it better to have been so busy simply *living* the moment?

You did not cease to exist on a day when you went to school and were out of sight. You are no less real to me today, my Wee Man. A picture is merely a bonus.

A year ago today, I woke up with music in my head. It's still there now. How could it be lost, simply because you and I are the only ones who can hear it?

232. Grief work
Tuesday 19 August 2003

Barbara Hummel tells me they have an expression in Germany that translates as something like "grief work". The idea is that just the simple process of being sad can be a tiring business in itself, even when you don't appear to be doing anything.

Are you feeling better today?

No, the pain that I had yesterday is just as bad as it ever was, or ever will be. No one can cure that. Though in time I might learn how to live with it.

It's the Remembrance Assembly at the school in the morning. That will be a time for "grief work", Jamie Man. Barbara has lent me a CD that was recorded by the people of Dunblane after sixteen of the primary school children and their teacher were killed by a man who went crazy with a bunch of guns. I remember that day in March 1996 when we first heard the news. Dunblane is not so very far away from here. You expect things of that kind to happen in places like America. But not in a small Scottish town. Everyone was walking round in total disbelief.

Dunblane was in the headlines just before you started school. Kyle was in P2. That was in the days when we used to gather at the school gates with all the other parents of the wee ones. I think the "Bairns of Dunblane" would be about the same age as Kyle now. But I guess for each of those families the "grief work" must still be just like yesterday.

233. Remembrance day
Wednesday 20 August 2003

I listened to the songs on the Dunblane CD while I was making breakfast this morning and I cried all the way through. They too will never grow old…

There was a quiet about the school when I stepped inside the building an hour later. Something of the same stunned hush of the day of those dreadful shootings back in 1996.

A Remembrance Assembly. Your P7 classmates returning after just one day at Grantown Grammar. I sat with Bryce's Mum. She said that Bryce had travelled on his own on the bus to school yesterday. Then James had sat with him on the way home.

Mr Whyte welcomed the new wee ones into the nursery and P1, and then he spoke to all the children in a very simple way. He told them it was okay to remember the good things about their friendships with you. It was a sad and thoughtful occasion. But there was comfort too, knowing that you weren't forgotten.

Mrs Rennie, your class teacher in P4, read the words of the song that I wrote for them, "Hold on to the smiles". It was an important day for her too. It would have been the 29th birthday of *her* son who died. It sounded strange to hear the words read like that, without the music. The school too seemed strange. So full of children but without *you*…

I met Margaret the dinner lady in the staff room afterwards. I'm glad she was there on the bus for your last ride to Inverness, though it's still a sad memory for her now, I know.

One way and another, I didn't see much of the inside of the house for the rest of the day. Everywhere I went I seemed to be bumping into Mums from your P6–7 class. Well, I guess it was that kind of day. And no doubt the housework will still be there tomorrow.

234. New routines
Friday 22 August 2003

So the first week of term is over. In the past, Saturday would always be an early morning, scurrying through breakfast to get the two of you out for the bus to Inverness at 7.45am. But now it looks like Mum's going to be driving down to pick Kyle up on a Friday evening instead. Every day cries out for new routines to paper over the holes and cracks in the life we had before. At the moment, I don't think either Kyle or I is up to great debates, or disagreements. Generally speaking, if a thing works, we simply go with it.

By and large this week we've merely continued the habits of the holidays. Kyle has come home and we've spent most of the time doing things together. He seems keen to share in making the dinner and—now and then—even some of the washing up! After that, there's been homework, walking or biking in the woods, playing games, watching videos and reading more of *Earthsea* to fill up the space until bedtime. Inevitably those patterns will change in time. But for now he simply needs the two of us to be close.

Evenings always tended to fall into one of two patterns. There were the quick, slick ones for Scout nights, Music Club, Carrumba practices, or whatever. And then there were the more leisurely, stay-at-home evenings. Often there would be some video that the three of us would carry on watching over dinner. *Young Indiana Jones* had gone down well with both of you. *The Tenth Kingdom* was another well-worn favourite.

Reading aloud was a further special treat for Dad. We always had at least three books on the go at once. One for reading with you. One for with Kyle. And one for the three of us together. Who knows how many books we must have worked our way through over the years? What a privilege, all that watching and listening and sharing of stories with my children. Surely the best and closest of times. Some of the images that I dreamed might stay with you for the rest of your lives…?

235. New mornings
Friday 22 August 2003

Mornings were inevitably a more chaotic affair, with two boys to get sorted out and ready to leave the house at different times, for different schools. Now it's not like that. We've had to find a new morning routine too, to fill in the unaccustomed gaps. Most days this week before school, Kyle and I have sat on the sofa and watched the latest video together while he eats his breakfast. At the moment it's Series 6 of the *X-Files*. Mulder has just fallen into a time warp in the Bermuda Triangle and found himself on a ship back at the start of World War II. I wonder how he's going to get out of this one!

236. Hard to go on
Saturday 13 September 2003

In the James Michener book that I've just started reading I've met a word I'd never heard before:

> ANOMIE *is the emotional state of mind we are apt to fall into when we are wrenched away from familiar surroundings and thrown into perplexing new ones. The two key words...are* <u>disorientation</u> *at first, followed by* <u>alienation</u> *if it continues long enough.*

I certainly feel like I've been thrown into perplexing new surroundings. Sometimes the days seem long and very empty. There are jobs that ought to be done, each one clamouring for my attention. To think about all of them at once is to stare into space without achieving anything. I tell myself that a single step forward is a sufficient measure of progress come the end of the day. Take your time. The rest will wait until tomorrow.

As I struggle on through a continuing stream of chance encounters and long conversations, it seems more important than ever not to rush the partings. In an over-busy world of unfulfilled promises, isn't it all too easy to lose sight of what really matters? Are a few extra minutes so very much to pay to show that we have time for one another?

It's not easy to take up the threads again when the treasured companion is missing from the script. I hear one story after another of friends of yours who are finding it hard to return to activities that they previously enjoyed with you, Jamie Man. Times when you "kept each other right." And me? Where do I start with a list of all the things that used to have meaning because I shared them with you? Carrying the accordion case to Music Club on my own? Getting the skis down out of the loft without the prospect of your company on a winter expedition? No glowing, rosy face alive with enthusiasm for the next big construction project in the snow? Sometimes it's so very *easy* to see why it can be so *hard* to go on.

you made a gingerbread house with Eoghann

P2

P1

you drew a picture of Eoghann

P5 *you wrote:*

Eoghann shares his playpiece.
He is my friend.
He plays with me.

"A friend is someone ...

... who shares things with you

... who likes and plays with you

... who has the same interests as you

... who comes to yours and cheers you up

... who sticks up for you and doesn't lie to you"

Jamie

"I like friends, don't you?"

TO FORGET A FRIEND IS SAD
from The Little Prince by Antoine de Saint-Exupéry

"I do not want anyone to read my book carelessly. I have suffered too much grief in setting down these memories.....If I try to describe him here, it is to make sure that I shall not forget him. To forget a friend is sad. Not everyone has had a friend. And if I forget him, I may become like the grown-ups who are no longer interested in anything but figures..."

---

237. The poems that you enjoyed
Monday 27 January 2003

I seek always to remind myself that you liked to laugh, my Jamie Man. You were much better at it than I ever was. You had a face that enjoyed being jolly.

Back in the cold days at the start of this year, you came home from school with a new task for homework. You had to find a selection of poems that you liked. We searched the children's sites on the internet and—surprise, surprise—every single poem that you chose was a funny one, guaranteed to bring a smile to the face of a glum old Dad.

The titles alone tell the story. Things like "King Wastelot and the right royal rubbish dump" or "Never trust a lemon". And as for "The elephants bounced", well I'm sure just thinking about that one must be bringing a smile back to your face even now, Jamie Man. Or perhaps an idea for a new game with the Scouts?

238. The start of a new chapter
Tuesday 26 August 2003

Wow! The second week of term is upon us already. Everyone is settling in to their new classes and their new timetables. The holiday headlines, the good and the bad, have been exchanged and discussed at length. The Landmark Centre is not quite so busy now. And in another week's time, it will be quieter still once the English schools have gone back as well. Yesterday Kyle was off with the others on their bikes all evening. It's good to see him getting out with his friends once again, even if the house does seem so very silent and empty after he's ridden away up the drive.

So what does September hold in prospect for us now? The passing of summer, if the cold or wet weather comes quickly? Or a golden, peaceful time if, like last year, we have those glorious, mild days that stretch right through to the end of October? Whatever happens, I don't expect the leaves will stay on the trees all the way into November like they did last year. Already the lawn has a sprinkling of dry, shrivelled birch leaves. Even the pine trees have been shedding their needles this dry summer.

The page is turning, Jamie Man, whether we like it or not. So where will the new chapter lead us?

239. The director's chair
Thursday 11 September 2003

People in America call today "nine–eleven" now. For us it marks two months. This morning I came out of the bathroom and saw the director's chair straight ahead of me in the lounge. It's been standing in the same place there all summer. But for some reason on this particular day, I noticed it specially. As if for the first time.

The director's chair has become the place where I put the things that I want to keep safe. Until it's the right time to look at them again. Or to sort them out. All kinds of oddments have accumulated there, day by day. Letters and cards. News-paper cuttings. School certificates. Photographs. Recorders and whistles. The tuning pipes for your guitar. The wooden fish and the begging dog carvings that we made together all those years ago.

With everything that's piled up there now, it had become quite hard to see the chair itself. It was only this morning that it came back to me that the canvas of the seat had torn again. Do you remember when that happened, Jamie Man? And how you laughed about it at the time?

It was the Wednesday evening before you went away. We were having our grand picture show and you'd brought the chair through from your bedroom. Suddenly in the dark, there was an almighty ripping sound. It gave both of us such a fright. Especially Dad, who happened to be the one sitting on the chair at the time! And then every few minutes after that, there was a bit more. *Rip! Rip!* You thought it was so funny. And we joked together that you might have to res-cue me when I dropped right through.

We knew the chair was getting old. What it really needed was a new canvas seat but that would be a tricky job. I'd mended it a few times with carpet tacks but that only made it tighter. All the more ready for the next rip. And so when the canvas tore almost all the way along the line of tacks that night, I think we both knew it might be the end of the road.

The director's chair came from my Nan. Grandad's Aunty who brought him up all on her own when his mother died. She was a special person for me when I was your age, Jamie Man. Born on Valentine's Day, 1900. As old as the century. She saw the world progress from horses to men on the moon. From steam trains to supercomputers. Wowee zowee!

It was sad that night to think that the director's chair might be beyond repair this time. For now though, it's taken on a new role in life—or death—as the place of safety for some of the most important keepsakes and reminders of another very special person.

240. A new look for the stick pile
Monday 1 September 2003

I've run out of space in the garden. Before I can go any further with the excavation of the tank, I have to have somewhere else to shift the earth to. The only possible place I could think of was over on the stick pile. So today I set to work clearing the space. Rocks and stones to the right. Kindling for the stove to the left. Fence wire and other junk to the back. It's not a matter of a simple bit of tidying up, however. The stick pile was *your* private realm. The place where you modelled and remodelled year after year. A motorway for your cars across the stones. Your own mini drystone wall. The den down in the heart of the pile that you showed off so proudly to Grandma and Grandad when they came to stay.

What should I feel? Yes, in one sense every stick and stone shifted out of place is another step away from the shape of the world of your games. And yet, on the other hand, I know this is exactly the kind of job that would have had you out there, chivvying me along and joining in with spade and rake at my side. And there's no doubt about it, I've been aware of your presence alongside me in the garden so very strongly today.

So what have we got to show for it, you and I? Some of the old fence posts that you had for your road on the patio, with a couple of sheets of corrugated iron to make a kind of three-sided pen. And I've dug it, and I've raked it, and I've flattened it. So that all that's left to do tomorrow now, is to bang in a few nails and we'll be ready for action.

I could have done with an extra pair of hands on the job today though, Jamie Man. Especially when I was trying to bend the corrugated iron. I miss my willing little helper standing on the other end to hold things down. It's very hard to manage both sides of the seesaw all on your own, you know.

241. Ski slope on the move
Friday 12 September 2003

We're well into September now and still the weather continues to hold fine. Which means that most of the housework and sorting out indoors remains undone, while I press on with the work outside. Does that sound at all familiar, Jamie Man?

My hopes of using the trolley for shifting the earth have come to nothing, so it's back to the old wheel barrow. Have you seen the size of the heap of earth over on the stick pile now? You must be really chuckling at some of my antics, taking a run up to tip the barrow out up on the top! It's hard work but it has made more space. And now at last—ta-da!—I'm ready to start digging down in the hole once more. That's real progress for you!

242. The Jamie Fund is launched, again...
Wednesday 17 September 2003

I'm back in my time machine again today, Jamie Man. But this time it seems it's the world that's catching *me* up for a change. There's an article on page three of the *Strathy* with the headline:

> *Falls plunge boy's family launch memorial fund.*

Strange. I thought we launched *The Jamie Fund* nearly three weeks ago! Oh well, never mind. Better late than never. Most of the article is based on quotes from the e-mail I sent them just after the beginning of term. And they've used my photograph of you in the Gang Show kilt too. What a fine, smiley gent!

They wanted to put a picture of me in the paper as well. I said I thought they ought to concentrate on you. So they used an *old* photo of me from last year instead. That's not quite what I meant!

243. The tank takes shape
Wednesday 17 September 2003

Our big excavation has reached another milepost today, Jamie Man. Time to shift off the wooden sleepers. And I've had the camera out for before and after pictures in honour of the occasion. Basically what we seem to have now is a rectangular, drystone tank measuring about 4ft by 5ft. I think there must have been five sleepers across the top for the lid originally, though the middle one is missing and the two outer ones are quite badly rotted. The two across the hole are in remarkably good condition though, for all that time underground.

It looks like the tank itself will be quite a work of art. I'm still not sure about the long-term plan. That rather depends on how deep it turns out to be. And to a certain extent, what I find at the bottom of the hole too! One thing's for certain though. They don't build 'em like that anymore, Jamie Man!

244. A Jamie Fund meeting
Wednesday 26 November 2003

We had a meeting at the Church Hall today to talk about where we've got to with *The Jamie Fund*. And to discuss ideas for the big *Jamie Weekend* we're planning in January. When we first set up the fund, I spoke of the general aim as "making things happen for young people," and that's still the best way I can think to describe it.

You wouldn't have wanted to see money wasted on some useless, flashy memorial. I know you'd have preferred to leave behind something of benefit to the friends that you grew up with, and all the other young people who will follow on in years to come. That's why we're looking to see how we can tie in with the kind of things that Kyle and his friends have been talking about in the village Youth Action Group. I'm sure that you would have been joining in with those discussions before very long, Jamie Man.

These things take time though. All sorts of folk have to be consulted. Plans have to be made. We need to be patient and see how it all develops. And in the meantime think about other ways that we can add to the fund. Like with our *Scrapbook* here maybe.

245. Down in the tank
Saturday 20 September 2003

The work on the tank is much easier now that the sleepers are out of the way. No more stretching down from above. I've got the old washing-up bowls out again, just like when you were there. But now I have to jump down into the tank. Shovel earth into the bowls. Climb back out again. Wedge the bowls in the wheelbarrow. And then trundle them along to the stick pile for emptying. Filling up the barrow itself is out of the question now. The tank is too deep at the one end. And the stick pile heap is too high at the other. I hope you realise, I wouldn't be doing all this for just anyone, Jamie Man!

I'm about 4ft down into the tank now. I haven't hit the bottom yet but I have found the pipes. The inlet comes in from the direction of the other tank that was filled up with concrete. I'd expected that the outlet would run straight out the other side down into the dip in the woods. In fact, it goes off to the right and runs away towards the Crannich, presumably to that third, or even fourth tank in Mrs Cormack's garden. Drains, big time!

246. Making a start on the clothes
Saturday 20 September 2003

Mum brought a kit bag full of your clothes down from Inverness a couple of weeks ago. Like so many other jobs around the house, I've known what needs to be done. One day. When the time is right. When the weather breaks. When the digging outside is finished. When I feel ready for it. Oh, yes, I've found all sorts of very good reasons why *tomorrow* is so much better than today. Waiting for that extra little push that starts things rolling. A reason. A deadline. Or just getting a bunch of tough jobs over in one go.

This week, Mum and I have an appointment with the Procurator Fiscal in Inverness, just round the corner from Save the Children Fund. So all I need to do is to sort the clothes out before Tuesday. Then I can take them with me on the bus and deliver them to the charity shop beforehand. And then I can give Mum her bag back at the meeting too. Simple? Hardly!

Even just taking all your clothes out of the wardrobe and the chest of drawers seems like another betrayal. Okay, not the old socks and the worn-out school joggers maybe. There are some obvious candidates for the textile bank here. But there are also unique things, so close to you that I could never possibly let them go. Like the tatty, faded blue Carr-Bridge Primary School sweatshirt that everyone signed on the last day of term. The old Cubs jumper with the arms loaded with badges that you worked so hard for. Or the new Scouts shirt that you got in September, with its own growing collection of badges. The stuff in between? That's what'll have to be sorted out for Save the Children Fund.

247. Getting to the bottom of it all
Monday 22 September 2003

I think I've finally reached the bottom in one corner of the tank. Just as well really. Soon it's going to be difficult to climb in and out of the hole. I'm glad I moved all that earth down to the stick pile. I certainly wouldn't fancy getting buried down there by an avalanche! When I stand in the bottom of the hole now, my eyes are just about level with the ground outside the kitchen door! And the ski slope pile is another…5-6ft higher up?

I suspect the weather is going to break soon. It's getting chillier in the mornings and I'm even starting to wonder about turning on some storage heaters. According to Mr Weather Man, today is the official end of summer. The autumn equinox. Equal day and night. From now on Grandma and Grandad will be having longer days than us. I wonder though, can this summer ever truly be over? When does an echo stop, or a ripple end?

We did have some rain overnight but I'm still hopeful that the weather will hold long enough for me to get the whole of the tank cleared out. Then it can just stay like that over the winter and I'll decide what to do next when the spring comes. The poor elder tree beside the hole has dropped all its leaves in protest at my digging near its roots. I hope it's not asking too much to look forward to some new green shoots next year?

248. Doing what has to be done
Monday 22 September 2003

A day of digging in the tank and fitting new seals on the wood burning stove. Followed by an evening of snipping out name tags from the clothes for the charity shop. What a job! I reckon it must have taken almost as long to cut those labels out, as it did to stitch them all in in the first place! And then the sorting out. Folding and packing up into half a dozen or more carrier bags, ready to be crammed into Mum's big kit bag. Finally, at half past eleven at night, it's all zipped up out in the hall and ready for the morning.

Suddenly the bedroom seems painfully empty. Unnaturally tidy and utterly forsaken. Just the pitifully small pile of those best of all clothes that are simply too precious to be abandoned to the charity shop. Do I call it a job well done? I ask myself the question, if I take all this stuff to Inverness tomorrow, what will *you* have to wear, Jamie Man, when you get back…? Oh, God, sometimes it really feels like I'm simply waiting for you to walk in through the door again, full of news after a trip away…All I want to do is take you in my arms and welcome you home. Is that so very much to ask?

249. It shouldn't happen to a Dad
Tuesday 23 September 2003

It's half past midnight when I finally get to bed. The alarm is set for an early start en route to the meeting with the Procurator Fiscal…3.15am, I wake up to a blast from the radio.

Who am I? Where am I? What's going on?

I'm dragged out of sleep at the deepest and most confusing point of the night. And for what? The clock radio switching itself back on following a power cut! So I'm treated to one of those snatches of the BBC World Service so much beloved by night workers and insomniacs everywhere. The perfect start to the day, Jamie Man? I rather think not.

250. "A report has been submitted to the Procurator Fiscal"
Tuesday 23 September 2003

Here in Scotland we come across that phrase all the time: on the radio, on the television, in the newspapers. A sure sign that something unexpected, and probably unpleasant, has occurred. But it's always someone else, isn't it, Jamie Man. Criminal, or victim, it's always a stranger. What reason did I ever have to imagine that one of my own children would become the subject of just such a "report to the Procurator Fiscal"?

Then it happens, with all the media headlines and the tabloid sensation. One day, without warning, it's *your* front door, *your* telephone, *your* garbled family details, and *your* child's school photograph splashed across the pages of a Sunday newspaper. Public property. Instant celebrity for something you wish had never, ever happened.

Time passes. Everything goes quiet. The media move on to other feasts. And where are all those hungry journalists now on this anonymous, unreported day, so many weeks later, when I'm invited to come and hear the outcome of that selfsame "report to the Procurator Fiscal"?

No one here now to film my progress up the road where you and I walked for so many years together: to school, to the shop, to Music Club…No one to record a lonely wait at the bus stop where I haven't succeeded in catching a bus since that day in July when I said goodbye to you for the very last time. Or to sit and keep me company on that selfsame journey to Inverness that you took that day.

What does it matter to them if there is early snow on the hills at the Slochd and the roadsides are dusted with the first white of a winter that *you* will never see? None of that is news, my Jamie Man—except to you, and to me, and to some of those other folk who remember you as more than merely another, tiny statistic who was unwittingly responsible for selling a few extra newspapers one weekend in July.

251. Kindness in the city
Tuesday 23 September 2003

The previous time I came to this shop I was buying new seals and glue for the wood burning stove. I was chatting with the lady as she wrote out the receipt and we were trying to remind ourselves what the date was. She passed some casual, smiling remark about her children having started back at school the previous week:

> *...of course, everything goes when it's the summer holidays...*

And I froze. She looked at me in concern and asked if I was okay. I could scarcely speak, Jamie Man. Eventually I found sufficient words to explain about you. About being on my way to sort out the final details of a headstone with the masons that day.

That was all a month ago. Now I'm back on their doorstep again. And it's the same lady, who remembers enough to ask me how things are going. She's very sympathetic when I tell her about the meeting with the Fiscal. And my mission to Save the Children. Perhaps she thinks I only go into her shop on problem days. Or maybe that I'm just a total wreck all the time. But she insists on giving me the missing seal for the stove without charge. Sometimes even the City of Inverness is just another big village, eh, Jamie Man.

252. Here is the bad news
Tuesday 23 September 2003

I return from the meeting with the Fiscal and set about unpacking all the various items of comfort shopping. I've come through the day. Some ups, some downs. But I've survived. Pretty drained. And long overdue for an injection of good news. I switch on the radio for the weather forecast and the six o'clock headlines. *Good* news, did I say?

Top story, a school teacher who's been sent to jail for the manslaughter of a boy who drowned on an outdoor adventure holiday. We're treated to the usual comments about the need for improved safety procedures. They take the opportunity to recall the case of another boy, who drowned in freezing water in the Lake District not so long ago.

It puts me in mind again of the twelve-year old girl who died after falling from the cliffs at Arbroath the weekend before last. They said she was taken to Ninewells Hospital in Dundee, just like you, Jamie Man. There were rescue teams working to help her too. I didn't need much imagination to be with her parents.

My thoughts draw me further back too to the weekend after your funeral. A twelve-year old boy knocked down and killed by a police car during a chase down in England. Another youngest son.

I guess it's only natural to share the suffering of other families who've been forced to walk a similar road. Is it so much to ask, however, for just *one* story of hope at the end of a day like today?

253. The most difficult part of the day
Tuesday 23 September 2003

The meeting with the Procurator Fiscal wasn't easy. The photographs on his desk opened up a world that I had previously only visited in my imagination. A lot to face up to. I think Mum and I were both pretty drained by the whole affair.

And yet, strangely enough, perhaps that wasn't actually the most difficult part of the trip to Inverness today. I got off the bus at the Eastgate Centre and humped the loaded kit bag down the High Street. The clock tower on the corner of Church Street showed just two minutes to wait before the Save the Children Fund shop was due to open at ten.

One of the volunteers took me through to the storeroom at the back and I lifted out each of the carrier bags, one by one…and *that* was the moment when I lost it and burst into tears. The lady was very kind and understanding. She sat me down on a chair and held my hand till I was calmed down enough to explain why I was so upset. And why it had seemed so important to bring your things to Save the Children of all places.

I could have got a lift. Or asked someone to take the bags in for me. But that wouldn't have been right. No one else could have done that particular job in my place. Or that's how I felt about it at the time anyway.

The task of sorting everything out is inevitably going to be a long and painful process. Some things are just too precious ever to let go. But I think there is comfort to be had too when things of yours can go to a new home where they will be appreciated and put to further good use, don't you, Jamie Man?

Remember Big-E and Little-E, who went with Grandma and Aunty Iris. The Harry Potter tapes we gave to Cousin Alan. And all sorts of other small bits and pieces that I've picked out for some of your friends from school. That's surely the best of all, Jamie Man, the gift that can go to someone who will treasure it always. Because it comes from you.

254. Paul and Jan Betts
Wednesday 24 September 2003

There was a drugs awareness evening for parents last night. My first visit back to the Grammar School, where the rest of your class are now settling in to S1. The talk was presented by Jan and Paul Betts, whose daughter Leah died some years ago, after she took an ecstasy tablet at her 18th birthday party. Watching Paul Betts at work, it makes me feel quite shy and inadequate by comparison. When we were introduced afterwards the first thing he did was to throw his arms around me. I wasn't surprised. I guess he is someone who knows instinctively how it feels. I'm sure it would be easy for people only to see the flamboyant show-man. But perhaps that would be to overlook the fact that it might be possible to smile with one side of the face, while still crying out of the other.

255. Running the gauntlet
Thursday 25 September 2003

It's a silly thing I know, Jamie Man. But I still can't face walking up the road past the crowds waiting for the school bus in the morning. At the top of the drive. Outside the Village Hall. Down by the Spar. You wore your new sweatshirt just once, that time when you tried it on and came out to show me how big and grown up you looked. Now I can't leave the house until all the uniforms have disappeared off for another day. Three months ago the thing I dreaded most about you finishing at primary school, was how I was going to be able to distinguish between your black socks and Kyle's black socks when you were both wearing the same uniform for the Grammar School. How times change.

256. Finger doodling
Thursday 25 September 2003

Remember finger doodling, Jamie Man? Those busy little hands that always itched to find something to fiddle with when they came into the office? Or while they were at a loose end, in the middle of a conversation, or listening to a story perhaps?

While I was putting some things away yesterday, I came across the shiny-gold fastener that I bought for you in the shop up on Cairngorm at Easter. A cara-biner, the mountaineers would call it, like the snap clips they use for rock climb-ing. Of course, your little carabiner was never designed to carry the weight of a full-sized Dad. Nevertheless, it occurred to me that this might be just what I needed to see me through the drugs evening.

So I clipped my keys onto your golden carabiner and while I was listening to what Paul Betts had to say, I held onto that precious little ring of yours—my very own, original finger doodler. And that's where I've left it now. Fastened on with my door keys so that it can go with me whenever I leave the house. And when I'm at home, it'll be hanging on the usual hook by the computer. Which means I'll always know where to look to find my special finger doodler, Jamie Man.

257. Why "Man"?
Wednesday 6 July 1988

It was always Kyle Man and Jamie Man, from the moment that each of you was born. But do you know what, in all those years since, not one single person has every asked me why. Would you like to hear where it came from, Jamie Man? It goes right back to when Nicola was just a wee girl and we were still living in Pitlochry. She had a friend whose Daddy used to call him "Wee Man". That little boy's Daddy worked in the oil industry—until one day they sent him out onto a rig called *Piper Alpha*. That was something I could never forget.

ECCLESIASTES III

To everything there is a season and a time to every purpose under the Heaven

A time to be born and a time to die…

---

258. A time for change
Thursday 25 September 2003

Today has been edgy and unsettled from start to finish. Too many challenges in the space of too few days. It feels like I've been one step away from a short circuit. Caught between running off to hide in a dark corner and rushing out to do everything all at once. Eventually I found myself stumbling into some sorting out in the lounge. No plan. No purpose. Just impulse. Perhaps that's the only way the job was ever going to get started.

At first I was merely gathering up all the cards and letters that people had sent. I'd been thinking about it for some while. But…well, how do you know…when? Would Kyle be upset because it was too soon? Or was he already wishing that I'd taken them down weeks ago? Is there ever a right time to throw out the last flower? It sounds like such a simple question…until you're the one who has to decide how and when to ask it…

I put the cards in a box for now. Then I just…carried on. Taking this and that through into your bedroom to be sorted out later. Hoovering the carpet—when did *that* last get done? Perhaps if the pine table and the benches were up the *other* end by the window…?—Better light for Kyle with his new 3-D jigsaw puzzle. And then if the drop-leaf table moved along a bit…I could bring the keyboard in from the office…

I think you'll get the picture, Jamie Man. In the end, a little sorting out turned into a full-scale change round. It still makes me sad to think of moving things from where you would remember them. But I have to organise the place for Kyle now, don't I.

I've begun to sort through the photographs too, so that we can get prints of some of the best ones to go up on the wall. Kyle says he'd like to have pictures of you to put up in his bedroom. Like the one of the pair of you with the dinosaur glider that we built and took down to the field by the school to fly.

I got to thinking that the walls in the lounge could really do with being repainted before starting to reorganise all the pictures in there. But now *that* definitely is a job for another day, Jamie Man!

259. Small dates that come and go
Friday 27 August 2003

The primary school journey is marked by an endless succession of notes home about this, that and the other. The latest event or activity goes up on the calendar. The day arrives. It passes. Another small scene fades off into the obscurity of childhood history. These days when I pull a piece of paper out of the scrap box, I'm forever stumbling across old notes, or bits of homework put out for printing or scribbling. Previously trivial snippets of information, almost forgotten, that now clamour to be retrieved and stored away with all the other treasures in the new, shiny files that I bought in Inverness.

I gathered up a whole list of small dates in our *Scrapbook*, didn't I, Jamie Man. Were they really so special? Well, I guess not every child is fortunate enough to be able to go downhill skiing with the school, or orienteering in a forest just down the road with the Scouts. But generally speaking, they're mostly just the sort of thing that any parent would find familiar—sports day, swimming gala, interschool quiz team and the rest.

I can smile when I cast my mind back to the fun you had down at the Village Hall last summer with Tricky Ricky the Magician. Or messy printing and painting on the *Art Works!* days. And if I should happen to shed a tear for the junior

chanter competition at Nethy Bridge Highland Games in August—the appointment that you *weren't* able to keep this summer—it doesn't mean that I don't still
rejoice for the many small dates that brought you so much joy.

260. The sponsored walk
Friday 26 September 2003

Today would have been your first ever shot at the annual Grantown Grammar
sponsored walk, wouldn't it, Jamie Man. Eight miles of fun, blisters, glowing
cheeks and aching bones. Kyle was quite tired by the time he got home. According to him, he and his friend had run much of the route. Just as well Friday is
early closing day for the school! We sat on the sofa for a while after he got in and
watched some more of the *X-files* together. When we reached the end of the epi-
sode, Kyle began to droop and…snore, *zzzzzzz!* I guess he was asleep for about an
hour, while I sat nodding a little myself as I pictured you striding out with all the
others along the paths and across the fields…

261. Comfort shopping
Tuesday 23 September 2003

In the opening chapter of *The Lord of the Rings*, when Bilbo is speaking to Gan-
dalf before he leaves the Shire, he talks about giving up the ring:

> *After all that's what this party business was all about, really: to give away lots of
> birthday presents, and somehow make it easier to give IT away at the same time.*

I'm sure Bilbo's not the only one who tries to smooth over something unpleas-
ant by wrapping it up in bright and jolly paper. I guess we all do that at times.
Some people go in for comfort food. Hmm, that's not really me, is it, Jamie Man.
But I suppose there has been a certain amount of comfort shopping over the past
few months: videos, DVD's, games and so on. And if I've missed the likes of
Wallace & Gromit and *The Muppets* and *Narnia*, then maybe there has been some
consolation in settling down with Kyle to watch *The X-files* and *Babylon 5* and
The Lord of the Rings.

So what of these trips to Inverness? A shopping list like a box of allsorts. My
attempt to disguise the more unpleasant business of the day? Does it succeed,
wrapping up a meeting with the Procurator Fiscal, a visit to the stone masons, or
a delivery to the charity shop? Do I forget?—Of course not. Or no more than
Bilbo ever forgot that he was letting go of the precious.

262. Big Ben
Friday 19 September & Sunday 26 October 2003

Kyle got the 3-D jigsaw puzzle of the Big Ben clock tower the day we went to Aviemore for his very last check up with the orthodontist in September. He spotted it in the charity shop. It had only just come in. They hadn't even priced it up yet.

So that became one more thing to keep us busy this past month. Slowly piecing together all the walls and gothic decorations. This morning Kyle had a sudden renewed burst of enthusiasm to get it all finished before the end of the October holidays.

Well.... we've certainly completed all the different flat bits now...However, we haven't quite sorted out yet how we're supposed to turn all these floppy sheets of foam plastic into something resembling a famous London landmark! Hmmm...how to push *this* side in...without *that* side unzipping itself again...?

Help, Jamie Man! I'm sure you would have been full of suggestions. And a few clever ideas are definitely what's required here. Getting it all finished before back to school tomorrow suddenly looks a whole lot more doubtful. Meantime, we're taking a break for a bike ride down to Tesco's. The days are getting shorter for cycling now and Big Ben will still be there when we get back...

263. Two hands
Wednesday 14 January 2004

When Grandma and Grandad came in the summer, they brought a jigsaw puzzle with them. A gift from a friend. A picture by the Dutch artist Escher—two hands drawing one another. They reckoned it was more my kind of thing.

There is something rather calming about the slow, repetitive discipline of a jigsaw puzzle when all around is going crazy. So, that's how I was occupying my hands through many of those late-night discussions, reminiscences and reflections back in July. It proved to be quite a challenging puzzle, largely because of its very simplicity. So much light and shade, and not a lot else. But I did succeed in the end. It turned out that there were actually three pieces missing. Well, I suppose that's always the risk with a second-hand jigsaw. But perhaps also a somewhat apt outcome—in the circumstances.

That was all six months ago and now we're in the final stages of preparation for our big *Jamie Weekend*. A time for music and celebration, plus the presentation of the Royal Humane Society certificate to Andrew Dale. Yes, some things—like courage and friendship, or love and support—should never be allowed to slip from our memories. But perhaps others are best not revisited. *Two hands?*—too many associations. I took the jigsaw puzzle and gave it to some friends yesterday. I don't need to keep that picture in the house any longer. That was all six months ago.

264. You never know who you might meet
Wednesday 1 October 2003

I managed to snatch a few minutes before lunch today to scrape out the final six or eight bowlfuls of earth from the bottom of the tank. Yes, the big dig is finally completed…or at least for this year, anyway.

Climbing in and out of the hole turned out to be okay in the end—with the inlet pipe sticking out of the wall providing the critical step up. For a while, I thought they'd put wood across the bottom of the tank all those years ago. But now I reckon it's actually just hard-packed sediment. I'm glad it's old stuff though. I wouldn't fancy shovelling fresh sludge, even for you, Jamie Man!

You know what though. Right at the very end of the job there was still one further little surprise to be had. Just as I was scraping up the last few shovelfuls, I thought I caught a movement out of the corner of my eye. I peered around and finally I found it. A tiny wee frog, no bigger than a match box, hopping around at my feet. Strange that, coming across life down in the bottom of the hole just as the job was coming to an end.

Our BBC *Supernatural* video described superstitions about toads found shut up inside graves, didn't it. There was a straightforward explanation of course. It's just that the baby toads hop in through the cracks when they're small, or they hatch out from eggs that have been laid in there, and then they grow too big to be able to escape later on.

I'm not sure whether this particular frog had hopped in along one of the pipes, or through a gap between the stones, or maybe just fallen into the open hole by accident from above. The frog pond outside the back gate has been dried up almost completely over the summer, so we haven't seen so many frogs this year. Do you remember the big one we found up on the Main Street that time, Jamie Man? I carried him back here to safety, with him trying to hop out of my hands all the way! I wonder. Did you send me this tiny fellow to remind me of that? Or maybe of Fwoggie, who's turned up so often this year?

Anyway, I lifted the wee frog up out of the hole, just in case he was stuck, and he sat and watched while I was finishing my digging. He was there so long, I went inside to fetch the camera. But by the time I got back, he was nowhere to be seen anymore.

A year in the life of a BIG excavation.
July 2003: clearing the earth with you. August 2003: ready to remove the sleepers. October 2003: empty at last. April 2004: a lot less stones...but a sleepy frog!
May 2004: filled in and rolled flat. July 2004: Digging on into the ski slope.

So the job is finished. That promise is fulfilled. And I've been out taking the last of my photographs recording the progress of our archaeological investigation. Sad to say, I don't think it's going to be practical to keep the tank as it stands. It's just too deep. But it would be a shame to see all that fine stone go to waste. I guess the first challenge for next year will be how to dismantle the whole thing without getting buried under a heap of rock! I'll have to give some thought to what I can build with the stone too. Something to remind me of the many hours we spent digging together over the years, my Jamie Man.

265. A Fwoggie postscript
Easter 2004

At the end of my wrestling with giant rocks, and still more bowlfuls of earth and sand and stones, I'm lifting out one of the very last big boulders to reveal…a sleepy frog, disturbed from his slumbers. Still coated entirely in his camouflage of grit and betrayed only by the slow blinking of his shiny black eye. I fetch the camera to take his picture close up and then carry him outside the back gate to the safety of the Frog Pond. Thank you for my Fwoggie Fwiend, Jamie Man.

266. Time for the wood burning stove
Wednesday 24 September 2003

Mr Weather Man was quite right. The autumn equinox has signalled a time for change. The weather has turned decidedly cooler this past couple of days. Snow on the hills yesterday morning even. Brrrr, it's quite early in the year for that kind of thing! And there was a cold wind to go with it too when I set out for the meeting with the Procurator Fiscal.

I was saying to Kyle this morning how it's always the same story at this time of year. We get out of bed and shiver and complain because the temperature outside has dropped below five degrees. And yet come the spring, when the thermometer begins to creep back above zero again, and the snow and ice are on the way out, we'll be stepping out of the house and declaring, "my, isn't it mild today!"

But at least I've managed to get the wood burning stove all spruced up for the winter. Fresh black paint and new seals—you wouldn't think it was the same stove, Jamie Man. It's a messy, unpleasant business getting it cleaned down and squeezing round to reach into all the awkward places with the brush. And the new paint certainly makes a pong in the house the first few times the stove is lit as well. But the job's done and now we can at least look forward to a nice, warm lounge once again this winter.

Do I write about such ordinary, everyday things for myself? Trying to pretend that nothing has changed? Or is it for you, because I know that you were someone who took genuine delight in the simple jobs and routines of life? I think I write for both of us, Jamie Man.

267. New Year's Eve and Christmas past
Wednesday 31 December 2003

A Christmas without you has come and gone. So where should I look to find my comfort at a time of cold days, long nights and a sadness that lingers?

How about an afternoon at Loch an Eilein on Christmas Eve with Kyle, following in the footsteps of your sponsored walk with the Scouts in June? Or the watchnight service here at the church in Carr-Bridge, with all its bitter-sweet associations from the year now ending? Or our visit to the cemetery afterwards with the torch, at one o'clock in the morning, to wish you a Happy Christmas before the drive up to Inverness?

I returned to Carr-Bridge towards the end of Boxing Day, waking up here the morning after to the first sprinklings of snow. A tenuous dusting that melted away in the midday sunshine. Only to return the following morning in a blizzard that progressed to thick slush in the afternoon. And then to hard ice after dark, as the temperature plummeted to around minus 12 or 13C for the next two nights.

Which brings us now to the final day of the year. The wind has returned and all at once it's ten degrees warmer. So—as always—it feels colder, with this sudden rush of damp air from the west. Five days in a row with the weather unable to make up its mind. Every possible example of the worst kinds of snow. Little joy there for the keen cross-country skier, or the eager wigloo builder, Jamie Man.

But then on my way back through the cemetery today, I came upon a small bunch of flowers with a note left by your friend Jasmine from P7, companion of those Friday afternoon walks around Landmark after school. This unhappy year draws to a close with the most genuine of reminders that you are not forgotten.

268. A return to Loch Vaa
Saturday 27 December 2003

Mr Whyte's kind loan of their second car over Christmas has made many things possible. At midday today, in the brief window of warm sunshine between snowfalls, I returned to Loch Vaa, scene of our famous bike lock adventure.

The only time I ever went right round the Loch there, it was with you, Jamie Man, sometime last summer. On that occasion the Loch was so full that we had to pioneer our way round higher up, through all sorts of heather and bushes and trees, across fields and over fences. This time though, the level was right down and I was able to make the complete circuit on the shingle beside the water's edge.

I had the small camera with me and I drifted along snapping the occasional picture, in a mixture of reminiscences and tears. On the far side of the Loch, I happened upon a strangely-shaped stone. White and quartzy. For some reason it reminded me of the little woolly sheep that you gave me once. The same sheep that's looking out at me now from alongside the computer here. I carried that piece of stone back with me in my pocket and afterwards I brought it up to cemetery for you. A poor substitute for all those exciting diary souvenirs that should have been this year, Jamie Man. But an enduring reminder of one happy summer's day when you and I walked around a quiet Loch together.

269. Go placidly
Friday 26 September 2003

There's a writers' meeting in Edinburgh tomorrow and I'm trying to decide whether I should go. It's a long day, there and back on the train. But the programme is all about getting your work published, so maybe I ought to give it a try…? When I was at school, there was a poem called "Desiderata" that was very popular for a while. It even made it onto *Top of the Pops*: I think it was probably written for times such as this.

---

from DESIDERATA
by Max Ehrman, 1927

Go placidly amidst the noise and haste
and remember what peace there may be in silence…

…do not distress yourself with imaginings
Many fears are born of fatigue and loneliness…

…With all its sham and drudgery and broken dreams
it is still a beautiful world
Be cheerful. Strive to be happy

---

270. Setting out for Edinburgh
Saturday 27 September 2003

It's almost nine o'clock in the morning and I'm all ready to go. Well, as much as I ever will be anyway, Jamie Man. I had a sudden chill earlier on, just as I was opening the curtains in the lounge. This is probably going to sound very silly, but for the first time it actually struck me where I was going today. Or rather, where I was going to go past on the way. In that instant, as I put my hand up to let the light into the room, I caught a glimpse once more in my mind of a photograph, on a desk in the office of the Procurator Fiscal.

I've checked the map now. How could I possibly ever have forgotten? The main railway line south crosses right over the path between the House of Bruar and the Falls. I've just had a few four-lettered thoughts, in great big, hard-edged letters.

Carr-Bridge Primary School
Carr-Bridge
Inverness-shire
PH23 3AF
1/7/03

The Wildlife Park Team
Highland Wildlife Park
Kincraig
Inverness-shire
PH21 1NL

Dear All,

Thank you for such a brilliant day out at the Highland Wildlife Park yesterday.

My favourite part was at the very end when we went to see the otters swimming around in their pool. I thought it was really interesting watching them swimming and running around.

The birds of prey looked really strong with their sharp beak and talons.

I am glad we got to see the wildcat babies because it is rare for wild cats to have babies in Scotland and I think that they are funny when they are playing around.

The arctic desert with Hedwig, the snowy owl, and Arny and Solo, the Arctic foxes, was really good because you had tried mixing two types of animal, fox and owl. I think where it is possible this should be encouraged so the animals live more with animals they would live with in the wild.

I think the wolves system of order is alright, if you are the Alfa male but if you are the bottom wolf them it must be pretty hard to get food.

I hope you all, and the animals, keep well. See you some time soon.

Yours sincerely

Jamie Gasking, P7

---

271. On the train to Edinburgh
Saturday 27 September 2003

We've just passed the entrance to the Highland Wildlife Park. You can see it from the window of the train, just south of Kincraig. That's where we were going to take Grandma and Grandad in the summer. And you were going to be the big guide, passing on all the things you'd learned on that school trip on the last Monday of term. Now, as we head on by, it's hard to escape the incessant, nagging thought of how very different everything might have been, if it had only rained on that Friday, eleven days later. Or you'd just driven on past the House of Bruar. Useless, empty thoughts. Too late to turn the clock back now. We're already speeding on towards Kingussie, where you came so often with the school in years gone by, to take part in reading and singing at the Festival.

272. At the Kingussie Festival
March 1998

Nicola has your mark sheet for the solo verse-speaking at the Kingussie Festival in 1998. I remember going over the poems with you when you were learning your words and then going down to listen and applaud. "Hello's a handy word", "If I were an apple" and "Porridge is bubbling". The adjudicator gave you a *VERY GOOD* for each part. She said you'd found the fun in the poems and had spoke very clearly, even though you had a bit of a cold on the day. Didn't Jasmine win the competition that time? I think she might have done.

That was in the spring when you were six years old. Somewhere around the time when you and Eoghann and Bryce planted your trees at the back of the school. Sarah McWilliam was in P1 then and she too remembers the Festival that year. She sent me a copy of the photo that was printed in the *Strathy*. Don't you all look *so* young!

Carr-Bridge Primary 1 and 2, who won the "own choice" action song.

You didn't have to worry about remembering words for Mr Big when we did *The Piper* at the end of November that year. That was a silent part. All mime. But there were plenty of other occasions for testing you on your lines. The songs for the Gang Show. Willing Hand no. 2 in *Beauty and the Beast* at the school last Christmas, and all the other bits and pieces of acting and singing, Jamie Man. It's strange how someone who could be so content with his own company, nonetheless gained and gave so much pleasure from being part of the team in every one of those countless, different shows up on stage.

273. Passing ships
Sunday 28 September 2003

Normally it's quite good having space to yourself on a train ride. Yesterday though, I sat at my empty table and watched the familiar scenery slipping by, feeling very alone, with the approaching Falls of Bruar weighing heavily on my thoughts. But then at Kingussie a young woman got on with her baby and made a beeline for the two seats opposite, where she launched immediately into conversation. It reminded me so much of Grandma when she goes travelling—always on the lookout for someone new to talk to.

Her husband was with her, but he seemed to prefer to find a seat further back on his own and stare out of the window, while I was hearing all about his family. They were from America, living in Dublin for a couple of years, and had just popped over to Scotland for a few days break. Now they were heading for Edinburgh on the way back to Ireland. Before we reached Bruar, she knew all about you, Jamie Man, and she understood why I was watching out of the window as we came up to cross the path to the Falls.

When we parted on the platform in Edinburgh I still didn't even know her name. But I did make sure I thanked her for her company, which had meant so very much to me on that particular journey. I said goodbye to them and walked out of their lives. Passing ships. But one of those occasions when American lack of inhibition had scored particularly well.

Mum told me that when she and Nicola were coming past Bruar on the train, a lady sitting nearby had announced very loudly to her travelling companion:

Wasn't that terrible what happened with that wee boy…

Mum was too upset to say anything at the time, so the speaker never realised how close to the truth her words had come that day. You never know who might be listening, do you, Jamie Man.

274. A serious case of culture shock
Saturday 27 September 2003

I reckon you could probably fit the whole of Carr-Bridge into Waverley Station in Edinburgh. As I started up the stairs towards Princes Street, I felt like a visitor arriving from another planet. One that moved in slow motion. I ducked into the big shopping centre out of the rain but there was hardly room to stand up, let alone find a quiet corner to perch for lunch. I ended up back in the station, on a bench on one of the far-flung platforms. I really can't remember when I last saw so many people in one place. Certainly not on the way up the street to the Spar! Lights, glass, mirrors everywhere and a wall of sound.

So what of that writers' meeting? Was it worth a fourteen hour round trip? Time will tell, I guess. There were speakers from various areas of publishing in Scotland, each saying how difficult it is for an unknown writer to get their first break these days. Tell me about it!

I did manage to speak to a literary agent afterwards. And she said she would be willing to read the first few chapters of *Super Max* to see if there was anything she could do to help. No promises, of course. There never are. But it would make the whole trip worthwhile if…

275. Nicola's 17th birthday
Sunday 28 September 2003

Big sister Nicola is seventeen years old today. Imagine that, Jamie Man! Sometimes it seems like only yesterday when I was carrying her in the backpack along the side of the River Tummel below the dam at Pitlochry. Like I remember wild man Kyle, up on his feet and walking at eight months old—giving us all heart attacks diving head first from the bed into the top of his cot! I suppose all parents like to hold on to little things like that. Does this one ring a bell, from when you were very small?

You're standing on my foot, Jamie Man.

Oh no I'm not. I'm just resting my foot on it...gently!

Now all at once here's my little girl, so grown up, towering over her poor wee Dad when she wears her high heels, like at the funeral.

It's been a misty morning. Other years there've been sunny birthdays, and wet birthdays, and windy birthdays—even a snowy birthday on one occasion, I seem to recall. But today, Nicola sits with me on the sofa with a sad look on her face and tells me that she just wants to stay sixteen years old—the way that *you* would remember her, Jamie Man.

Once again it was difficult to know what kind of birthday card to draw. In the end I came up with a gang of slugs, who all looked a lot like the one you drew in wax crayon on the cover page of your *Slug Story* that she read so well for us at the funeral.

I gave her a hug and reminded her that it was only natural to feel sad after what had happened this year. But you would still have wanted to see her smile on her birthday. I didn't say, but at that moment it suddenly struck me that I was sitting at the very same place in the room where I'd been when I asked the doctor my question—"are you sure?"

276. A time for giving, a time for taking away
Thursday 11 December 2003

According to the calendar, five months have passed. Whether I drag my feet or not, time moves on. Yesterday Cousin Alan celebrated his eleventh birthday, which means he's the same age as you now, Jamie Man. Nicola's birthday is already fading into the past. And in just a couple of weeks Kyle will be fourteen years old and Christmas will be upon us yet again.

I'm onto the second draft of our *Scrapbook* now, beginning to stitch the patchwork together. There are fewer and fewer interruptions. The telephone seldom rings these days. Scarcely anyone but the postman comes to the door now. Everyone has so much else on their minds. So much to look forward to. So much to prepare for.

For myself, I seek for nothing more than a pathway through this dark and narrow valley of the year. Christmas time? How am I to reconcile a festival that celebrates the arrival of a child bringing new hope to the world, when my thoughts still remain so firmly bound up with the loss of a precious son?

277. A gift from the children
Thursday 11 December 2003

This evening Kyle and I went up to the Primary School for the children's panto-mime. An essential and cheerful part of the traditional run up to Christmas. It was hard not to feel like some kind of slightly embarrassing and unwelcome rela-tive at the party—the one whose attention would insist on lagging behind in the past, seeing not Cinderella, Buttons and Prince Charming up there on the stage, but rather the cheerful face of a dear Willing Hand no. 2 from last year's *Beauty and the Beast.*

Nevertheless, the children of Carr-Bridge Primary School did have a gift for us which might yet turn out to be the kindest Christmas present of them all this year, Jamie Man. Towards the end of the piece, when happy ever after was all sorted out, Zoë, playing Cinderella, began to sing the song that I wrote for them at the start of this new school year. And with the rest of the cast joining in on the chorus, they sent us home with a reminder once more to "Hold on to the smiles".

278. Headstone decision
Monday 8 September 2003

I've just posted off the order to the stone masons, Jamie Man. It's not an easy business finding just the right words for a headstone. We tossed around all sorts of slightly different ideas.

And then there's the stone itself. Shape? Colour? Rough, sanded or polished? I found myself trying to picture what *you* might have picked. This natural grey conjures up so many thoughts of you in the garden. Pacing up and down along the stepping stones in the middle of the latest story. Constructing a wall on the stick pile. Excavating the tank.

The first words of the inscription proved to be the most difficult of all. In the end, we came down to something very simple and straightforward:

With love for Jamie Colin Gasking, Our smiling son and brother.

I think that says it all, Jamie Man. I hope you like your stone.

With love for

Jamie Colin Gasking

Our smiling son and brother
who died at Bruar Falls, Perthshire
on 11th July 2003
aged 11 years

One of our stars is fallen
But his footsteps still light the sky
One of our smiles is sleeping
But his story still fills the days
One of our tunes is silent
But his music can never fade
One of our loves is missing
Till the next time the piper plays

At the cemetery, with the Scottish Crossbill.

279. The day comes
Tuesday 7 October 2003

It's felt like I've been on an emotional roller coaster these last few weeks since the meeting with the Procurator Fiscal. Catching up with one thing after another.

Today I was going into school to deliver the very last of the kilt photos—the one for Mrs Kirk. I'd been edgy and restless all morning and so I decided to go for a long walk round the woods beforehand. I went up past the new car park extension and along behind the Landmark tower to the railway line. Then round into Ellan Wood and in at the back gate of the cemetery…

…where, to my surprise, I came upon a heap of earth on the edge of the path and a headstone standing in place. It wasn't there when I went through yesterday. They must have been working on it this morning. Some unexpected extra news to share with Mrs Kirk.

280. Leaves grow and tears fall
Tuesday 7 October 2003

We've had a steadily improving day after a wild and wet night. The sun came out and the wind dropped to give us the very best that October has to offer. The trees are a riot of autumn golds, yellows and reds now. The guilder rose tree just inside the front gate has really sprouted this year and the deep crimson dripping from the edges of the leaves is like nothing I have ever seen on it before. I hope you have the chance to enjoy all the different shades that autumn has served up for us this year, Jamie Man.

281. Our smiling son and brother
Tuesday 7 October 2003

I went back up to the cemetery with Kyle after he got home from school this afternoon to show him your new headstone. It's strange. You wait. You talk about it for so long. But somehow, you never quite imagine that it will ever really *happen*. But, there it is. Our tribute to you. And a very special gift for you from "Uncle" Colin, who also gave you a middle name all those years ago.

> *With love for Jamie Colin Gasking*

The stone seems so very stark just now. The polished surface on the front is darker and rather more speckled than I'd imagined it would be. And the inscription is so very glossy. I guess I've simply never had cause to consider what a gravestone might look like when it's brand new. But autumn and winter, spring and summer—I imagine the edges will soften in time.

I wonder, is this a bright step along the way, or a dark one? Is it all very final? Or something lasting that can never be erased? I suppose that all depends on who is doing the looking. And how the symbols are interpreted...

I'm glad we had the chance to go up there quietly together like that, however. Then home for a thoughtful dinner before Kyle disappeared out with his skateboard once more. One foot in the past, and the other stepping out into the future with his friends. That's the way it has to be now, isn't it, Jamie Man.

282. Weeping in the washing up
Wednesday 8 October 2003

I was browsing along the shelves of CD's last night. Pop, classical, instrumental, musicals, films—*nothing* that quite matched the mood of the moment. Then I remembered a song that always meant a lot to me when the three of you were very small. I put it on in the kitchen and cried into the washing up as I listened again to the familiar words of "For your babies" by Simply Red:

> *Your face is just beaming...*
> *...I don't believe in many things*
> *But in you, I do*

Beaming. That's a good word for you in smiley mode, Jamie Man.

After that, with the CD player on repeat, I had Gerry & the Pacemakers with "You'll never walk alone" three times over while I finished the rest of the dishes.

After Kyle had gone to bed I sat up late into the night gathering together the songs for my *Weeping in the washing up* collection. It includes another special anthem from those early days of being a Dad and sleepless nights: "Everything I do, I do it for you".

There's a Diana Ross song too, with a line that I always liked, about being a hero. Now when I listen to it though, I find my thoughts dwelling on the line that follows:

> *Every time you touch me I become a hero*
> *I'll make you safe, no matter where you are*

Mr Whyte would understand, I'm sure. I did try so hard, Jamie Man. But all my best efforts were not enough to make you safe. What's that other song? "If I could turn back time"...?

283. All aboard for the *Jamie Weekend*!
Thursday 18 December 2003

Here's another big team effort, Jamie Man. Mrs Banks wrote the letter. Mr Whyte got loads of copies printed at the church. And then all sorts of other folk have been out delivering them round the village this week, along with the church Christmas newsletters.

> *We would like the weekend to be a child-friendly time for the whole community to join together and celebrate the happiness Jamie brought into our lives. There will be a Ceilidh with music and entertainment, plus a Raffle on Friday evening, when Andrew Dale, from Castle Douglas, who went to Jamie's aid on the day of the accident, will be presented with a Royal Humane Society Award for bravery.*
>
> *Events suggested for Saturday include a Children's Art Competition, "Draw a picture to make us smile", plus a Grand Auction of donated items, and we hope to offer soup, teas and home-baking to make a community day of it.*

Mrs Banks is organising the music for the Friday evening. We've been practising our tunes at Music Club—even the wrong notes will be polished specially bright for the occasion! All sorts of other people have said they'll sing, play or whatever. I'm hoping that we might even have a sketch or a song from some of your friends from the Gang Show. I like to think that it will turn out to be just the kind of weekend that you would have loved to be a part of, Jamie Man. A time to remember. Truly a time to rejoice.

284. Back to the future
Saturday 11 October 2003

It's a strange kind of time travelling that allows me to stand and look at a brand new headstone at the cemetery in the same week when I've finally been starting to catch up on TV and newspaper reports from three months ago.

2003 seemed once to promise so many reasons for celebration. Instead, I've seen the bus set off for the Grammar School with one seat empty. I've visited the Registrar for the first time since you were born. I've met the Procurator Fiscal for the first time ever. And I've had the brown envelopes in the post telling me how much less Child Benefit they need to pay me because I only have one son and not two to look after now.

Perhaps I am coming a little closer to catching up with the world. Though I suspect that my poor, fragile ship will always sail a tiny bit more slowly than everyone else's in the days ahead, no matter how fast the current seeks to drag me along.

Yesterday I cycled to Aviemore for the shopping once again, with all the now-familiar flashbacks and chills from three months ago. And that fear of coming home to a message—any message—on the answerphone. There are images and associations there now that I expect to be branded into my consciousness for the remainder of my days.

285. Stumbling
Saturday 11 October 2003

I slept badly and woke early. I've stumbled through much of today without purpose or direction. And yet, for all that absence of clear thinking or planning, there was one brief period in the day when I did find myself in exactly the right place, at the right time. Between one o'clock and one thirty on the eleventh day, three months on, I was there with you at the cemetery, taking the first photographs of your new headstone.

Maybe I am closer to catching up now. But I'm not quite there yet, Jamie Man. There's still one more giant hurdle to be faced. The day is coming when I will have to follow in your footsteps and walk up that rough path to the Falls of Bruar…

I said goodbye to you for four days and it turned into a lifetime. None of us knows what the day ahead holds. All we can do, is to try to make every parting worthy of a last goodbye. And promise only what we honestly expect and intend to deliver.

I do regret deeply the time and the manner of your death, my Wee Man. But I will always rejoice in the kaleidoscope of the life that you allowed me to share with you. My sadness I carry with me for all time. But recrimination would be a vicious and unforgiving partner. I have no desire to venture down that dark and destructive road.

A LETTER UNDER THE STONE FROM LOCH VAA
Tuesday 24 February 2004

Dear Jamie

Hi Jamie, Jasmine here, just thought that I would write a letter to you explaining that I will never forget you! I really miss not having you around because if I was upset you would always be there for me with a shoulder to cry on. And at school if I had done a small talk or play in front of the class or even the whole school, when it was over you would come over to me and say something that would make me feel so good inside, like that was great Jasmine or that was amazing. And it wasn't just me that you would be kind to because it was everyone that you knew, even if they treated you like dirt you would always be there to help them. Jamie I will never forget you because you will always be remembered for being loving and caring to everyone.

I better go now but I will be in touch soon!

Love Jasmine McInnes

X X X X X

286. First snow
Tuesday 21 October 2003

The garden is white for the first time today. And now there's melting snow glistening like jewels on the wire of the fence in the sunshine. The coming of the snow reminds me of laughter, of shining red noses, of endless wet gloves and clothes, and of building snowmen and a wigloo. I ache for the satisfied exhaustion at the end of a skiing expedition in the woods with you. You would have been delighted by the appearance of snow in the second week of the October holidays. This winter I'd been thinking it might be the time for new skis and boots, now that you were getting bigger...

Richard was coming over at lunchtime today to go up to Inverness with Kyle. About half an hour before that, Kyle suddenly decided he wanted to go outside. When I next looked out of the window, there he was pushing a giant snowball across the lawn. I went off to put a new film in the camera and by the time I got back, he'd built a complete snowman! It was that kind of snow—ideal for rolling and stacking. He'd got some twisty branches from the stick pile for the arms and was busy adding a face with some stones.

I was just taking some photos of Kyle and his handiwork, when Richard came jogging down the drive. So I was able to snap a quick one of the pair of them with Mr Snowman before they dashed off to Inverness. Another classic picture to go up on the wall, I think, Jamie Man.

287. Jammy fingers
Tuesday 21 October 2003

I was watching the Wallace & Gromit *Cracking Contraptions* video again over lunch today, Jamie Man. And afterwards I read a little more of your *Sands of time* summer holiday book while I was drinking my coffee.

When I stood up I was suddenly reminded of the final video that you were watching before we set out for the bus stop that Thursday. It was *The Muppets take Manhattan*. Another favourite for the aspiring animator. The tape is still part-way through, at the place where you left it to carry on the following week. When I pulled the video out from the shelf today, I found that there were even still jammy fingerprints on the case from your lunch that day. A wee, sticky reminder from *Jim Jam*, *Jammy Dodger* and all those other favourite pet names that Nicola loved to give you.

288. Reflections
Tuesday 18 November 2003

I date this for your 12th birthday, Jamie Man. But in truth it speaks to all your days. I started out pondering on what you might have learned in your short life. But soon I found this turning about. What lessons had *I* learned from life with *you*?

Losing you has caused me to re-examine each and every aspect of the world I find around me. What is it that truly matters? That's not an easy riddle to unravel. We pick up so many unnecessary habits along the road. So much excess baggage. How should we compare the value of a clean house, or an expensive car, or the admiration of society, with that of a loving smile, or good companionship, or the unqualified trust of a child…?

What lessons did you teach me then, Jamie Man? What would I write on *my* school worksheet? The list grew longer and longer. Would you like to see some of my favourites?

289. Good news
Sunday 19 October 2003

I had a telephone call this evening from Andrew Dale. He'd just arrived home from holiday to find my letter waiting for him. I'm rather glad he hadn't heard from the Royal Humane Society, because it meant I could be the first to give him the news that he's been awarded the certificate for his bravery in July. We talked for a long time and it only served to confirm what I already believed. That

Andrew is a very special person and I could not have wished for a better companion for you in those hours at Bruar.

DAD'S WORKSHEET

Mr Big??

Jamie taught me that ...

... imagination is the toyshop of the mind

... a small person may be someone who is on the way to growing big inside

... holding hands is a lot more than not letting go

... once hugged, never forgotten

290. Stepping outside for a while
Tuesday 21 October 2003

It was late afternoon by the time I'd finished my long talk on the phone with the Factor from Atholl Estates today. My thoughts were racing. I picked up the camera and wandered up to the cemetery, where I stood in the first snow of the year, waiting for the moment when the final light of the day would strike your headstone. Then, at the last minute, the sun dipped below the treetops, just a instant too soon. Oh, well, Jamie Man. Don't worry. It'll come back. You'll see the sunset again come springtime.

And there were other photos while I was waiting. Patterns of the trees and the sunlight catching the polished surface of your stone. I don't know how the pictures will turn out. But at the time it seemed like there were red and orange flames flickering behind the words of the inscription. As if they were burning somewhere deep inside the stone itself. Like a fire within your heart, Jamie Man. Don't ever let that fire go out.

291. Snowdrops and crocuses
Tuesday 21 October 2003

While I was standing there at the cemetery, stamping my feet to keep them warm, I got to thinking about snowdrops and crocuses as the first signs of the spring in years to come. An idea for that little garden around the headstone? Next year's project perhaps?

It was growing dark by the time I'd made my way home through the woods. Anne Mitchell was just finishing up in her back garden as I was coming down the drive. She called me over and told me that she'd been potting up bulbs this afternoon. Then she handed me a tub of snowdrops and another one of crocuses. She said she'd thought we might like to have them to plant for you…up at the cemetery.

Was that just a comforting shiver of coincidence? Or was it *you*, Jamie Man, sending me a message on this "anniversary" of the funeral?

292. Counting the days
Tuesday 21 October 2003

Yes, it's a whole three months now since we gathered at the church. By contrast, my visit to the Falls of Bruar last Tuesday is still so fresh in the mind that I've counted its passing first by the day and now by the week. When I look out of the window here today, I see that the world that merely a week ago was bright with autumn colours is now closer to the monochromes of winter. Bare branches stark against the new snow.

Three months ago, I stood in the glare of summer sunshine in a village where the whole world seemed to be arrayed in black and white. That day now grows more remote, as measured by the clock and by the calendar. For now, we do continue to register its receding outline by the month. But in time, that will come to be by the year. Today I turn to look ahead into the face of winter. And I set my clock to start a new countdown. First by the week, then by the day. On another Tuesday, four weeks from today, you will be twelve years old. Will be? Would have been? One fateful moment of ill-chance has decreed that—in the eyes of the rest of the world at least—you should never take that next, simple step forward.

293. "Only" in my memory?
Tuesday 21 October 2003

For the past few days, Kyle has been watching the video of *Titanic* over again. Yesterday he was coming to the end of the film while I was laying the wood burning stove. And he'd just reached the point where they return to the old lady who has been recounting the story of the ill-fated voyage. Her words mingled in my mind with the logs in my hands—those logs that you had helped me to stack at the back of the house. And the tears started to run down my cheeks once more. Of her Jack, the old lady says:

Now he exists only in my memory.

Only? I don't think that Kyle was aware of the tears. But when the stove was done, I went and sat with him on the sofa as we listened to the song over the closing credits.

Every night in my dreams I see you, I hear you…

I miss you, Jamie Man.

My heart will go on?

Perhaps it will. But never, I suspect, in quite the same way as it did before.

294. Bryce's song
Friday 9 January 2004

Bryce has given me the words of a song that he's been writing for you, Jamie Man, to the tune of a record that was in the charts recently. He's still working on it and he says he'd like to write his own tune for it one day. But this is what he's got so far. It's quite sad. I think it shows how much your best friend still misses his special companion:

CHANGES
by Bryce Hope

You were my best friend
In every way
Wish I could go back
And change that day
You gave me everything
I didn't need
But now I need you
So hear my plea

    (Chorus)

Why did this happen
At the given time?
You're everyone's friend
Including mine
You were so generous
You'd give your life
So that some others
Could live without strife

    (Chorus)

---

295. Holding on to your story
Thursday 18 September 2003

Each new story idea and plot twist was always lobbed back and forth with you and Kyle. No manuscript could claim to be finished before it had passed the all-important reading-aloud-to-the-boys test. I couldn't have asked for a better pair of story consultants. You were familiar with Karbo Karbonevich, the hero of the latest, half-finished novel. And you'd heard the first scenes of *The Bridge Builders* script that I was working on too.

So what can I say now of those strangely prophetic words that I read to you back in April–May time? From the opening scene on the island when the old man, Jonas, is talking to his granddaughter, Kristin, and recalling a saying of his own grandfather:

The one who is lost is the one whose story is forgotten.

The focus of my life changed in the space of a single phone message that day in July. Script, novel and everything else went on the shelf. But those words of Jonas stayed with me. And your plans for a holiday diary too, Jamie Man. Could I make sure that your story would not be forgotten?—I could certainly try.

296. News of *Super Max*
Tuesday 21 October 2003

My self-addressed envelope came back this morning from the literary agent I met in Edinburgh. My first inclination was simply to leave it unopened. It would just be the sample chapters returned, plus the usual rejection letter. But why did it have to come *today* of all days, when thoughts of a funeral three months ago already held my world poised on a knife edge? In the end though, I decided I'd better open it, bad news or not.

…and it wasn't at all what I'd expected! The agent said she'd actually *enjoyed* reading the beginning of *Super Max*. And now she wants to see the rest of the story, plus samples from the other novels as well! I sent *Super Max* first because I think that was your favourite of all the stories, the one that I always imagined would say "dedicated to Jamie" inside the cover. For a Wee Man who never once ceased to believe that it would really happen…one day. I wonder if that day is any closer now?

You never had any need either, to outgrow the open, childish joy of having a silly little catchphrase from a story like *Super Max* immortalized in your very-own, Jamie e-mail address:

hushyandshushy@…

297. My butterfly
Tuesday 28 October 2003

I was in the office talking on the phone to Grandma and Grandad when there was a sudden commotion amongst the vertical blinds. I looked over and saw that it was a butterfly fluttering against the window—a Red Admiral.

Just a week ago, Kyle was out building a snowman on the front lawn. But now the weather has gone warmer again. And with the sun shining in through the window this small stowaway had decided it was time to go off and do…whatever butterflies do. I reached over and opened the window to let it flutter out, with a running commentary for Grandma and Grandad on their speaker-phone at the other end. It made me think again of the verse on the rhubarb card from Mr and Mrs Banks. And I hoped that this intrepid butterfly would manage to find some joy in its late October excursion, no matter how brief.

298. Back tracking
Tuesday 14 October 2003

When I cast my thoughts back over the past few weeks it seems now as if the pieces of the jigsaw needed to be fitted together in the correct order. A natural progression, retracing the steps, filling the gaps. Headstone. TV reports. Newspaper articles. Andrew Dale. The Procurator Fiscal. A new school term. The summer holidays. A funeral service…

…all built up upon the foundation of those final, precious moments with you at the church that Sunday night. And the priceless final week that you and I had together before you went away, my Jamie Man.

Can I claim any credit for planning things that way? Not in the least. Most of the time, I'm working blind. I guess the route at each new turning and hope that one day I might happen upon a way out of the maze. Meantime, I just go on, one step at a time.

It's the start of the October holidays. Kyle and Nicola are off visiting Nan for the week with Mum. The moment has come for my first visit back to the Falls of Bruar.

299. Turning point
Monday 13 October 2003

The autumn colours in the garden are quite spectacular just now. Better than I'd ever imagined after this long, parched year. The weather forecast for tomorrow is good too and perhaps the trees at Bruar will prove to be equally fine. I hope so.

I always looked forward to the autumn colours of Perthshire. My first introduction to Pitlochry was on a frosty October morning when I got off the overnight train and walked out through Faskally Wood for an interview at the Freshwater Fisheries Laboratory. A magical spot to live and work. Nicola's birthplace, five whole years before you began to twinkle, Jamie Man. I suppose if life has to come to an end anywhere, then Highland Perthshire must be one of the finest places on earth for it to happen. So I tell myself.

Today has the feeling of a turning point. There is a heavy sense in the air as if autumn is close to the very height of its beauty for this year. That sense was so powerful this morning that I felt compelled to get the camera out again and go round the garden taking pictures of the trees, to remind me of this unique moment in a unique year.

It's sad to think that you won't be there, stepping out of the house each morning to go for the school bus, striding through the fallen leaves and marking the changing yellows and golds of our big sycamore tree above the playhouse. Then the frosts, the days growing ever shorter towards midwinter, the first snows of the year…Or will you?

300. Benedictus
Monday 14 July 2003

The morning of the Book of Condolences, I was talking to Mrs Banks on the phone and she told me how she'd been listening to one of her music CD's. Playing it very loud, ignoring the neighbours and thinking only of you. It was the *Requiem for the armed man,* by Karl Jenkins. She promised to lend it to me when I got back to Carr-Bridge.

When I came to listen to the CD myself, one track stood out above all the others: the "Benedictus". Such a simple, haunting melody but definitely one of those pieces for my list of "music I wish *I'd* written". More than that, Jamie Man, with all the associations from July, I always imagined that if I went to visit the place where you fell at Bruar, then the "Benedictus" would be the music that I would hear there, coming to me on the breeze.

301. Requiem for the day
Tuesday 14 October 2003

These last few weeks I've been listening to a collection of classical and requiem music—the Karl Jenkins with others like Debussy, Satie, Fauré, Ravel, Allegri, Tallis. Last night I made a copy on cassette, so that I could have it on the journey to Bruar. As we approached the turn off for Calvine, the opening theme of the "Benedictus" began to play. And then as we swung round into the House of Bruar itself a few minutes later, the voices of the choir swelled up to join in for the first time.

I sat there in the car park with the hot tears coursing down my cheeks. While the music, the place, and all my thoughts of you, blended together in one of those seamless moments that simply defy all description.

There is one single hymn on my requiem collection: "The day thou gavest Lord is ended". Back in Carr-Bridge, at the end of my day today, there was one further piece of the jigsaw that I needed to slip into place. A final act to bring this most important of chapters to its proper conclusion. I picked up your big Tony Dixon whistle and walked slowly up through the woods to the cemetery. And there I sat on the grass with you, as I set about working out the notes for the "Benedictus". The sun was beginning to set, reflecting off the surface of the head-stone. Was that your voice I imagined I heard so faintly, joining in from afar? I wish I could say for certain that it was. For all the deep sadness of this day, it seemed as close as I could come to the most perfect ending.

302. Full circle, 1985–2003
Tuesday 14 October 2003

Today I stood on the edge and looked down into that split second that changed the course of both our two lives for ever, Jamie Man. Prior to that moment, I had had no image of the place in my mind, beyond a single, obscure photograph at the Procurator Fiscal's office. Only when I came to stand at the place today, did I realise how well I knew that particular spot alongside the Falls of Bruar.

I was transported back to the year before Nicola was born. The Tayside '85 International Orienteering Championships were taking place in Highland Perthshire. Teams from all over the world were camping out on the front lawns of Faskally House at the head of the loch, alongside the Freshwater Fisheries Lab-oratory. And Matt, who worked in the office, had had the bright idea of asking the organisers if our little band of lunchtime joggers could join in on one of their races.

Which is how we found ourselves lining up to compete with orienteering folk from all sorts of different countries. I remember I started alongside a man from Sweden. The race set off at a wide dog-leg bend on one of the forest tracks, a short way north of Blair Atholl. And while the competitors waited for their respective start times, they could stroll over and enjoy a spectacular view of the neighbouring Falls of Bruar.

Any one of us that day who cared to glance in that direction, might just have noticed the narrow pathway a little lower down the cliffside, leading to a view-point.... Today I came full circle to that same corner in the forest track and looked out again at that self-same view. Remembering events of 1985. Remembering events of 2003.

Everybody cries. And everybody hurts sometime…[REM, 1992]

303. This place where we don't belong
Tuesday 14 October 2003

I guess I'd pictured all kinds of ways that this day might go. Few of them proved to be close to the reality, Jamie Man. I don't think I ever anticipated the crushing weight of the feeling that—as far as all the *other* visitors to the Falls of Bruar today were concerned—you were already just a piece of invisible history, in the past and forgotten.

There are new, bright-yellow safety warning signs all the way up the path now. But none of them gives the slightest hint that our Jamie Man lost his life, simply because he happened to go walking at the Falls of Bruar. That would be…too alarming?

I wasn't prepared either for the stark, industrial tourism of the modern-day House of Bruar, so very different from our days in Pitlochry. I had the overwhelming feeling that I didn't even deserve to be stepping in through the door. When I did venture to go in, I stood in the shop there and tried to picture you walking around that same place on an ordinary summer's day back in July. Just another eleven-year old, anxious to find some small thing that you could afford to buy for your Mum. A child whose name had never appeared on the front page of a tabloid newspaper. A boy wearing the same unremarkable clothes that I remember now from a photograph on a desk in the Procurator Fiscal's office…

…and I recall so clearly too, the sharp taste of those raspberries that you bought for your Mum at the House of Bruar that day. The only thing that came home to me from a fateful stop for a rest on the road to Perth.

304. The Falls of Bruar
Tuesday 14 October 2003

But this Bruar of today is a place of two worlds. And if I lost you in the cold, clinical world of cash registers and souvenir goods, I found you again, my Jamie Man, in that other slow and quiet world of the Falls themselves. In an offering of gentle sunshine and soft breeze rustling through the gorge, with the sprinklings of autumn colours on the birch and the larches, and the steady, peaceful murmuring of the water below. All those things that I know you would have loved so much more than the crude, modern concrete.

And as I stood at that spot, high above the waters, a solitary bird suddenly swept in from above, with its plaintive, mewing cry like the sound of a young cat. Then, rising once more, it was joined by a second, and a third.... Until finally I watched as five young buzzards swooped and chased one another around the sky. Like primary children at play. High above the hard and unforgiving rocks of a Highland gorge.

But I don't want to talk any more about the Falls of Bruar. I have had my time of telling everyone our story. The rest is a tale that is yours and mine to keep, Jamie Man.

ALL MEN HAVE STARS
from The Little Prince *by Antoine de Saint-Exupéry*

"All men have stars," he answered, "but they are not the same things for different people. For some, who are travellers, the stars are guides. For others they are no more than little lights in the sky. For others, who are scholars, they are problems. For my businessman they are wealth. But all those stars are silent. You—you alone—will have the stars as no one else has them...In one of the stars I shall be living. In one of them I shall be laughing, when you look at the sky at night...You—only you—will have stars that can laugh!"

305. The day after
Wednesday 15 October 2003

A mere two days since I took the camera out into the garden. I felt then that the big sycamore and the other trees were close to the height of their autumn best. This morning I look out and I see that the stones of the drive have begun to collect their first carpeting of gold. There is no wind. And even as I watch, one by one the leaves are drifting lazily down in the cool sunshine. One good, hard frost—or another burst of wind—and I shall be out there once again, collecting them all up by the armful for another passing year.

Two years ago today, Jamie Man, we set out to ride to Loch Vaa and we had a silly adventure with a jammed bike lock and a broken key. The following summer you were big enough to ride all the way to Aviemore and back. And I was able to sit and watch in the sunshine while you and Kyle went on the go-karts.

He was the wild racing driver. You were the cautious one, perfectly content to potter along behind and be lapped.

This summer Kyle and I cycled all the way to Lochindorb together. And we went for long walks in the woods with Monty Dog. We read a new Harry Potter book to an ending that you could not be there to share with us. And we struggled to learn how we should live in a house with a room that will never be filled again and the echo of your lost footsteps everywhere we turn.

Yesterday when I returned from the Falls of Bruar, the only post in the box was a letter from the Procurator Fiscal with the conclusions of his enquiries. Today there is only one letter again, this time from the Royal Humane Society, confirming what they told me on the telephone—that Andrew Dale is to be awarded the certificate of commendation for his courage in going to help you. I can't think of a better time to present the certificate than on our *Jamie Weekend* in January.

So your story is not forgotten, my Jamie Man. Many people suffer. We are not alone. In time perhaps we can share some of our *Scrapbook*. And I guess that the same words can go out to anyone who is looking back, like us, through sadness and tears:

> *Hold on to the smiles*
>
> *Hold on to the fun*
>
> *Hold on to the times of laughter.*

306. Closing words
Friday 11 July–Monday 21 July–Tuesday 14 October 2003

So that really is our *Scrapbook* for the summer and autumn of 2003. Words written through my tears and signed with my love. It's not the end, Jamie Man, never that. But I think it's time for a wee rest now. Or perhaps another walk in the woods together...?

Our final week together—scenes from a lifetime.
The shed, the log pile and the ski slope. Landmark tower. Our BIG excavation.
Varnishing in the playhouse. Waterslides at Landmark. The loft and the go-kart.

EPILOGUE
Sunday 11 July 2004

A year ago yesterday, Jamie Man, we said goodbye. You'd been watching *The Muppets take Manhattan* over lunch. And you left the video to finish when you came back. For a year since then I've wondered how I could ever bring myself to rewind that tape.

This afternoon I sat and watched the rest of the film for you, from the point where Kermit wakes up in hospital after an accident. He's lost his memory and the doctor advises him to go out and start a new life for himself. Later, when he's got his memory back and all is well again, the movie closes with Kermit's final line:

What better way could anything end, hand in hand with a friend?

And then, over the closing credits of the film, the Muppets all join to sing:

Saying goodbye. Going away.
Seems like goodbye's such a hard thing to say.
Touching a hand. Wondering why.
It's time for saying goodbye.

Saying goodbye. Why is it sad?
Makes us remember the good times we've had.
Much more to say. Foolish to try.
It's time for saying goodbye.

Don't want to leave. But we both know.
Sometimes it's better to go.

Somehow I know we'll meet again.
Not sure quite where and I don't know just when.
You're in my heart. So until then.
It's time for saying goodbye.

0-595-33091-6

Printed in the United Kingdom
by Lightning Source UK Ltd.
102827UKS00002B/58-1008